Plato's Stranger

SUNY series in Contemporary Continental Philosophy

Dennis J. Schmidt, editor

Plato's Stranger
An Essay

Rodolphe Gasché

Published by State University of New York Press, Albany

© 2022 State University of New York

All rights reserved

Printed in the United States of America

No part of this book may be used or reproduced in any manner whatsoever without written permission. No part of this book may be stored in a retrieval system or transmitted in any form or by any means including electronic, electrostatic, magnetic tape, mechanical, photocopying, recording, or otherwise without the prior permission in writing of the publisher.

For information, contact State University of New York Press, Albany, NY
www.sunypress.edu

Library of Congress Cataloging-in-Publication Data

Name: Gasché, Rodolphe, author.
Title: Plato's stranger : an essay / Rodolphe Gasché.
Description: Albany : State University of New York Press, [2022] | Series: SUNY series in contemporary continental philosophy | Includes bibliographical references and index.
Identifiers: LCCN 2022005553 | ISBN 9781438490335 (hardcover : alk. paper) | ISBN 9781438490359 (ebook) | ISBN 9781438490342 (pbk. : alk. paper)
Subjects: LCSH: Plato. Dialogues. | Other (Philosophy) | Strangers.
Classification: LCC B395 .G226 2022 | DDC 184—dc23/eng/20220706
LC record available at https://lccn.loc.gov/2022005553

10 9 8 7 6 5 4 3 2 1

For Samuel Weber

Contents

Acknowledgments	ix
Introduction	1
1 Theaetetus	19
2 The Sophist	51
3 The Statesman	111
Notes	163
Bibliography	203
Index	209

Acknowledgments

In 2015, I presented a first outline of chapter 2 of this book under the title "Europe and the Stranger: Some Reflections on Plato's *Sophist*," as a GSSSH Distinguished Scholar at Koç University in Istanbul. I thank Megan McDonald for providing me with a first opportunity to try out my thoughts regarding the project. On the invitation of Prafulla Kar to give the Fourth Balvant Parekh Memorial Lecture in 2015 at the Balvant Parekh Centre for General Semantics and Other Human Sciences at Baroda, India, I read another early draft of the second chapter under the title "Europe and the Stranger." The full text of this lecture has been published as a monograph by the Balvant Parekh Centre. Subsequently, on the invitation of Juan Manuel Garrido, a revised version of this lecture was delivered in 2016 as a keynote address under the title "The Stranger in the *Sophist*," at the Universidad Alberto Hurtado in Santiago, Chile. This early draft of chapter 2 was published as "Europe and the Stranger," in *The Journal of the British Society for Phenomenology*, in a special issue on "Phenomenology and the Idea of Europe," under the direction of Francesco Tava (vol. 47, no. 3, 2016, pp. 292–305). It was also republished with the same title in *Phenomenology and the Idea of Europe* (ed. Francesco Tava, London: Routledge, 2017, pp. 88–101). Finally, I wish to thank Cesare Casarino for inviting me to deliver a keynote lecture at a 2018 symposium at the University of Minnesota on "Political Ontology for the Present," where, under the title "The Art of Citizenship: Some Reflections on Plato's Statesman," I was able to test part of what has become the third chapter of this book.

I thank Josef Miller for reviewing and correcting all my Greek transliterations. A special thanks is due to my research assistant, Bryan Counter, whose help has been instrumental in the preparation of this manuscript for publication.

Introduction

Philosophy, as the Greek heritage of the West, comes into being with Plato. The self-questioning associated with Socrates was instrumental in laying the ground for the attempt to find a way out of the one-sided and bipolarly opposite reflections by earlier thinkers—especially the Ionians and the Eleatics—on *what is*. The very form of philosophical reflection beginning with Plato involves such self-criticism in a fundamental manner. Of course, this does not mean that Platonic philosophy can simply be reduced to such self-criticism, but the establishment of the specific topoi that make up this philosophy, especially after Socrates' turn away from the philosophy of nature, is intrinsically tied to it. However, although it is broadly recognized within the living tradition of the Platonic legacy in the West, self-criticism has been a rare commodity in its history. Nevertheless, some of Plato's dialogues have bequeathed on the West an even more formidable challenge: the challenge of not only being open to criticism from strangers, but allowing, or rather explicitly inviting, criticism of oneself by a stranger. If self-criticism is a rare thing, openness to such an unheard-of request is an even rarer thing. It presupposes tying, in a constitutive way, one's own identity to the intervention of a stranger, which in the same breath bestows upon him or her a unique status. Yet, this is precisely what is staged in the *Sophist* and the *Statesman*, two late dialogues of Plato—that is, in works that are an integral part of the philosophical corpus of the Western tradition. Thus, this makes self-criticism, and the relation to oneself as one implicating otherness, an essential feature of Western philosophy. Self-criticism demands that one be other to oneself—ultimately, a stranger to oneself—and thus prepares the ground on which a foreigner or stranger can be invited to accomplish what normally one shies away from doing, that is, critically uprooting oneself. Undoubtedly, the Western tradition has not always lived up to—or, rather, has more often than not ignored—this unprecedented beginning in Greek thought at its own core. But, I hold, when in the *Sophist* and then again in the *Politikos* Socrates withdraws and falls silent, leaving the word to the *xenos eleates*—a radical stranger, since nothing whatsoever is known about him except that he is from Elea and hence, as the occasion demands, is familiar with Eleatic thought, but is not in any way necessarily an adherent of Parmenides himself—Socrates (meaning also Plato) allows a stranger to call into question the foundations of all Greek thought hitherto, and in particular one of its several tribal streams, that is, the thought of Parmenides. With the *Sophist*, Greek philosophy becomes grounded on what the Stranger himself, though denying it—that is, also affirming it—calls a parricide, the parricide of the *patrikos logos*, "father Parmenides," one of the major fathers of philosophical thought in Greece so far. Although one may argue that the new way of philosophizing sketched out by the Stranger in the two dialogues where he heads the discussion (namely, his doctrine of "the greatest kinds"—that is, of the minimal intelligible building blocks of philosophical thinking and speech—and his discussion of the nature of the statesman) is not entirely new, since it has some antecedents in earlier Platonic dialogues—particularly in the *Theaetetus*, as we will see—the dramatic dimension of having a stranger explicitly develop a conception of philosophizing that is other than native, and that breaks with any native authority, has *in all its radicality* to be taken seriously.

The *Theaetetus*, *Sophist*, and *Statesman* form a cycle: the dialogues take place over two consecutive days at the same location, and the protagonists remain identical throughout, except for a stranger who joins them for the last two discussions, in which he figures as the principal examiner, thus replacing Socrates, who remains silent throughout both. The topic of the first dialogue concerns the nature of knowledge. Attempting to answer Socrates' question of what knowledge is, Theaetetus proposes three definitions: knowledge is perception; knowledge is true opinion; and, finally, knowledge is true opinion with an account. Socrates refutes the first "sensualist" definition as self-contradictory, in that it implies that one can simultaneously know and not know something.[1] But in the course of the examination of this definition, both Socrates and the young Theaetetus arrive at the conclusion that, rather than being generated in sense-perception, knowledge is generated by the soul, which highlights what is "common" to sense-perceptions and its objects. The second thesis—that knowledge is true opinion—is found lacking because it is unable to explain satisfactorily how false opinion arises, a question intrinsically intertwined with it. The third attempt at defining knowledge—as true opinion with an account or an explanation—falls short of its expectation as well: indeed, if giving an account means only to express in words, to enumerate the elementary parts of a known thing, or to furnish the differential mark of some particular thing, this is not sufficient to define knowledge if knowledge is not primarily to be about sensible objects, but instead about what the soul focuses on as what is common to all things.

Since the question of what a philosopher is has been raised at the beginning of the *Sophist*, Socrates asks the Stranger in this dialogue to elaborate on the differences of the philosopher from figures such as the sophist, the statesman, and the madman, under whose appearances he manifests himself to the common folk in the cities. In the *Sophist*, the question of knowledge raised in the previous dialogue is pursued not only with regard to the knowledge in which the sophist pretends to excel, but also by way of showing knowledge to consist in the definition of its object: that is, in finding, through a process of division, the genre or class to which its object belongs. In the *Statesman*, the Stranger makes a similar attempt at defining statesmanship.[2] Before moving on, however, let me first provide a succinct description of what the *Sophist* is about. If pinpointing the sophist by way of a definition is an ardent task, it is so particularly because he rejects being classified as an imposter who simulates wisdom, an allegation he counters by arguing that there is nothing such as false pretense or falsehood. Untruth presupposes Non-being. However, in order to counter his definition as a sayer of untruths, the sophist calls on Parmenides, who argued that, in distinction from Being, it is impossible to speak of Non-being, and thus that there is no falsehood in what he teaches. To come to grips with this claim, the Eleatic Stranger therefore faces the task of showing how deceitful imitation and false statements are possible, a demonstration that involves a refutation of the whole tradition of pre-Socratic philosophical reflection in Greece, including above all that of Parmenides' doctrine on Being and Non-being. The refutation, which is compared to a parricide, must show that in addition to Being, Non-being also, in a way, *is*. The Stranger accomplishes this by way of a turn to language, to Being and Non-Being as discursive forms—more precisely, forms belonging to the order of the eidetic building blocks of discursive speech. In his doctrine of "the greatest kinds," which comprise Motion, Rest, Otherness, and Sameness, Non-being is everything Being is not, and becomes part of the greatest kinds insofar as it names Otherness. Some of these "kinds," or forms, connect with all other kinds, whereas others only blend with some of them. It is this understanding of the interconnection between them—and lack thereof—that allows for the possibility of discursive truth and untruth. Falsehood is not a statement about Non-being in the sense of the not existing, but is rather a statement that connects discursive forms that are incompatible. With this conclusion, the sophist's hiding behind the cover of Parmenides is dispelled, and he can be pinned down as a deceptive imitator of knowledge that he does not possess.

In order to define the statesman, the dialogue about him takes as its departure an inquiry into knowledge, which is separated into practical and theoretical knowledge. The statesman's art is found to reside in the theoretical arts, specifically in the injunctive arts that are instrumental to all engendering of something, as opposed to the discriminating arts, which are limited to judging the validity of an insight. Yet, when the process of division along these lines leads to the conclusion that the statesman is a shepherd in charge of the well-being of featherless bipeds, the Stranger interrupts the division to recount a myth to Young Socrates, his present interlocutor. This tale describes the age of Cronus in which the god, like a shepherd, nurtured human beings in all respects, in contrast to the present age, in which he has withdrawn and in which human beings must care for themselves, invent ways of living together, and rule themselves, including the art of statesmanship as an exclusively human art. If, at this point in the dialogue, the Stranger evokes the art of weaving, it is in order to be able to proceed to another mode of division, as a result of which the statesman—now recognized as possessing the human art for the ordering of human beings into a commonwealth—can be neatly separated off from all of those who have, or pretend to have, a part in the actual governing of a state. Already, before the Stranger brings up the myth, the question had been raised in the dialogue of the shortness or excessive length of certain developments, which leads in the second part of the dialogue to an inquiry into "true measure." This is the knowledge that, in addition to true opinion, the statesman must possess if he is, as will be shown, to weave the contrary virtues of human beings into a lasting social web. With this knowledge, which is specifically that of the statesman, the class finally has been found in which he is at home.

It is my firm conviction that examining the role of the Stranger in these late Platonic dialogues, as well as what already in the *Theaetetus* foresees his arrival, is not merely an academic exercise. It is also this, of course, but more than ever it is a question that concerns the thick of current debates. If what, since Plato, is called philosophy would prove to require a constitutive place and time for the Stranger, and if Plato's deferral to a stranger of the inquiry into a truly democratic policy is not accidental, such an examination of seminal texts in the history of Western thought and politics cannot but be important. In spite of the historical neglect by the West of the exigencies that come with this founding concern of such canonical texts, this concern confronts the West with demands that determine it from the beginning.

From the start, my reading of the trilogy is predicated on the contention that the Stranger, in the last two dialogues, is not merely a dramatic figure in the same way as the other protagonists, including the several other strangers that appear in the dialogues. What characterizes him is not his dramatic or literary function alone which, in these dialogues, is kept at an absolute minimum.[3] Instead, the distinctive role that he plays in the dialogues in question is theoretical. The status he enjoys as a stranger is philosophical. As a stranger and a foreigner, he himself is an argument, as it were, within the argument that is made in the dialogues themselves. Indeed, as a stranger he is intimately implicated in what will be established henceforth in these dialogues as philosophy and statesmanship. But such implication also lodges a space and time of otherness in philosophical and political thought, one in which the presence of the other forbids any unifying closure.

Hannah Arendt reminds us that it was the Romans who, after having established their political existence on the founding event of the Republic, wanted to provide themselves with an equally authoritative and binding foundation in matters of theory, thought, and poetry by turning to the legacy of Greece, and thus invented, if I may say so, Greece as an authority in spiritual matters. Therefore, one may wonder: is it not the legacy of the Romans that has bestowed upon Europe the idea that Greece is not only its origin but also, in this capacity, a unified origin?[4] Indeed, the concern—if not obsession—with beginnings is not Greek but Roman in essence. As Arendt also reminds us, only the Romans had a god of beginnings: Janus.[5] Without the Romans, what happened in Greece might have remained without consequences as far as Europe is concerned; but it is also the case that the Roman legacy bestowed upon Europe a conception of Greece as a unique and unified event not unlike the founding event of the Roman body politic. But was Greek civilization indeed a phenomenon so unified that it can be construed in terms of a beginning that remains authoritative and constitutive for a tradition throughout the history of the West? Let me refer here to the subtitle of Christian Meier's book *A Culture of Freedom* (in the original, *Griechische Anfänge—Anfang Europas?*). Its English translation, which gives the subtitle as *Ancient Greece and the Origins of Europe*, does not render the question posed by the subtitle, namely, whether the multiple beginnings of Greece are the beginning of Europe, and even more generally, what exactly the relations are between Greece and Europe.[6] The subtitle of this book, written for a cultivated but broad audience by an eminent historian of Greek political thought, bespeaks the multiple beginnings comprising Greek civilization and, in doing so, suggests that Greece is the beginning of Europe, not as a unified origin, but precisely by virtue of the plurality of the beginnings that make up its history and culture. The specific form of cultural formation without monarchs that characterizes archaic Greece, and that is maintained throughout Greece's history, is the unheard-of frame for the progressive political consolidation of increasingly broader segments of the population. This process, accompanied by a mode of thinking whose focus concerns the form of the *polis*, is punctuated by an array of radically new beginnings. Among the most important of them, I mention Cleisthenes' far-reaching reform of the *phylai*, the divisions based on kinship, a reform that amounted to a refounding of Athens in 507 BC. Fifty years after his modification of the institutional structure of the *polis*, as a result of the introduction of the equality (*isonomia*) of both aristocrats and the bulk of the citizenry, Athens was the first in Greece to make another beginning with the introduction of democracy. Another example of these new beginnings is when, with the victory at Marathon over the Persians—a power of continental dimensions—the tiny Greek city states, under the guidance of Athens, achieved hegemony over the whole of the Mediterranean.[7] These multiple beginnings of Greece entrust the beginning of Europe, and more generally the West, with a heritage that, because of its manifoldness, is not—unlike the Roman heritage—unified and imperial. As emphasized by the title and, in fact, by Meier's study as a whole, the plurality of beginnings in Greece is the result of a culture that pivots around a concern with freedom, not in the sense of private free space, but as that which brings its citizens together in a common space, and as the incentive (or chance) for living a way of life entirely different from that lived by all its historical neighbors. Even though these neighbors were recognized for their high cultural accomplishments, the Greeks despised them for their despotic structures. As Meier points out, Greek history and culture are characterized by "something unique in world history" of which no other example can be found in the preceding history of the world, namely, "a grand experiment in living life, under difficult circumstances, without a single ruling force," and this also means a life devoted to making such a life "possible and to secure it, producing themselves everything they needed for it."[8] The following reflections on Greek philosophy take off from the assumption that Greek philosophical thought, like its history and culture, is not a unified but rather a multifaceted and complex phenomenon, in order to bring into relief one among its beginnings that yields to the concern with freedom from rulership not only in the domain of thought, but in that of political life as well. This form of philosophical and political thought at the beginnings of Greece could, precisely because it has not been heeded, perhaps be construed as an inheritance in wait for the (future) beginning not only of a certain Europe, but also, in more general terms, of the West.

I do not question the claim that Greece is the origin or, at least, one of the most important beginnings of Europe. I do wish, however, to reconsider here what of Greece has been construed as the origin of Europe or the West, in light of the *Sophist* and the *Statesman*—two of Plato's late dialogues that, because of their complexity and difficulty, have not received as much attention with respect to the question of Europe as other Platonic discourses—in order to show that even within Platonic thought (commonly considered to be the source of Platonism, that is, the practice beginning with Aristotle of interpreting Plato's thought as a two-world doctrine, a practice which, essentially, has commanded Western philosophy) new starts are made. More precisely, these starts are radically innovative to the extent that they demand a systematic interrogation not only of the tradition of philosophical beginnings in Greece but also of what in Greece was considered to be one of the most heinous crimes, namely, a parricide intimately linked to these novel beginnings—in our case, the parricide of a father of Greek philosophy. Significantly enough, the author of this new beginning of philosophizing *within* the Platonic dialogues in question—in short, within Greek philosophical texts themselves—is a stranger. Let us not in the following ever lose sight of the amazing fact that Plato, a Greek thinker, charges a stranger to uproot this Greek thing that is philosophy from the bottom up; for, indeed, if Greece is the prime beginning of Europe, the task of self-questioning is precisely what has been bequeathed to Europe. Throughout the dialogues, this stranger is simply referred to as the Stranger (*o xenos*). Although that which is strange or foreign does not yet constitute a fundamental concept of classical philosophy, and even less so a concept of the Other in the sense of the human other, the prominence of the Stranger in these Platonic dialogues, as well as the radical overhaul of all philosophical thought to which he proceeds, represents another beginning in Greek thought itself that, even though its legacy is perhaps the least attended to, I propose to consider as the beginning of a certain Europe, another Europe or a Europe to come.[9]

In the *Phaedo*, Socrates recalls that as a young man he had an extraordinary passion for the natural sciences as they were developed at the time by the Ionian philosophers. From its rational account of nature, in particular by

Anaxagoras, who had come from East Asia to Athens, Socrates hoped to find the answers to all questions. But, as he confides to Cebes, this wonderful hope was soon dashed when he realized that Anaxagoras made no use of reason as a principle, and instead explained everything by way of air, ether, and water. It is at this point that Socrates decides to abandon physical investigations, and begins instead to work out his "own makeshift approach to the problem of causation"—in short, what is generally referred to as "his second sailing" or "second best journey" (*deuteros plous*)—by having "recourse to theories [or, more precisely, to the discourses or *logoi* of others], and use them in trying to discover the truth about things."[10] By thus cross-examining the thoughts of others who claim to know what things are, Socrates pursues his quest for knowledge throughout the dialogues. In the *Theaetetus*, the whole problematic of Socratic midwifery further dramatizes this dependency on others whose thoughts or speeches on philosophical matters he helps to deliver in order to subject them to the art that is his own—that of cross-examination, or the elenctic art—to judge whether they are genuine or nonsense. Now, the others whose speeches about the nature of things Socrates examines are fellow others, or citizens of other regions within Greater Greece—some foreigners, no doubt, if from a different city than Athens, but never complete strangers. In Plato, it is never unimportant who the protagonists are that, for having expressed certain opinions regarding philosophical or political subjects, and hence an alleged knowledge about them, are to be cross-examined. Therefore, it certainly cannot be indifferent if a total foreigner is introduced in two dialogues. Compared to all non-Athenians or unnamed protagonists who appear in Plato's works, the Stranger in the *Sophist* and the *Statesman* is expressly referred to as *the* Stranger. His anonymity, his lack of facial and bodily characteristics, or even of all resemblances—that is, his lack of a specific "look"—and even the uncertainty regarding his origin, is the way in which Plato provides him with the features, however negative, that paradoxically make him into a concrete personality.[11] As a *xenos* he is, in a way, a concretely and fully determined dramatis persona.

Let us also remind ourselves that in the *Phaedo*, in the context of the question regarding the immortality of the soul, Simias and Cebes ask Socrates, now that he is about to leave them for good, who would be capable of charming their fears of death away. Socrates tells them that though "Greece is a large country [. . .] which must have good men in it, [. . .] there are many foreign races (*barbaron gene*) too."[12] There are plenty of "good men" among both foreigners and Greeks who could accomplish the task of which, so far, Socrates has been in charge. In one of the few places in the dialogues where Plato compares Socrates' own rhetorical skills to those of chant-singers, speechmakers, and magicians (*epoidos*), Socrates recommends that his students should ransack both Greece and foreign countries in search of an enchanter who, after his imminent death, could dispel the spell that has been cast on their inner child. But Socrates acknowledges here also a similarity between, on the one hand, the philosophical help he provided to his students and, on the other, the arts of enchanters. Indeed, in the *Euthydemus*, the same word for enchanting is used to characterize the art of persuasion as an *epoidon techne*.[13] In anticipation of the Stranger's declaration in the *Statesman* that barbarians (that is, non-Greeks) are not another kind of species than human beings, Socrates thus acknowledges in the *Phaedo* that among foreign others are men as skilled as native Greek others. The question that arises therefore is whether, after having examined the *logoi* of numerous others about philosophical matters—and specifically, in the case of Theaetetus, a young Athenian lavishly praised by his teacher for his outstanding intellectual abilities—without however arriving at a satisfactory answer regarding the nature of knowledge, Socrates is not thereby driven at the end of the *Theaetetus* to welcome a complete stranger, listen to him, and let himself and the other participants be enchanted and persuaded in complete silence through the two following dialogues.

But why must Plato make room for a *complete* stranger who, rather than being another interlocutor for Socrates to grill, instead examines in turn the personalities of Theaetetus and Young Socrates, if not even that of Socrates himself, and is in fact invited explicitly to do so by his Athenian hosts? At this juncture, it may be warranted to recall that ancient Greece knew different types of strangers. In Athens, the numerous *metics*, or *metoikoi*, were settlers from abroad representing a significant source of manpower and skilled labor. Having a recognized place in the *polis*, they enjoyed both privileges and duties, unlike other permanent foreigners who had not attained the status of *metics*. Distinct from those two categories of strangers were the temporary foreign visitors welcomed by the city, and not only protected by the laws of a specific institution—that of hospitality (*xenia*)—but also accorded rights and privileges during their short stay that normal citizens were not granted. The Platonic Eleatic Stranger is, as will become evident in the chapter on the *Sophist*, modeled after this latter type of foreigners. Since they were not resident aliens, they remained entirely strangers to the city, strangers who, as in the case of Plato's Stranger, were protected, and could thus be asked to perform tasks that could not be expected from any ordinary citizen.

In his response to Theodorus' introduction of the Stranger, Socrates not only greets the stranger as being possibly "a kind of refutative god" but also as one who "come[s] to look us over and refute us who are poor in speeches" (216b5–7).[14] Only a complete stranger is in the position to do such a thing. In other words, if the Stranger is not just an other whose *logos* is the object of investigation but, in a reversal of roles, is invited to question the Athenians themselves, Socrates included, is this not due to a complete change regarding the status of philosophical speech, a change of which the Athenians all by themselves are thereby incapable? Could it not be that for such a speech to unfold, one that will not be cross-examined, but that develops into a definitively positive doctrine in the process of a radical interrogation of all philosophical efforts hitherto—a doctrine regarding the philosophical *logos* itself, and the specific art of statesmanship—Plato can entrust this task only to a complete stranger? Does not Socrates' silence throughout the two dialogues, and his closing remarks at the end of the *Statesman*, where he thanks the Stranger for also having drawn (besides his definition of the sophist) a perfect picture of the true statesman, confirm that the Stranger's speech differs from that of the previous Socratic dialogues?

The *Sophist* is part of what is commonly called a trilogy—a form the Greeks were deeply familiar with from the festivals of Dionysius—that, in addition to the dialogue in question, comprises the *Theaetetus* and the *Politikos*, or *Statesman*.[15] If the presumed chronological order of the three dialogues is correct, and if there is no good reason to doubt it in spite of a difference in style between the first and the two other dialogues, it is not least because at the end of the *Theaetetus* Socrates tells his interlocutor that he must go to the portico of the King Archon to meet the indictment that has been drawn up against him, but that they will meet again in the morning of the following day.[16] That the location where the three consecutive dialogues occur remains the same—an unnamed gymnasium—is further proof of their trilogical character. Faithful to the appointment made on the previous day, all those who participated in that conversation have arrived once more. Yet, though no hint whatsoever has been given the day before that an additional participant would join the group, Theodorus has this time brought a guest with him.[17] How and when he met this guest is left unexplained. As only a stranger can arrive, the new participant arrives unexpectedly. We learn only a little bit later that on their way to the meeting Theodorus and his companions already had a conversation with him; yet it is not specified what this conversation was about, except that it was a subject matter closely allied (*paraplesion*) to the one that Socrates at the beginning of the dialogue invites him to explore. Theodorus introduces his guest as "a kind of stranger, who in birth (*genos*) is from Elea, a comrade of the circle of Parmenides and Zeno, and a man very much a philosopher" (216a3–5).[18] Throughout the two dialogues that take place after the inquiry the day before into the nature of knowledge—the *Sophist* in the morning, and in the afternoon the *Statesman*—the Stranger, to whom Socrates passes on the word while maintaining his silence, remains a stranger, anonymous, without a patronym, with no specific features to characterize him, and no indications of who he is. Yes, he is said to be from Elea, but Elea is a faraway place, *to ekeí topon* (217a), thus making him all the more a foreigner. The reference to Elea serves Theodorus primarily to present the stranger as a philosopher, and is indubitably an indication that he is thoroughly familiar with Parmenides' thought, a qualification that he must have if, in order to pinpoint the sophist, he will ultimately have to refute Parmenides. But whether he is in fact from Elea or not is perhaps not so decisive since, as we will see, one of the sole things that the Stranger, though implicitly, eventually reveals of himself is that he is not only at home with Parmenidean thought, but also with the whole, mostly anonymous, past of Greek philosophizing (242c9ff). His origin, as Jean-Luc Nancy observes, thus reaches back to an "anonymous genealogy."[19] Throughout the two dialogues, no effort is made to ask the Stranger to identify himself. He is allowed to remain a stranger, the *xenos Eleates*, distinct from the homogeneous group made up by the other participants in the conversation of the previous day.[20] Needless to say, in due time (that is, when reading the dialogue on the sophist), we will return in greater detail to the question of his identity, or rather his non-identity.

Now, although nothing in particular in the *Theaetetus* predicts the arrival of the Stranger on the following morning, I wish hereafter to discuss what it may be in this dialogue that anticipates, if not calls for, the dramatic introduction of a stranger in the two subsequent dialogues of the trilogy. In short, through a kind of proleptic reading of the *Theaetetus*—that is, by way of a reading that understands certain passages of this dialogue as inviting to be read from the later dialogues as an anticipation—I wish to explore why, and with what necessity, Plato must resort to a stranger in the two later dialogues.[21] The fact that the questions raised in the *Theaetetus* will find an answer only in the *Sophist* and the *Statesman* is something that has, of course, not gone unnoticed. Seth Benardete, for example, calls the coming of the Stranger a "godsend," but the question of why it must be a stranger remains unanswered.[22] Could it be that, given the very nature of the (seemingly aporetic) problematic of the *Theaetetus*, only a complete stranger is in the position to do what Socrates has not been able to accomplish himself?

The question of who the Stranger is has been an undeniable issue in Plato scholarship. In this context, one need also remind oneself that the Stranger joins the group of discussants the day after Socrates has been solicited to appear at the porch of the king, and shortly before he is condemned. Both dialogues—the *Sophist* and the *Statesman*—acknowledge in various ways, both obvious and not so obvious, Socrates' looming trial and his death. But does the Stranger, by filling in the place that Socrates occupied in Plato's dialogues until now, become only Socrates' double, foreshadowing his death? In the *Theaetetus*, "the Platonic Socrates is, as it were, on the way to becoming double," writes Auguste Diès.[23] The question of whether the Stranger is a double of Plato or Socrates has been repeatedly asked, not without some grounds, given that in both the *Theaetetus* and the *Sophist* the questions of physical resemblance (between Socrates and Theaetetus) and the homonymy of names (of Socrates and Young Socrates) are raised. But by precipitating the identification of the Stranger in this manner, the commentators circumvent the question of why Plato resorted to the dramatic device of introducing a stranger in the first place, rather than someone from within Athens, or one of his own disciples. Casting him as a double of the Platonic Socrates diminishes his role as a distinct dramatic persona, and thus also the innovative nature that his teaching is supposed to signify. If Plato introduces a stranger, is it not because only a *stranger* is, according to him, in a position to address and solve the theoretical (and political) problems that have arisen in the first dialogue of the trilogy? Does Plato, with the introduction of the Stranger, not hint at a new kind of speech, a mode of philosophizing unlike that of Socrates who, at the very end of the *Theaetetus*, observes that his "art is only capable of so much and no more" (210c6)—that is, on this occasion, of emptying Theaetetus of all the wind eggs regarding knowledge with which he is pregnant, leaving him at the end of the conversation "as barren as Socrates himself?"[24] If he were only a double of Socrates or of Plato himself, why would Plato so forcefully stress the Stranger's thorough, if not plain, otherness from the homogenous group of the participants, which remains the same throughout the three distinct dialogues of the trilogy? Is one not to assume that by just calling him *xenos*, or Stranger, Plato wished to leave the Stranger other than all those present, and not identifiable through any resemblances? If the Stranger, who resembles no one, is nonetheless compared by Socrates at the very beginning of the *Sophist* to a god, is it not precisely to make him more thoroughly other?

By addressing him throughout the dialogues as *o xenos*, as "Stranger," Plato makes him a dramatis persona different from all the others, one whose dramatic personality is to be a stranger.

It is a commonplace, not only in popular belief, but in much of the humanities as well, that Plato is the author of a doctrine of ideas that are situated in some heavenly place beyond the actual world, and are the object of intellectual contemplation. This stereotypical conception has a long history, and can be traced back to Aristotle's interpretation and critique of Plato's so-called Theory of Ideas, and in particular to Neo-Platonism. From the vantage point of this historically powerful tradition, Plato is also associated in a highly questionable way with the sage, whether Greek or Oriental, and thus all that which in Plato's work seeks to break with the authority of the wise men and their withdrawal from the actual world cannot make itself heard or become fruitful. Indeed, the common understanding of Plato as a theoretician of Ideas—a stereotype that not only marks the average opinion about his work but also pervades many of the more intellectual approaches—categorizes him as a thinker who, at the origin of Western thought, has taught us that abstinence from political life and exclusive devotion to theoretical contemplation—star-gazing in all its forms—is what is really worth pursuing. What I intend to do in this essay is to bring out a different Plato, one who, because he does not fit this representation, has until relatively recently been largely ignored or treated as puzzling. As I will show in a reading of the trilogy, Plato sketches out here a conception of philosophy and politics rather different from the one still prevalent not only in much of Plato scholarship, but above all in our intellectual culture, in which Plato's take on politics is largely determined by what he says about the philosopher-king in the *Republic* and the laws in the *Nomoi*. This novel conception of thought and the political, precisely because it has been ignored, could perhaps constitute a historical starting point in our tradition for thinking today in new ways about philosophy and political ontology.

An equally prevalent commonplace is that it was in Greece that philosophy and politics were invented. Although, historically, this is largely correct, the contention in question remains just a commonplace until the meaning of this invention has been fully established. In advance of the discussion of the three dialogues, a few remarks on the meaning of the invention of the philosophical and the political may thus be warranted. To do so, it is necessary to recall that Greece is a culture of freedom, and that it is this concern that is at the origin of the inventions in question. In the *Sophist*, the Stranger calls philosophy "the science of the free" (253c9). Among the several implications of this statement, let me first emphasize the one that concerns the invention of philosophy in Greece. Philosophy is the science of men who have discovered that thinking can be freed not only of the fetters to which it is subjected by the necessities of a certain public life, as is the case with the sophist, but more generally those that are imposed on it and frame it by the authority of kinship or native privileges in all possible forms. In other words, philosophy is the discovery that thinking can be changed, that it is possible to free it from restrictions not only by ingrained forms of thinking, such as myths or tales, but also by "exterior" forces such as traditions, venerable authorities, or native self-evidences that, from within thinking, restrict the logic of its unfolding according to rules of their own.[25] Philosophy is the discovery by the Greeks that one can think differently not only as regards subject matters, but with different forms of thinking as well—different, that is, from what is the case with particular customary thinking.

Moreover, the Greeks also discovered that the way one lives together with others is not limited to the modes and habits inherited from the tradition, but that it too can be changed and improved. In the same way as the unheard-of abstraction associated with philosophy—its concepts and ideas above all—allowed for a novel mode of thinking apart from established beliefs, the introduction of the equally highly abstract concept of equality (*isonomía*) between the various groups of the *polis* made the transformation of the political institutions possible. Further, as Christian Meier observes, Solon's realization that certain happenings in the *polis* stand in a cause-effect connection—such as the exploitation of the peasants by the powerful, the resulting enslavement of the former, and the resulting civil war—and that they are aspects of a total event rather than isolated phenomena, led him to the conviction that "the citizens had the potential of turning the fate of their cities to the better." Meier writes: "Solon's specific discovery consists not so much of the (unpleasant) lawfulness [according to which such phenomena inexorably lead to calamity], but of the recognition based on these laws of the (highly pleasant) possibility that the human being can intervene, and change things towards the better."[26] With the notion of *eunomía*—that is, the idea of an ameliorated lawful constitution of the *polis* (*isonomia*) for which its citizens have the ultimate responsibility—there arises in Greece, and for the first time in history, a concrete sense of an alternative to existing political conditions.[27] In the same way that the Greeks became aware that thinking could be freed from the grip of nativeness, they also discovered that the realm of the political, insofar as it concerns life together in the *polis*, is a realm excluded from that of nature and its eternal laws. For the latter, Zeus continues to be in charge, whereas another goddess, one of the Morae, the goddess of Good Government—Eunomia—presides over the practical realm where change for the better can occur only at the initiative of the entirety of the citizens to transform it. In the late Platonic dialogues of the *Sophist* and the *Statesman*, Plato thus advocates for a radical break with modes of thinking aligned with traditional beliefs and forms, however authoritative they may be, as well as with a conception of statesmanship that in principle must be able to ignore the authority of the law as representative par excellence of the power of the customary and the traditional in order to make just decisions.

It is a stranger who, in two of Plato's late dialogues, brings these two Greek discoveries home to the Greeks. Is this simply a paradox? Apart from the coziness, but also violence, that tribal representations represent, and apart from the deterrent burden that responsibility for the *polis* brings with it for every individual, are there more fundamental reasons for this dramatic staging? In *Democracy and the Foreigner*, Bonnie Honig has forcefully argued for the "intricate relation between democracy and foreignness," claiming that democracy as a form of political togetherness, rather than being enclosed in the national, is in its essence and impulse "always about living with strangers," and is therefore inherently cosmopolitical.[28] A democracy is something different from a state or a nation. It is a political order—a *politeia*—and consists of a mode of rule in which foreignness has a constitutive role to play. Aiming at "rethink[ing] democracy in non-kinship terms, as a politics among strangers," Honig asks "whether democracy itself [. . .] might require not just the (re)construction of the national [. . .] but also the violation of the national," precisely by "presuppos[ing] and requir[ing] some deep relation to foreigners."[29] There is, first, the curious "figure of the foreign-founder" in the history of the concept of the political, which compels one to ask whether every foreigner is not potentially in the position of a re-founding function.[30] And, further, there is the foreigner putting "foreignness to work on behalf of democracy by modeling forms of agency that are transgressive, but (or therefore) possessed of potentially inaugural powers."[31]

By according a stranger the principal role that hitherto had been the privilege of Socrates, Plato inscribes into the very texture of philosophy a role of the stranger that has nowhere else its equal. To recognize this is not to celebrate some European or Western superiority, but instead to advocate a kind of thinking that is not simply or inconsequentially open to foreigners, but that acknowledges their constitutive role for all self-identity. It is to recognize what in any event is always already at work in any self-enclosing identification, namely the differentiation from others, outsiders, and foreigners, who are thus openly welcomed for their singular work. In no way does such recognition imply the uncritical adoption of a stranger's equally conditioned views, but instead fundamentally mitigates the self-centeredness and blindness of one's cultural formations to others by the presence within them of the foreigner. Rather than providing any sort of comforting superiority over others, such a conception confronts Western thought with itself, and inscribes at its core a face-to-face confrontation with its own expectations, with its idea, or with its concept—in short, it inscribes self-criticism as a unique institution. It is this, an essential vulnerability characteristic of Western thought, which has been decried from within the West by the conservative forces as self-destructive, and, paradoxically, as the source of the arsenal of tools that has allowed European and non-European anti-Europeanists to make the accusation of Western self-centeredness.

In the *Sophist* and the *Statesman*, Plato has a stranger establish what philosophical thinking is, and who a true statesman is. Indeed, when realized in conformity with their essence, the true philosopher and the true statesman break with ethnic privilege and as a result are, in a way, foreigners. This is also the reason why only a foreigner or stranger can bring home to his hosts that which the Greeks themselves invented but did not heed, namely, the realization that both thinking and the ways of living together can be changed for the better. Only a foreigner, it would seem, is capable of persuading natives—who are blinded by the divisive and colorful diversity of "the many-headed sophist" (240c5), who claims for himself the title of a philosopher, as well as the very large chorus of politicians whose "genus is of every kind of tribe" (291a8)—that they have the power to change things from ground up.

As should be obvious by now, this essay is not conceived as a philological contribution to Plato scholarship. As it is in genre an essay, it has a much freer form, characterized by its repeated recommencements to bring into relief one particular concern—that of the Stranger—which, needless to say, not only has methodological implications for the presentation of the argument, but also for the argument itself. The *intentio recta* of this essay is to show that the problematic of the Stranger in Plato's dialogues engages our present historical moment and the potential of future of our Western culture.

Although my reading is based on the current standard translations of the dialogues, only on a few occasions do I touch on textual uncertainties or issues of translation. Nor, furthermore, is this essay a study on the trilogy in a critical dialogue with existing interpretations of decidedly difficult and puzzling passages in these late Platonic texts. I do not, in a technical sense, take issue with previous interpretations, and only rarely take issue with the place they occupy within the history of the interpretation of these classical dialogues. This, of course, does not mean that I have not greatly profited from the scholarship in question. Without it, I could not have written this essay. But my approach is, of course, not disinterested: I read the dialogues in question not only in terms of an anti-Platonist interpretation of Plato, resisting all absolutization of particular aspects of his philosophical concerns, such as his theory of the ideas; I also, on occasion, resist Plato's self-interpretation. In addition, in my reading I highlight the dialogues' seemingly non-philosophical textual and dramatic (if not theatrical) nature, with the recognition that these aspects demand to be read in a strong sense—which is also to say that, while recognizing the fine contributions it has made to the clarification of delicate technical problems in the dialogues, I pay little attention to the analytic tradition of their reception—basing myself above all on scholars within this particular tradition of interpretation. My approach to the dialogues proceeds on the assumption expressed by Julius Stenzel of the indissolubility of the connection of the literary form of the dialogues and their philosophical content, and the impossibility of dealing with one without taking the other into account.[32] Indeed, rather than merely being of the order of artistry, the dramatic staging of the arguments in the dialogues—which concerns the time and place of their occurrence, the protagonists' characters, their knowledge, and so forth—is intrinsically interwoven with the arguments. I also give priority to those commentators who argue for a shift of direction in Plato's late work as opposed to the first and second periods of his writings. In the later dialogues, I hold, and in the *Sophist* and the *Statesman* in particular, something fundamentally new occurs in Plato's work, something strange or rather alien to Socratism. For this reason, I also consider that the fact that in these dialogues Socrates is replaced by a stranger as the head of the discussions is anything but fortuitous; on the contrary, this is tightly interwoven with Plato's mature philosophy, and will thus be given appropriate attention in this study.

Precisely because my focus in this essay is on three of Plato's later dialogues, with the contention that in the triptych a new philosophical vision is elaborated by Plato's Stranger, the reader may expect a more systematic comparison of these later works with Plato's earlier ones. Regarding issues such as Plato's early conception of the ideas and its recast form in the *Sophist*, or the status of the philosopher-king in the *Republic* compared to that of the statesman in the homonymous dialogue, I certainly could not avoid meeting that demand, at least to some extent. But my reading of the three dialogues seeks to bring the dramatic role of the Stranger, as well as what it is that Plato has him accomplish, onto center stage. Therefore, my prime interest here is not so much the way that this new vision compares with Plato's earlier one—which would have led to a quite different study—but instead how the Stranger relates to the whole of Greek philosophy, including that of Plato himself. In other words, in order to show that it is fundamentally the task of a stranger to bring philosophy into its own, not only "Plato's Stranger" but also "the Stranger's Plato"—rather than the historical Plato—had to occupy center stage.

If the title of this book is *Plato's Stranger: An Essay*, this is also to indicate that it is a book-length essay, an attempt at articulating a problematic that is not only of theoretical, but also, at this moment of history, of some cultural and political interest. Not only do I develop certain issues in the dialogue well beyond the space that they are granted in Plato scholarship, but I also introduce some new threads into their weave. If I have taken what some may judge to be unwarranted liberties, it is because of what I hold to be the topicality of these dialogues: in my view, they contain highly topical resources for the reinterpretation of the West's heritage. If, for example, one takes into account that "our world is and will remain more and more mobile, and will 'produce' more and more strangers," the Platonic Stranger holds in reserve some food for thought.[33] On more than one occasion I venture risky interpretations of certain passages and topics that may go beyond what seems to be textually and philologically allowed. For such audacities, there may not always be the "literal" support in the texts that some may believe to be indispensable. Furthermore, these risky interpretations may on occasion also seem to interpret Plato otherwise than he might have understood himself. Yet, I risk the contention that the concerns I have brought to these Platonic dialogues are not simply arbitrary, but that even there where the dialogues do not seem to offer explicit textual evidence for the points I make, these extrapolations are nonetheless in tune with the spirit of their text.

Chapter One

Theaetetus

Compared to the rich settings in the context of which some of the other Platonic dialogues are narrated—such as the *Symposium*, the *Phaedrus*, or the *Republic*, for example—the dramatic background for the gathering in the *Theaetetus* is alluded to in an extremely economical fashion as an unnamed palaestra, though the time of the dialogue's occurrence is clearly indicated at the very end, and the parties involved are identified in the introductory scene by profession, origin, age, and so forth.[1] Although these characteristics of the personae involved in the introductory conversation are highly significant for the work, and even though the dramatic power of the dialogue is still remarkable, its dramatic dimension is mainly restricted to the twists and turns of a discussion that is pursued, as A. E. Taylor observes, "with a system and strictness we have not yet met in any of the major dialogues."[2] In this, Taylor continues, the dialogue has "features that show that we are near the point at which dialogue will become mere conventional form for what is in reality an essay on a set theme."[3] The reference is, of course, to the two dialogues that follow chronologically, the *Sophist* and the *Statesman*. For what interests me hereafter—the discursive events that announce or make the introduction of the Stranger in those dialogues dramatically, if not also theoretically, necessary—certain and at times unexpected twists and turns in the argumentation of the *Theaetetus* will require particular attention. Indeed, rather than a randomly or merely colorful event—if there could ever be something of the sort in Plato—the arrival of the Stranger in the later dialogues is prepared and staged here with inexorable discursive necessity.

In distinction from the two other dialogues of the trilogy, the *Theaetetus* is held to be an aporetic dialogue because at the end its guiding question into the nature of knowledge does not seem to receive a conclusive answer.[4] Undoubtedly, given the numerous aporetic dialogues, especially Plato's early ones, this fact is perhaps of no particular significance. After all, the dialogue in question is dominated by the refutation of Theaetetus' three responses to what knowledge is.[5] As demonstrated by his first response, whose refutation also takes up the bulk of the dialogue, knowledge is considered in this dialogue only as the sensible knowledge of individual things. Although Theaetetus' two following answers acknowledge that knowledge cannot be reduced to them, the issue of objects of thought is only briefly touched upon. As becomes clear in the *Sophist*, it is only with respect to intelligible things that the nature of knowledge can find a conclusive answer.[6] But it is not only knowledge that fails to receive a satisfactory resolution in the *Theaetetus*; one is also left without an acceptable account of what true opinion is. And yet, even though the aporetic nature of the *Theaetetus* is still debated by a number of scholars, is it not noteworthy that the two following dialogues, in which the Stranger leads the discussion, more completely cover the question of knowledge, as well as that both arrive at a fuller conclusion—first, in the *Sophist*, through a deeper understanding of what an "account" is as regards the nature of knowledge and, second, in the *Statesman*, regarding the role that "true measure" plays in knowledge as true opinion? Indeed, only once "*logos*" is understood—something with which the *Sophist* is concerned—can the nature of knowledge in an emphatic (that is, philosophical) sense and the art of statesmanship, respectively, be determined.

First, however, a few words about the participants of the dialogue are warranted. First among them is Theodorus from Cyrene, a mathematician who taught at Athens and who, though having been a friend of Protagoras, has turned away from, in his own words, the "bare speeches" of philosophy to devote himself exclusively to pure mathematics. He has historically been known for having contributed to further developing the Pythagorean theory of the irrationals, to which Plato also alludes at one point. Three of his students—among them the brilliant Theaetetus, praised by his teacher for his aptness for mathematics—join Theodorus and Socrates. While the two other young men remain silent throughout the dialogue, including the Young Socrates, Theaetetus became one of ancient Greece's most important mathematicians and a foundational member of Plato's Academy, where he taught solid geometry; he will be asked to be Socrates' respondent. Now the fact that Socrates, who in a dialogue about the nature of knowledge professes a lack of knowledge concerning knowledge (in the famous stretch concerning his art of midwifery), also faces two mathematicians cannot, of course, be accidental. On the contrary, this arrangement indicates that what in this dialogue will be at stake is the status of mathematical knowledge, which Plato praised in particular in the *Republic* as a propaedeutic to philosophy, but which as a propaedeutic cannot be identical with philosophical knowledge itself. From the beginning and in a dramatic fashion, the dialogue presupposes a difference between mathematical knowledge and the knowledge of the philosopher, but Socrates wants to find out what that knowledge is, in a crisscross examination, from the very young and especially gifted Theaetetus.

Socrates' proposition to investigate the nature of knowledge is triggered by the elderly Theodorus, a venerable authority in mathematics who, when asserting the physical likeness between his student Theaetetus and Socrates, invokes a standard of beauty, and hence a knowledge which, however authoritative he may be as a scientist, he cannot have since he is not competent in the art of likeness, which is that of the painter.[7] The "small point" (145d7) that Socrates wishes to investigate together with the young man is one that, as he holds, he cannot adequately solve by himself, and that requires a dialogue resembling more a kind of play (*paidia* as opposed to *paideia*) between him and his respondent.[8] Throughout the debate we are reminded several times that it is together with his interlocutor that Socrates wishes to arrive at a conclusion on the issue under investigation. Even though the dialogical nature of the dialogue may be on the way of fading into a formality, the theme of arriving together—be it in playful fashion—at the conclusion of the problem that nags Socrates becomes all the more important. The "small point" that Socrates is puzzled about, and which in no time at all is qualified as one of the hardest questions, concerns knowledge (or science, *episteme*) and its relation to wisdom (*sophia*). More precisely, what is in question is whether professional competence, such as that of Theodorus, merits to be called a knowledge capable of, or identical with, wisdom, or whether it is just knowledge of a technique.[9] If Socrates asks Theaetetus what knowledge is, it is in view of a knowledge that would merit to be called wisdom, and by which one is to become wise.[10] Now, it is at the precise moment when Theaetetus answers Socrates' question of what knowledge is by assimilating it with perception (*aisthesis*) that the need for an examination in common (*koinei*) of the thesis arises explicitly (151e5–6). As is demonstrated by Socrates' instant retranslation of Theaetetus' response that knowledge is perception into a statement made by Protagoras, the immensely popular and self-declared sophist of the Periclean age—namely, that man is the measure of all things, the term "man" referring not to mankind or human beings as a species, but to each singular individual[11]—the assertion in Protagorean terms that what appears to me is also what *is* for me, has the purpose of stressing that, thus understood, knowledge is (hopelessly) individual, private, and non-communicable. As Taylor comments: "Protagoras denies that there is a *common* real world which can be known by two percipients. Reality itself is individual in the sense that I live in a private world known only to me, you in another private world known only to you."[12] The seemingly disproportionate length of the rebuttal of Theaetetus' first definition of knowledge can no doubt be explained by the necessity of, first, overcoming such a purely private conception of knowledge by elaborating on it in togetherness, a possibility that all by itself is already a refutation of the thesis. Distinct from this performative dimension of the debate, Socrates' invitation of Theaetetus to join him in an inquiry about the nature of knowledge is precisely in order to argue for a conception of knowledge that is shared by all and established together through thinking, rather than through private perception. With this call to examine together the nature of knowledge, and to thus arrive in common at a conception of it, it is obvious that the target of the inquiry is also the knowledge claimed by the wise man or sage who, in this case, is Protagoras as he is portrayed by Socrates in this dialogue.[13] As is evidenced by the *Theaetetus*, Socrates himself is incapable of knowledge, and is thus lacking the authority of a sage, but as is also intimated from the beginning of the investigation, knowledge can emerge from conversation and unrelenting cross-examination. Knowledge is not something one possesses privately. It is not of the order of a secret doctrine communicated in whispers to some disciples, but something discovered together. This insistence on arriving together at an understanding of the nature of knowledge stresses the logical—that is, discursive—nature of philosophical examination. Discursivity implies a step-by-step form of argumentation, along with which an interlocutor can closely follow, and that anyone can follow with the mind (*sunakolouthein*), a process by which the intelligibility of the argument is secured.[14] Unlike what is the case with the sage, for Plato in the *Theaetetus*, philosophical knowledge is not the result of the solitary contemplation of some unsayable truth, but emphatically of dia-logical "praxis."

Notwithstanding the centrality of the question of knowledge in the dialogue, it does not take center stage in my reading.[15] This question will be considered only within the limits of what I will seek to develop hereafter. Given the concern of this chapter—the role of the Stranger in the subsequent dialogues, and his accomplishments—I am interested in the fact that the investigation in question is framed from the beginning by an interrogation of authorities who make claims of truth. Indeed, each of Theaetetus' three responses to the question can be retraced to "great and amazing men" (210c8) of contemporary Athens, or of the past. Theaetetus' answers to the question of what knowledge is, rather than expressing his own thoughts, are, as Jacob Klein has noted, "the thoughts of other people, who are, as it were, the fathers of Theaetetus's thought."[16] But Theaetetus' answers to the question of what knowledge is do not draw only on past authorities. Socrates is quick to retrace his first response—that knowledge is perception—back to Protagoras, but the fact that a mathematician could suggest that knowledge is perception (*aisthesis*), or sensible awareness, already indicates an uncritical acceptance of popular opinions, and perhaps, more fundamentally, a lack of awareness of the essence of the mathematical itself. Be that as it may, when in his second response he asserts that knowledge is true opinion (*orthe* or *alethes doxa*), he takes the authority of common sense for granted, and in his final answer he calls on hearsay as a self-evident power to determine what is the case. If Socrates wishes to inquire into the nature of knowledge, it is, admittedly, because he has no answer to the question, whereas others seem to know what it is. Rather than being an authority about anything, he has to turn to the *logoi* of others who pretend to know what knowledge is, and to examine by means of the art of cross-examination—that is, Socrates' elenctic art—whether the answers given to the question hold up or are, in terms of his claim to midwifery, mere wind-eggs. Socrates' affirmation that he is not wise and does not know anything, as well as that his art is only an art of midwifery, signifies that knowledge is something to be established in common rather than something that one alone possesses in distinction from others. At issue here is therefore also a conception of wisdom that differs from that claimed by the sages, in that it is produced together with an other, that is, in public (rather than in secret), and through what is agreed upon as a result of conjunction in a dialogue. In the *Theaetetus*, the other to whom Socrates turns in order to find a viable answer to the question of what knowledge is, as we have seen, is the gifted young mathematician Theaetetus. Yet, none of the three answers that Theaetetus provides to the question—namely, that knowledge is perception, that knowledge is true opinion, and that knowledge is true opinion with a definition or an account (*meta logou*)—prove to be valid, and thus the dialogue ends, seemingly without a satisfying conclusion. No Platonic doctrine regarding knowledge is proposed that could pretend to any authority. However, throughout the refutation of these three propositions regarding knowledge, a number of things will have happened or become clear. It will have been established that at least true opinion and the ability to give an account are essential to knowledge. But furthermore, the discussion and refutation of the three propositions regarding knowledge have also implicitly revealed in watermarked fashion, as it were, an art, and hence a knowledge in search of itself, one that is actively *at work* in the examination, and is distinct from all the so-called knowledges under investigation. But there is at least one more positive outcome to the dialogue: having had to surrender all his answers to what knowledge is, all of which were grounded on unsustainable assertions by authorities, Theaetetus has, as Benardete writes, become "as barren as Socrates himself," barren in wisdom, that is.[17] Theaetetus thus becomes the ideal interlocutor for the Stranger, who in the *Sophist* develops a theory regarding discursive truth that is based on the parricide of Parmenidean philosophy whose own authority, in turn, is grounded on prestigious predecessors. Finally, not pretending to know anything since his abandonment of Ionic philosophy (see the *Phaedo*), Socrates, as noted, turns to the speeches of others to inquire into the nature of, on this occasion, knowledge, with Theaetetus recognizing that they have failed in their quest. Theaetetus has thus not only become an unprejudiced interlocutor for the Stranger's take on an ultimate authority over Greek thought, but in his reaching out to others, Socrates can now also reach out to an other who is a complete other—the Stranger—and pass the word on to him.

Theaetetus' first response to Socrates' question is that knowledge is perception. This is a response, as Socrates is quick to point out, that follows from Protagoras' thesis in his book entitled *Truth* that "Man is the measure of all things," a book and a thesis by one of the most important sophists and thus a figure with whom Theaetetus, admittedly, is quite familiar. Both Theaetetus and Protagoras are saying the same thing, Socrates contends. His answer is thus not his own but is based on the authority of one to whom Socrates refers as a wise man, as "someone all-wise [*passophos tis*]" (152c8–9), and who has confided a secret doctrine regarding the meaning of his famous statement to his elite students. Withholding the truth of his doctrine from the crowd of ordinary men to which, according to Socrates, he himself and Theaetetus belong, and in contempt of having whatever in common with these others—if not with others generally—tints his authority even with an authoritarian sway of sorts. The hidden principle of his doctrine, Socrates makes clear, is that "the all [is] motion and there (is) nothing else beyond this" (156a7)—in short, that all is in flux. Consequently, to refute the statement that perception is knowledge requires taking on not only Protagoras' man-measure doctrine but also its underpinnings in the Heraclitean flux theory.¹⁸

Before sketching out a more detailed exhibition of Socrates' rebuttal of Protagoras, it needs to be pointed out that the refutation is not just any refutation. One of the remarkable aspects of the *Theaetetus* is Socrates' consistent effort to construe his adversary as an opponent worthy of the name. From the beginning Protagoras is characterized as a wise man, and even (though certainly not without irony) as "someone all-wise," and as such not likely to proffer nonsense. But there is more. Since the nature of wisdom is at stake in this discussion, the debate concerns, indisputably, the status of the knowledge claimed by all wise men. Of the doctrine that Protagoras confided in secret (*en aporretoi*) to his disciples, leaving all others in the dark, Socrates says that it is "actually a not trivial speech" (152d2)—not a banal, but a remarkable thesis.¹⁹ "It says, 'After all, nothing is one alone by itself [. . .] nothing is one, neither something nor of any sort whatsoever. But all things—it's those we say are the things which are (not addressing them correctly)—come to be from locomotion and motion and mutual mixing; for nothing ever is, but (everything) always becomes'" (152d2–10). If, according to Socrates, Protagoras' thesis is not trivial, it is first because "all the wise," from "the tip-top poets of each kind of poetry, Epicharmus of comedy and Homer of tragedy," to Heraclitus, Empedocles, and Protagoras converge on this speech regarding what is, with the one exception of Parmenides (152e1–5). This assumption that all is in flux makes Protagoras only the last exponent of a powerful tradition that has dominated Greece and that reaches back not only to Homer but to "still more ancient" opinions about the nature of Being (179e4). But if the proposition in question has to be taken seriously, it is also because by stating (though incorrectly, because self-contradictory) that all that *is* is change, or that everything begins with "sweeping being (*pheromenen ousian*)" (179d3)—that is, with perpetually changing Being—Protagoras' thesis reveals itself as the diametrical counterpart of the Parmenidean statement that only Being is, and is at rest, a second current in Greek thought whose main if not sole representative is Parmenides of Elea. This parallelism—as a result of which Protagoras' doctrine appears, however negatively, to be on par with that of Parmenides, whom Socrates has excepted from the whole tradition that Protagoras belongs to—is further highlighted by Socrates' observation that if, according to Protagoras' theory, "there is to be nothing that is one itself by itself, but always to become for something," then "'be' must be removed from everywhere" (157a13–b2). In short, what distinguishes the Protagorean thesis from that of Parmenides is that, rather than Non-being, as in the case of Parmenides, it expels Being from its speech, and does so as radically, as in the case of the former. What we will be interested in hereafter is that both positions, which represent the two tribal approaches to philosophical thought so far in Greece, have their basis in a movement of removal, or forcing out (*exairein*) or away, either Being or Non-being. Both are doctrines that rest on expelling the contrary other of what they assert, change or unchangingness, respectively. Socrates' deeper point in his refutation of Theaetetus' take on knowledge in his first statement—and, through it, of the philosophical underpinnings of Protagoras' man-measure doctrine—is not only that these theories force upon their defenders' contradictory and devastating affirmations but, as we will see, that they radically purge their positions from having a place within themselves for any otherness in any meaningful sense. In this context, it will be important to draw attention to two notions of otherness throughout the dialogue. For the time being, however, let us note that by excepting Parmenides from the tribe that considers everything to be in motion, Socrates not only construes the Protagorean view as representing the exact contrary of Parmenides' position, but he thus provides it with a dignity of its own, on par with that of the latter. Do we not already learn here, in an oblique fashion, a first reason why Socrates will eventually shy away from taking on Parmenides in this dialogue, even though he holds out the prospect of doing so, bequeathing it to the coming Stranger as an even more formidable task than that of taking Protagoras apart? Unquestionably, the contrast with Parmenides is instrumental to establishing that the flux theory is to be taken seriously, and to justifying its lengthy and complex refutation in the dialogue.[20] Thus, this contrast must be maintained throughout the process of refuting Protagoras. However, by establishing a reverse symmetry between the two figures, Socrates has also made Parmenides an easy target of Protagorean criticism. In Socrates' words, "if one stops something in one's speech [as Parmenides does with Being], whoever does (makes) it is easily refutable" (157b8–9). To do justice to Parmenides, even though he too is to be impugned, requires a shift of perspective. Desiring to bring his examination of knowledge to a close, Socrates therefore has to defer this task of examining Parmenides to the Stranger. Let me draw attention to the following as well: by excepting Parmenides from the venerable tribe of the streamers, the former is, in this very move, construed as the binary opposite other with respect to this tradition. Yet, even though Socrates acknowledges that Parmenides must be taken to trial as well, is his gesture of refraining from a parallel examination of the latter not, paradoxically, his way (at this moment) of recognizing otherness in a strong sense, as well as an implicit anticipation of the significance that the Stranger attributes in the *Sophist* to the category in question?

In any event, Protagoras, having been raised to a level of recognition comparable to that of Parmenides, were it only for the sake of justifying the debate of his theory, must consequently be counted among the "dreadfully canny and wise" (154d10), or among those qualified as "dreadful men" (164d4)—that is, luminaries such as Homer, above all. When Socrates wonders: "Who, then, would still be capable, should he dispute against so large an army and so great a general as Homer, of not proving himself to be ridiculous?" (153a1–3), it is made clear that challenging Protagoras' authority is a formidable task, one that requires challenging basically all of Greek thought up to that point, literally and philosophically, with the exception, of course, of Parmenides' philosophy—in short, a task that comes with the risk of making oneself look like a fool.[21] The risk that Socrates runs here, by taking issue with the Athenian past from Homer to the more contemporary Protagoras—the first installment in the battle against all handed-down authority that the Stranger concludes by confronting Parmenides in the *Sophist*, and the sacredness of the law in the *Statesman*—is a risk that, as we will see, is not only worth taking but inevitable if certain questions are to find satisfactory answers.

I wish to pause here for a moment, and ponder Socrates' contention that the homo mensura formula is not a trivial matter, not only because his exposition of the complexities of the flux theory that underpins it seem to betray a great respect for it but also because he provides protection for it at, in Ronald M. Polansky's diagnosis, a "very vulnerable spot."[22] This has erroneously been construed by some as Plato's endorsement of the Protagorean formula. It is true that Socrates unfolds Protagoras' conception in great detail, drawing out its many implications, and by ventriloquizing the dead Protagoras (165e8–168c2), he even lets him come to his own defense.[23] If the refutation of Theaetetus' first definition of knowledge is to be adequate, it requires a full exposition of Heraclites' theory that subtends Protagoras' tale (*mythos*) (156c5). However, the exposition of the full array of the implications of the theory in question is in no way to be confused with its endorsement.

But there is more at stake here. The problematic of memory—called upon to argue that what one has perceived, and what one remembers, can also, when one closes one's eyes, no longer be known because it is no longer seen—serves Socrates to conclude that it is impossible that perception and knowledge are identical. They must be different (*allos*), he avers.

But at this same moment he also makes Theaetetus aware that they have arrived at this conclusion "in the contentious way of contradiction [. . .] gain[ing] an agreement in light of agreements about words (names)," and while professing wisdom and claiming to be philosophers, behaved exactly the same way as the professional disputants or "dreadful men," without accomplishing anything except a victory through mere words (164c8–d4).[24] If at this juncture Socrates excludes all sophistic or eristic refutation of the thesis of the identity of perception and knowledge, it is because in such refutation "the Protagorean myth [also gets] lost and perishe[s]," as well as because of Theaetetus' assertion that perception and knowledge are the same (164d12). The thoughtful nature of Protagoras' formula requires more respect. It deserves to be taken seriously as a thesis, and to be refuted on philosophical grounds. Yet since "the father of the other myth [*pater tou heterou mythou*]," that is, of the secret myth that links the homo mensura formula to the flux theory and beyond it to the doctrine of the initiated, is no longer alive and cannot himself come to its defense, the task incumbent on the philosopher is to come to the assistance of his opponent "for the sake of the just [*tou dikaiou heneka*]" (164e2–8).[25] However much irony goes into Socrates' defense of Protagoras' philosophical assumptions, it is noteworthy that the respect he shows the latter takes place in the name of justice. The philosophical approach to an opponent is intimately tied up with such respect. Coming to his assistance by strengthening his doctrine in his absence is the philosophical way of doing justice to him or her. In other words, the systematic reconstruction of Protagoras' thesis, with all its ramifications, is in no way an endorsement of the thesis, but merely the respect shown to an opponent who is to be philosophically refuted. But Protagoras, furthermore, is not just any opponent, but one whom Socrates recognizes as having rendered an indisputable service to clearing the way of philosophy by already fearlessly breaking up inveterate beliefs and opinions, even though this was done only in a negative fashion. For this, Protagoras deserves recognition.[26] Philosophy, in distinction from eristic sophistry, pays tribute to the otherness of an other by reconstructing the full complexity of his or her adversary position before all refutation, and renders honor to such otherness through the refutation itself. As opposed to eristics—that is, verbal disputation exclusively intent on refuting the opponent—the Socratic elenchus or cross-examination is a kind of refutation in view of a mutual agreement that maintains respect throughout for the other.[27]

In response to the question of what knowledge is, Theaetetus held that knowledge and perception are the same. With an eye on what will interest me in the following, I wish to point out that during the refutation of this statement, Socrates rephrases the issue under examination at one point by asking "whether knowledge and perception are after all the same or other [*tauton e heteron*]" (163a9–10). In the process of refuting the statement, he concludes that "one must say each of the two (is) different [*allo*]" (164b12).[28] Knowledge and perception are thus recognized as different, each one being something else, but are they, therefore, *other* (*heteron*) with respect to one another? Before pursuing this issue any further, let us heed the fact that Socrates' query not only introduces the difference between the same and the other, but also, as should already be evident, makes what I hold to be a crucial distinction between two kinds of otherness: otherness in the sense of *allos*, and otherness in the sense of *heteros*, a distinction to which I wish to pay attention in the following. To my knowledge, this distinction has drawn little interest in Plato scholarship, but putting aside the fact that the ancients did not always rigorously observe conceptual distinctions—which, rather than for stylistic reasons, might in this case have been furthermore encouraged by the frequent synonymous use of the terms in ordinary language—I believe that *allos* and *heteros* are generally operative as distinct terms in the *Theaetetus*. Furthermore, I am of the opinion that Protagoras, as he is presented by Socrates, makes a sophisticated rhetorical use of these notions, making *heteros* (which his system of thought rejects) not only into a foil against which his universe of *alloi* comes into full view, but also makes a strategic use of *heteros* to be able to conceive of *alloi* as having, in a strict sense, no opposites.

So, let us restate with Protagoras that, apart from motion and its infinite distinct manifestations—the manifold *alloi*—there is nothing other beyond it, and since nothing is ever itself by itself, nothing can for this reason ever be determined as something other (*auto heteron ti*) (153e1) than movement. Since "Being" would represent something stable, "'be' must be removed from everywhere" (157b1–2) in order for there to "be" infinite distinctness and nothing whatsoever identical to itself, but everything everywhere and at all times "other," and "other" than itself. Up to this point, when speaking of the consequences of Protagoras' thesis that the beginning of everything is motion, Socrates has consistently characterized the status of anything that is, or rather, anything that becomes distinct from another thing, and hence is "other," by means of the Greek term *allos*, whereas the something other distinct from motion and the infinite mass of *alloi* generated by it is referred to by means of the word *heteros*. For Protagoras, Socrates suggests, only others in the sense of *alloi* are conceivable, and anything different (*heteros*) from them is out of the question.

According to the dictionary, *allos* means "*another, i.e. one besides* what has been mentioned"; frequently it is used "with another of its own cases" as, for example, "*one man* says *one thing, one another.*" Only infrequently, and even then in the form of *alloios*, it means "of another sort, different," or "otherwise."[29] The conjunction *alla* or *all'*, signifying *but* or *except*, limiting or opposing words or sentences, provides perhaps the best indication of the highly general sense of the word *allos*. It refers to another among indistinct others, certainly others of the same kind, but still other in some other way—namely, different above all in a numerical sense. It is true that in ancient texts, including those of Plato, the two Greek words for other, *allos* and *heteros*, are often used without distinction, sometimes as simple synonyms, similar to what obtains of the English "else" and "other." It is even the case that Plato, for merely linguistic eloquence, may occasionally sacrifice the conceptual distinction between both concepts. But here in the *Theaetetus*, I contend, the two terms designate strictly distinct concepts of how to think what is other, as a consequence of which the "logic" that regulates their distinctive use must be observed in interpreting the passages in which the terms appear. A specific case in point is the introduction of the crucial problematic of the soul (184d4), where Plato raises the question of what the soul explores all by itself, independently of the perceptions of the senses and without any particular *organa* of its own. Here, the difference between the two notions of otherness operative in various contexts of the dialogue springs into view. The soul's concern is with what different perceptions such as hearing and seeing—that is, two unexchangeable and thus entirely distinct kinds of perceptions—each of a pair, have in common. "[T]hink[ing] something about both (*peri amphoteron dianoeisthai*)" (185a5) and, furthermore, already in terms of what later in the *Sophist* will be called *genera* (namely, Being and Non-being, Similarity and Non-Similarity), Socrates asks Theaetetus whether "each of the two (is) [not also] other than each of the two, but the same as itself?" (185a12–13). The term for "other" consistently used here is *heteros*, a term that specifically designates a modality of being of a pair of "things," according to which what is other is "the same as itself [*heautoi de tauton*]." "Other," in binary distinctness from the "same," is here clearly of the order of what I provisionally call a "categorial" determination of all things, and thus enjoys a status that contrasts with that of *allos*, or uniform otherness.

Allos as other, in a very general sense of "another" or "elsewise," refers to something that is different *simpliciter* or in an indifferent way, and must be distinguished from *heteros*, which designates a difference in relation to something other that is not exterior and indifferent to it, and for this reason is a specific or determined other, an other that differs from such-and-such another thing and stands in a binary relation of contrast or opposition to it. *Heteros* is an other of another kind. It is meant to be the different part of a binary. Yet, as already intimated, an other of this kind would in the case of the theory of movement be altogether other (*holos heteron*) (158e8–12) than movement—namely, it would be of the order of rest, something declared impossible by the theory in question. In short, for Protagoras, anything that differs from difference *simpliciter* is *heteros*, understood in the sense of being entirely beyond the manifold of the *alloi*, and for this very reason is inconceivable as such. Does this then mean that when Protagoras holds that there is nothing beyond motion, the flux theory makes it impossible to think otherness otherwise than elsewise? Is it thus a theory that entirely evacuates otherness as determined, qualified, non-indifferent difference—that is, as *heteros*—from its discourse? Is Protagoras' theory, as represented by Socrates up to this point, a theory of infinite "otherness" that, paradoxically, eliminates otherness in a strong sense from otherness as being nothing but what I will call from here on "elseness"? By otherness in a strong sense, I refer not to what Protagoras calls the entirely other because beyond motion, but to otherness as constituted by qualitative difference in distinction from the difference of *allos*, which denotes only the unspecified divergence of something else.

While explaining, in the course of the refutation of the first definition of knowledge, how Protagoras construes perception and what is perceived, Socrates helps his respondent understand the hidden-away truth of Protagoras' tale that Man is the measure of all things: since everything begins for Protagoras with motion, which is of two infinite kinds, locomotion (*phora*) and alteration (*alloiosis*), "and there (is) nothing else beyond this [*allo para touto ouden*]" (156a7), nothing is ever "alone by itself [*auto kath'hauto*]" (153e7) or "equal to itself" (155a5). Consequently, there is nothing that could ever be determined as something other (*heteron*) (153e1) besides movement. Otherwise, it would have an assigned place in which it would enjoy a certain stability of sameness, rather than becoming in a process of becoming. But such an entirely other would also lack all relation to that from which it supposedly differs. In fact, wholly other, such an other would no longer differ from anything else. Sharing nothing, and without relations, it would be meaningless in relation to the manifold elses in a universe in flux. But does the way the *allos* is conceived not run the same risk as such a wholly other? As difference *simpliciter*, is it not also without any relation to any other else which, in turn, does not possess any difference of its own? How, then, bring to bear upon a something else the elsewiseness that it as such signifies, and how to make this relation self-constitutive, and at the same time protect it from the fate that a wholly other suffers at the Protagorean hand? It is here that Protagoras' theory of the double nature of movement comes in, whose doubleness not only secures its sweeping universality but also serves to prevent the *alloi* from losing all relation of difference to one another and, as a result, becoming as nonsensical as a wholly other.

According to Protagoras' secret doctrine, which Socrates confides to Theaetetus, Motion not only consists of two species, but one of them has the power to affect, the other to be affected—for example, perception and what is perceived. Perception arises at the very moment something is perceived, and the perceivable is engendered at the moment there is perception. Now, "out of the association and rubbing of these against one another, there come to be offspring [*allele gignetai*], infinite in multitude but twins (double)—that which (is) perceived and that which (is) perception—which (the latter) (is) always falling out together with and (is) getting generated with that which (is) perceived" (156a10–b4). In other words, nothing is ever itself by itself, including that which affects and that which is affected (which are what they are only insofar as they affect something else, and are affected respectively by such a thing), but always only the result of "the association [of both] with one another [*allela homiliai*]" by which "all things become and become of all sorts" (157a3–4). Rather than ever being determined in and by themselves, all things, then, including the things that generate them, "always [only] become for something [. . . *alla tini aei gignethai*]" (157b1).[30] In short, since the offspring, generated through the two species of motion in the interaction of perception and the perceived, are always a pair, a pair of twins, each one of them is inextricably intertwined with its "other," thus providing each one with a minimal difference sufficient to be a something else or a someone else. The twin-structure of all things thus generated prevents the elses from lacking all relation to something else (and thus from being, like the entirely other, without any relation, and as a result nothing at all), but does not for that reason cause them to become others in the specific sense of *heteroi*, which recognizes both a qualitative difference and a sameness between others.

What so far has become manifest about Protagoras' conception of movement, and the exclusion of something entirely other for the benefit of elseness in the sense of unspecified difference, is predicated on the assumption of the identity of being and seeming—in short, on the postulate that perception is "without falsehood inasmuch as it is knowledge" (152c6). But since perception is not infallible, as dreams and hallucinations tend to show—indeed, "none of the things which appears" (158a3–4) through them have any being whatsoever—what kind of speech, Socrates asks, is then left (*tis . . . leipetai logos*) (158a6) for someone who, like Protagoras, wishes to assert that the negative evidence notwithstanding, knowledge is perception, and that what is perceived "is" also for the one to whom something appears, and is thus true? Let me note that Socrates poses this question only after having first acknowledged the genuinely perplexing difficulty of establishing firm criteria for the difference between waking and dreaming, or of showing evidence on the basis of which hallucinatory perceptions could be distinguished from normal ones, as a result of which "our soul insists that whatever its opinions are at the moment cannot be more certainly true" (158d4–5).[31] But is it not striking that once the Protagoreans are confronted with cases that put the asserted infallibility of perception into question, rather than responding directly, they arrogate to themselves immediately the role of the questioner?[32] In demanding that their opponents, who wondered what kind of speech is left to them, themselves answer their own question, they make the questioners speak for them as their surrogates. Is it not especially remarkable that, at the same time, when asked to account for the difference between true and false perceptions, they—or, rather, Socrates and Theaetetus, who substitute for them—are led to resort to the notion previously expelled, the notion of "whatever is altogether other [*heteron ei pantapasin*]" or "wholly other [*holos heteron*]" (158e8–12), by making anyone admit that what is wholly other cannot, for logical reasons, have anything in common with that from which it differs?[33] What reason compels the Protagoreans to return to the question of the other after having already dismissed it? Since the aim of the regression to the problematic of otherness is the rejection of anything stable, and since "Being" to begin with is that which is subtracted from all change, the return to the problematic of difference (in order to reject it) intends to eliminate all measure for distinguishing between the truth or falsehood of perceptions so as to be able to uphold that all of them *are* for the one who perceives them. No doubt, but is it that simple? After all, the speech that is left after it has been recognized that perceptions can be wrong is a speech delegated to others (Socrates and Theaetetus) who, in their (the Protagoreans') name, seek to discourse on elseness, and can do so only by introducing in their speech the category of thought and speech that is Otherness.

As a consequence of their assertion that what is entirely different or other cannot "have in any respect any power the same as the other" (158e9–10), the Protagoreans declare that it cannot be similar to it but, of necessity, must be dissimilar.[34] In lines 159a7–10, it is said that if the becoming similar of something to something else amounts to its becoming the same (*homoioumenon*) as that to which it is compared, it necessarily follows that when it becomes dissimilar it becomes other than it, not in the sense of elseness but of otherness (*heteros*).[35] Through Socrates' voice, the Protagoreans at this moment recall not only that they had previously established that the things that affect are in number as infinite as the things affected, but also that if one of these mingles with others (*allo alloi summeignumenon*), "it will not generate the same things but others [*ou tauta all'hetera genesei*] if it then mingles with something else" (159a16–17). In what sense is one to understand *hetera* here? From the context one must conclude that "others," having "the same things" as a correlate, rather than meaning entirely others, cannot but signify distinct and qualitative others. Could it be that the substitution here of *heteros* for *allos* is only for stylistic reasons? Had Plato kept the more philosophically cogent choice of word, in this particular case *allos*, he would have had to say that "*ou tauta all'alla genesei*," which linguistically sounds quite awkward.[36] But if the choice of the term *heteros* is intentional, revealing an almost inconspicuous shift in emphasis, what are the consequences? Does Socrates wish to make the Protagoreans admit something by speaking of otherness where they were expected to refer to elseness? Indisputably, this shift is in no way an endorsement of the altogether or wholly other, since the flux theory has no place for such an other to begin with. But by making this change in terminology, are the Protagoreans not forced, while arguing for a universe of exclusive elseness, to admit that to speak about it they must perfunctorily speak about it by means of categories that "subvert" their claim? Let us remind ourselves also at this juncture that, as Socrates suggests, for the Protagorean universe of motion another language (*allen phonen*) (183b3–4) would be required from which the verb and the word "being" has been removed, and with it everything in language that puts a stop to things in motion. For this universe of things in relentless flux there is only one kind of difference, for which I have coined here the term "elseness," a difference that has not only expelled all otherness but that is also constituted by "elses" that defy their own sameness.[37] In this case, and as regards the notion of otherness in a determined sense, the point is that rejecting the categories constitutive of speech amounts to surrendering speech within speech.

When, subsequent to the statement "that if something else mingles with something else, it will not generate the same things but others [*all' hetera*] if it then mingles with something else" (159a15–17), a sick Socrates is said to be dissimilar and other than the healthy one, it is in order to stress the radical difference between both.[38] They are *hetera* with respect to one another. The same is valid as well for the difference between the one who wakes and the one who sleeps. They do not resemble each other, and have nothing in common—they are entirely different, according to the Protagoreans. But are they not pairs or twins who, notwithstanding their reciprocal otherness, relate to one another insofar as they are twins, with the result that their respective otherness becomes determined by the fact that they are paired? The sick Socrates is not someone else, but someone other, in relation to the healthy one. The twinlike structure that had to be imposed on the elses, so as to ward off the threat to their intelligibility resulting from their complete isolation from one another, is thus revealed to be inconceivable without the category of otherness. And, at the same time, the Protagoreans are compelled to accept, unawares, that one can speak of elseness only through the category of Otherness.

The distinction between the two Socrateses, who are a pair of others rather than two elses, once again requires our attention. Each one of them in turn, when drinking wine for example, "generate[s], when paired, other things, about the tongue a perception of bitterness, and about the wine a bitterness coming to be and being born(e)" (159e2–4). In conformity with the theory that knowledge is perception, everything that these two different Socrateses produce in being affected, and everything produced by that which affects them, does not only therefore bring forth otherness in the sense of determined otherness but also things that could under no other circumstances ever be the same. It is at this point that Socrates makes the following remarkable statement:

> And just as I shall never become in just this way if I'm perceiving anything else—for a different perception is of the different, and it makes the perceiver a different sort and different—so that which affects me shall never generate the same and become of the same sort if it comes together with a different thing. For if it generates a different thing from a different thing, it will become a different sort. (159e7–160a5)[39]

If these lines are remarkable, it is above all because of the unexpected shift in language and conceptuality. Where one was expecting a conclusion emphasizing otherness or *heteros*, the massive usage of *allos* in the passage marks a return to the Protagorean equalizing problematics of numerical otherness. If this is so, it is because after the rejection of the notion of an altogether other, in this segment of the Protagorean argument the category of *heteros*—and thus the temporary acknowledgment of a determined or qualified other—has served to prevent elseness from being subject to the same fate as the wholly other. More specifically, by establishing the radical non-sameness of the two instances of Socrates, showing that both of these entirely different men also engender things that in each case are different from Socrates as an agent and that which affects him, otherness in the sense of *heteros* has unwittingly helped to secure elseness, free of inherent sameness, from relapsing into nonsense. Though elseness excludes any sameness whatsoever, because of the twin-structure of the elses that make up the universe in permanent flux, one remains nevertheless always "other" with respect to something else, and to itself.[40]

I return to the distinction between *allos* and *heteros*, elseness and otherness, in order to briefly reflect on the kind of relation involved in these two notions of difference. Both notions are notions of a relation to something different from something else, and in both cases the relata are of a different nature, as is the modality of that relation. The Protagorean argument regarding something wholly or altogether other, apart from its impossibility in a world in flux, proceeded on the assumption that such an other has no relation whatsoever to anything else. Of the order of a substance exclusively relating to itself, it is in its very sameness sufficient to itself. However, in its semantic distinction from *allos*, as we have seen, *heteros* designates an otherness due to a specific and determined nature of its correlate. As a result, the kind of relation it involves is one of opposition, contrast, contrariness, and so forth, a relation that by this very reason is marked by a certain necessity: for example, what stands in a relation of opposition is inevitably other. This, however, is not the case with elseness. What is elsewise, or *allos*, has no necessary relation to what it is distinguished from. It does not refer to a specific "other" that would shape its relation to itself. What is else than something else is else without any particular specificity of what it differs from. Anything else stands in relation to something else, but is only one among others, numerically different from it. It would, then, follow that the relation of something to something else is not only contingent but also undetermined, undifferentiated, formless, or inchoate. And, at first glance, this would seem to be perfectly adequate to the way all things in flux relate to one another.

But let us take into consideration an additional consequence, one that follows from the postulation that a healthy and a sick Socrates are two entirely different men, both in terms of how they experience something like wine and in terms of the wine itself that causes their experience. Since, as the Protagoreans ascertain, becoming takes place in the interaction of one being affected by a thing that affects one, with the result that the thing that affects one makes one always different and never the same, becoming implies that the being which acts (perceives) and the object that affects (the perceived) are bound together with necessity. For the Protagoreans, there is never one or the other alone, but both are always given in a pair and are always intrinsically intertwined to such a degree, indeed, that they never relate solely to themselves. One is or becomes always only for the other; never is one the same—that is, in distinction from, outside of, severed, as it were, from the pair. And the same obtains for the other: it is, or becomes always only for the one whom it affects, never for itself alone. And so, if nothing ever becomes itself, then, as Socrates puts it, "the only thing left is for us to be for one another (*allelois*) if we are, or if we become, to become for one another" (160b5–6). This essential linkage (*sundedesthai*) of the perceiver to the other (the object of perception) and vice versa—which, at this point, also provides the strongest reason for the Protagorean thesis that knowledge is perception—makes it obvious that the other is essentially to be understood in terms of the interrelation of the one and the other, the perceiver and what is perceived. Needless to say, in the relation of one with another which grounds relentless becoming, the other is not an entirely or wholly other but, by definition, an other of or for the one with which it is paired together. But precisely because of this togetherness of the one and the other, the latter is never a simple and punctual else anymore. It is an else that is constituted by a dependence on, and simultaneous activation by, another else that is its twin. The one and the other are thus necessarily interlinked in such a manner that none of the members of the pair are ever anything in themselves, because each one becomes this member of the pair only in relation to the other. Rather than a welter of punctual elses without any intelligible patterns, the Protagorean universe of flux, consequently, is made up by an infinitely great number of such pairs or twins of elses that themselves are in constant flux, and which prevent any one of the interrelated members to coagulate into something identically at rest. This conclusion could be reached only by preventing the punctual elses from folding upon themselves, thus becoming selfsame identities, with the ensuing risk of becoming entirely other to themselves with no relation whatsoever among themselves. The pattern of doubleness—pairs, twins—is the Protagorean answer to this risk. In my reading, to counter the possibility of the risk in question, which threatens the theory of flux from the very beginning, a passage through such entirely heterogeneous elses as the healthy and the sick Socrates became necessary. But since in distinction from elseness (*allos*), otherness (*heteros*) is indicative of a specific relation to an other, the recognition of the interrelatedness of one of the twinned elses to the other, and vice versa, is also the inevitable result of Socrates' demand that Protagoras give an account in speech, a speech delegated to Socrates and his interlocutor, for his theory of elseness.

If I have paid so much attention to the problematic of the other, and the difference between *allos* and *heteros*, it is not only because of the topical importance of the distinction. In the context not only of Plato scholarship but also of Plato's crucial role in Western thought, it is also because the concern with otherness in the sense of *heteros* is a concern in the *Theaetetus* that anticipates Plato's new take on the ideas in the *Sophist* where, rather than transcendent intelligibles in some *topos ouranios* as they are often held to be, they are rethought as the "categorial" building blocks of intelligible speech.[41] Even though they are apprehended only by the mind, they are not merely noetic objects of a knowledge that is no longer that of the senses, but in fact form the structure of that knowledge—knowing, judging, opining itself. As Socrates already seems to tell the young mathematician who is only familiar with numerical elses, no speech is possible without them, that is, without these common terms, the "category" of Otherness in particular. In the final refutation in the *Theaetetus*, of the thesis that knowledge is perception, the soul is said to be the "single look [*idea*]" (184d3) in which the corporeal perceptions of the senses converge. It is through the soul and the power of language that we grasp what all these perceptions have in common (*koinon*), such as being (*ousian*) and non-being (*me einai*), sameness (*tauton*) and otherness (*heteron*), numerical oneness or another number (*allon arithmon*), similarity (*homoion*) or lack of it (*anomoion*) (185c9–d1). Socrates thus makes Theaetetus aware of the fact that knowledge cannot consist in *aisthesis* but must be of the order of thinking (*dianoia*) and syllogistic inference. At the same time, by listing these *koina* or common terms, he sketches out a first, rudimentary and undeveloped, outline of the Stranger's doctrine of the "greatest kinds (*megista gene*)," or what the latter also calls *eide*, "kinds" or "looks," without yet distinguishing between all of them or bringing the "greatest" among them into sharp relief, nor, especially, discussing how they relate to one another.[42] In our dialogue, the things in common—being and non-being, sameness and otherness, oneness and plurality, and so forth—are never explicitly referred to as forms, but what are they except intelligible existences or ideas, even though the notion of "idea" is certainly undergoing here a transformation of sorts? Discussing the trilogy, a number of scholars have noted that in the *Sophist* the Stranger takes up and pursues a variety of issues left in abeyance or unsolved in the *Theaetetus*. Myles Burnyeat even speaks of "a division of labor between the *Theaetetus* and the *Sophist*."[43] Indeed, in the latter dialogue the debates about resemblance, the relation of part and whole, and the possibility of false judgments, for example, find more satisfactory resolutions. I add to this list the topic of otherness. In the same way as the other subject matters, the problem of the other itself can find a successful treatment only through the process of a radical critique and transformation of the Parmenidean theory of Being and Non-being, a task to which, as Socrates confesses in the dialogue, he does not rise.

What the refutation of Theaetetus' first response to the question about knowledge has proven is not only that knowledge cannot be perception but also that the theory according to which all things are in motion is not amenable to an epistemology to begin with: to hold that knowledge is perception is not only to identify it with something that is not knowledge, properly speaking, any more than non-knowledge (182e11–12), but that furthermore can never, in conformity with the assumption that all is in flux, be anything in itself. Now, consistent with the insight gained by refuting the first pronouncement—namely, that knowledge must be of the order of thought, and of "whatever the soul has, whenever it alone by itself deals with the things which are" (187a4–6), rather than the order of sensible perception—Theaetetus' next response is that the activity characteristic of the soul is that of representation (*doxazein*). More precisely, he offers that knowledge is true *doxa*, that is, a true representation, opinion, or judgment (*alethes doxa*), and is thus independent of sensation. In addition, he adds, seemingly without being aware of the irony, that should this response not prove to be satisfactory, he would "try to say something else [*allo ti peirasometha legein*]" (187b7–8). In any event, the response that knowledge is true opinion immediately raises the question of false opinion, and of how false opinion is possible. It comes, of course, as no surprise that the difference between both opinions, the true and the false, is expressed by the word *heteron* (187c1–8), since what is true and what is false are clearly different things. But when, in the process of explaining false opinion, Socrates eliminates a number of explications and he and his interlocutor agree, first, that false opinion must be something else than the belief that one knows what one does not know or, second, that it represents something that does not exist (Non-being, in short), false opinion is found to be *allos*

(189b4–6) than what it had seemed to be so far—not something other, but only something else. Before the identification of knowledge with true opinion is not so much dismissed but suspended, and before Theaetetus offers his last response about the nature of knowledge, according to which it is true opinion with an account, a third attempt is therefore made to explain false opinion.[44] Significant, of course, is that this third attempt of explaining false opinion proceeds on the basis of a further deepening of the notion of representation or opinion, which lays the ground for the passage from representation to what happens in thinking when understood as a conversation that the soul has with itself (189e6–190a7). Since this third explication of false opinion involves the problematic of otherness, a closer look at it is warranted. Socrates now proffers that false opinion is a certain kind of else-opining, as Benardete discerningly translates the term *allodoxia*, a term that, in the same way as the soon to be introduced *heterodoxia*, is a nominalized compound of an adjective and a verb.[45] "Else-opining" occurs "whenever someone makes an exchange in his thought of some one of the things which are for something else of the things which are and says it is that" (189c1–3). Else-opining as exchanging in thought one thing for another presupposes, as Socrates and Theaetetus agree, that both things together or in turn must be thought by the soul—in short, that both must be—otherwise one could not be taken for or as the other. Otherness is thus opined with respect to something that has being, rather than with respect to Non-being, and already implies, as will be seen, Other-being, a thought that will only be entirely fleshed out in the *Sophist*.[46]

What is noteworthy here is that already, early in the process of repudiating the thesis that false opining is the result of taking something for something else, on the grounds that in the soul's dialogue with itself it is strictly impossible to take one thing present to the soul for another thing that is equally present to it—a repudiation that involves the failures to explain false opinion through what Socrates qualifies as a *poros* (191a8) in the face of dilemmas such as the paradigms of the waxen block and the aviary—Socrates is soon led to replace the term "else-opining" (*allodoxia*) with what Benardete renders as "other-opining" (*heterodoxia*) (193c9). Is this simply an irrelevant substitution suggesting, as some have proposed, "that Plato considers '*heterodoxia*' only another way of saying '*allodoxia*'?"[47] From what we have seen so far about Plato's use of *allos* and *heteros* in the dialogue, this is unlikely. In my reading, the two terms designate two clearly distinct notions of otherness. But this does not mean that it is easy to substantiate the point, which may also require taking some risks. At any rate, careful attention to what leads up to the replacement of one term by the other is warranted.

Is it not notable that Socrates, when expanding on *allodoxia*, immediately recasts what Theaetetus believes to be possible—namely, the exchange in thought of "some one of the things which are for something else [*allo*] of the things which are and says it is that" (189c1–3), which is held to result in false opinion—in terms of an exchange of one specific and determined thing for another (*heteron de anth'heterou*) (189c4)?[48] Why is it necessary to reformulate the interchange that is supposedly at the heart of false opinion in this way? In his commentary on Socrates' inquiry into false opinion, Martin Heidegger emphasizes the character of *amphotera* (188b5–6) or "bothness" in opinion as a knowing of something as something.[49] As we have already seen, for one thing to be able to be exchanged for the other, opinion requires that both things which are to be exchanged be present in thought as things that are. Heidegger comments: "The object to which a view relates is actually twofold: something (the one), which is taken for something else."[50] Now, to exchange in opinion one thing with another, thus knowing something *as* something, is to know it *as* another. Heidegger avers: "In Greek terms: to the object of *doxa* there belongs *heteron—heteron*."[51] To take one of two things that are present in the soul for the other is not to take it for something else, but for something *heteros*—that is, something other in a specific sense.[52] It comes, therefore, also as no surprise that the examples in the *Theaetetus* that are evoked in this context are the beautiful and the ugly, the just and the unjust, the ox and the horse—that is, things that stand in a relation of opposition to one another or belong to different well-determined species. *Allodoxein*, Theaetetus said, would consist in setting down in thought, as a conversation of the soul with itself, "something other as an other and not as that (i.e., other) [*heteron ti hos heteron kai me hos ekeino*]" (189d10–12). No doubt, if the other for which a thing is taken in thought were just something else, a mere *allos*, exchanging it for the other might be possible but would also be inconsequential. *Allodoxia*, then, would be merely a concern with something else that has no relation to what it is supposedly exchanged for. But as Socrates is quick to point out, in the case of specific and contrary things or things that belong to specific species, the soul could never agree that one is the other, thus also excluding the possibility that the exchange in question could be the explanation of false opinion. With this, the idea that false representation could consist in mistaking or confusing one thing for another becomes highly questionable. So why did Plato, after the introduction of else-opining, replace *allodoxia* with *heterodoxia*, other-opining? Else-opining, I hold, is inconsequential, since what is exchanged in such opining are just things that are elsewise. By contrast, in the case of *heterodoxia*, things are other with respect to one another in a strong sense, and one cannot be taken for the other if this other does not have a distinct identity, like, for example, holding Socrates to be Theaetetus or vice versa. By turning after the introduction of the term *allodoxia* immediately to *heterodoxia*, Plato makes it unmistakably clear that something is other only if it is not just something else, something that is merely otherwise, but is determined in itself by belonging to one species as opposed to another, by having a distinct mark as a member of a species, or by standing in a relation of opposition to another equally determined thing.[53] In sum, *allodoxia*, opining as exchanging and taking one thing as another, has in essence to be *heterodoxia*.

Very briefly, I note that Theaetetus, after the failure of his second explanation of what knowledge is, offers a third definition according to which knowledge is a representation or opinion with an account. As we learn in the course of Socrates' refutation of this last wind-egg to which the young man gives birth, even though the notion of an account is not satisfactorily explained, there can be no knowledge without right belief and a *logos*. Although the problematic of Otherness is not broached again on this occasion, I contend that after the introduction of the notion of *doxa*, the setting is in place within which, in the *Sophist*, the question of Otherness can make a forceful return. If *doxa* is understood as distinct from mere apprehension as perception, and instead as belonging to the soul's dialogue with itself and, furthermore, consisting of a representation with an explanation in a process of going through something in view of something—thus indicative of a "logical" dimension of *doxa*—the concept of *logos* in the sense of speech and account, as it is unfolded in the next dialogue, is fully prepared.

At this juncture, let us remind ourselves that in the process of being refuted, Protagoras is referred to as a "father [*pater*]" (164e2)—the father of the doctrine or tale that man is the measure of all that is and, backed up by the whole tradition reaching back to Homer and beyond, that nothing is ever in itself, and what appears to one *is* for the perceiver, and therefore is inexorably what *is*. As a consequence, there is nothing such as falsehood, but only multiple "truths." Protagoras is also referred to as a father because, assuming he were still alive, he would come to the assistance of the thesis he generated every time it comes under attack. As said, Protagoras shares this narrative, or mythic account, with the dominant "tribe [*phulon*]" (160d8) of all the wise men in Greece up to then.⁵⁴ In passing, I wonder about the connection between this tribal nature of much of Greek thought on the one hand and, on the other hand, the designation of one of its major protagonists as a father. If there is a tribal and nativist dimension in this particular current of Greek thought, does this also entrust it with some sort of family structure, with the result that fathers father their doctrines like offspring? Is there also a deeper interrelation between a philosophy that emphasizes becoming and infinite engendering, at the exclusion of all permanence or rest, and the designation of the author of such a geneticist theory as a father? For the time being, let me say only that if Protagoras is called a father, it is because his statement that man is the measure of all things—a statement grounded on the philosophical assumption that all is in flux, and that there is no such thing as Being—is at the origin of much of the thought, including sophism, for example, in contemporary Greece. But since as a father figure Protagoras demands respect, and since no one else is willing to take the field, Socrates comes to the assistance of his orphaned thesis and, in the interim, makes himself, as we have seen, an advocate of it before finally subjecting it to a ruthless rebuttal. In his stead Socrates furnishes, as Monique Dixsaut puts it, "an apology of Protagoras."⁵⁵ And, indeed, the defense of his thesis is thorough to the point that some scholars have contended that he identifies with it. Yet, even though the expression does not occur in this context—Theodorus characterizes Socrates' relentless and unsparing critique only as too much of a "running down [*katatheomen*]" of his "comrade" (171c9)—is Socrates' refutation of Protagoras after his apology not also a parricide (in disguise, at least) of the father of one of the major philosophical strains in contemporary Greece? Is the apology of Protagoras in the dialogue not precisely a way of bringing Protagoras to admit that his own doctrine, when buttressed by way of a thorough exposition, is paradoxically forced to acknowledge the exact contrary of what it teaches, and thus to destroy itself by its own hands? Would this parricide of Protagoras by means of an apology not be therefore an administered suicide of sorts?

As we have already seen, Socrates excepts Parmenides from the venerable tradition of wise men for whom everything is in flux, as the one and sole philosopher who, with his thesis that only Being can be spoken about and that Non-being cannot be thought or said, inaugurated the other of the two strains in Greek thought. In our dialogue, Socrates refers to Protagoras' doctrine as only a tale, a qualification that has all the more weight since Homer is alleged to be the great "general" of the doctrine in question (153a2). Parmenides is excepted from this tradition, but as we will see, in the *Sophist* the Stranger qualifies Parmenides' doctrine in these very same terms as well, the implication being that with the Stranger, Plato confronts the whole of Greek thought so far, and opposes to it a conception of philosophy that is no longer narrative, that is also no longer native. The *Theaetetus*, in which Plato has Socrates undertake a parricide of sorts of one of the native fathers of Greek philosophy, before he invites a stranger in both the *Sophist* and the *Statesman* to complete the task, is thus the prelude for a process in which the whole of the philosophical tradition is taken on, and with it, all its figures in Greece. The fundamental gesture of this examination consists in putting the native nature of each doctrine, as well as the status of their protagonists as wise men and leaders of sects with their initiates, radically into question. Philosophical teaching and learning, rather than being an initiation into an esoteric doctrine, is to become from now on a process that, without authorities and no longer one-directional, takes place together. But what guarantees that, even if accomplished together, such togetherness and the philosophy it generates is not tribal in turn, and native once more? It is here that the Stranger comes in, the *xenos*, whose presence in the *Sophist* reveals that Greek thought has opened within itself a place for the foreigner and, in a way, for the other. He is not only in charge of dismantling the second tribal current of Greek philosophical thought but also of demonstrating that the transgression of all tribal and native approaches to philosophy will not itself be tribal.

In a way not unlike Socrates' contention that Protagoras' homo mensura theory lies at the core of sophist doctrines and practices, the Stranger in the *Sophist* successfully shows that Parmenides' assertion that one cannot speak of Non-being is, in a similar fashion, at the heart of sophism's claim that there is no un-truth, and that therefore everything goes.[56] But if Parmenides' theory lends itself also to a sophist appropriation, what, then, prevents Socrates in the *Theaetetus* from challenging the other father figure of Greek thought? And why does Plato, in the dialogue of the following day, have to bring in and encourage a stranger to finish the job of putting all of Greek thought into question by also dismantling Parmenides' philosophy? The answer to this question is all the more urgent since, before directing a final deathblow at Theaetetus' statement that perception is knowledge through a refutation of the Heraclitean flux theory, Socrates not only anticipates the necessity to also confront the complementary Parmenidean doctrine that all is at rest but explicitly promises such a debate, though it is only in the *Sophist* that this task will be performed by the Stranger, rather than by Socrates himself.

Before reflecting on the reasons offered by Socrates himself for the delay, as well as for his reluctance to kill father Parmenides in turn, let us first see how he sets up the need for a radical critique of this additional strain of Greek thought. After having submitted to Theodorus that the problem they have taken on, namely that everything is in motion and nothing is at rest, stretches "from the ancients who were concealing it from the many with poetry," to the sophistically trained orators in fifth- and fourth-century Greece who, aware of Protagoras' secret doctrine, openly proclaimed that all is in flux so as to appear even wiser to the shoemakers, Socrates, as if he only just now remembered, adds: "But I almost forgot, Theodorus, that different people, on the other hand, declared the contrary to this—'As the sort that is immoveable, there is "to be" as the name for the all'—and all the different things that the Melissuses and Parmenideses in opposing all of them insist on, that all things are one and it is at rest in itself without a place in which it moves" (180d10–e5). If Socrates pretends that he almost forgot that, apart from the ancients in the east of Greece, in Ionia, there is also a school, but this time in the West, in Elea, of implacable foes of change, it is perhaps just because of the overwhelming presence of the flux theory in the history of Greek thought. But his admission of having almost forgotten that there is a second native current in Greek philosophical thought may in itself also already be an indication of his final unwillingness to take on Parmenides' doctrine directly. If it slipped his mind, could this not be because of some innermost reluctance to critically engage the thinker? Undoubtedly, like Protagoras' thought, Parmenides' doctrine represents an extreme position, but it is also distinguished from the former, first, in that it does not contain an esoteric doctrine. Indeed, from the *Parmenides* we learn that Zeno's treaty, which was written in order to defend his master's proposition that all is One by stating in reverse that it is impossible that things should be a plurality, has not therefore the purpose of hiding the true nature of Parmenides' truth from the public.[57] The authority of Parmenides' doctrine is of another caliber and order than that of Protagoras. But there is another reason at the bottom of Socrates' hesitation that is revealed by his apparent forgetting, and which shows that, in spite of the fact that one strain of thought contends that all is in flux and the other that all is at rest, the two strains or tribes of philosophical thought in Greece are not simply symmetrical: the proponents of rest, for example, cannot claim to have ancient counterparts as do the flux theorists.[58] Precisely because of this impossibility of retracing his thought back to ancient sources and traditions, Parmenides' thought is considerably more refractory than that of Protagoras. Even though Parmenides' thesis is mythic, he stands alone, and Socrates refers to him as the one Parmenides, who is thus set apart within the tradition from the tradition itself. In a way, there is already a break in Parmenides with the past, a significant progress, as it were, that therefore does not allow for his thought to be treated the same way as Socrates treats Protagoras' thought.

By evoking Parmenides' extreme position just before proceeding to the final refutation of the statement that knowledge is perception, Socrates draws Theodorus' attention to the fact that both of them "have, without being aware of it, fallen into the middle [*meson*] of both, and unless we somehow manage to defend ourselves and escape, we'll pay the penalty, as those do in gymnasia who play at tug-of-war, whenever they are seized by both sides and dragged in contrary directions" (180e6–181a4). If Socrates finds himself in a tug of war between both schools of thought—one of which asserts that all is in flux, while the other has it that all is at rest—it is because he is still of the opinion that they are alternatives, and that one would have to choose one of the parties over the other. In other words, he does not yet realize, as does the Stranger in the *Sophist*, that scrutinizing both extreme parties may open a new space for thought that, in a way, would genuinely be in the middle.[59] Indeed, it is only with the rebuttal of Parmenides' doctrine regarding Non-being, for which Socrates is not yet ready, that such a middle position can truly be brought into view. From Parmenides' take on Being as rest, it follows that everything of the constantly changing world of appearances is of the order of Non-being. Only by rejecting the uncompromising distinction of Being and Non-being (the latter as that which totally lacks existence) does the possibility of an intermediate world become conceivable. With the new understanding of *logos* and *doxa* that the *Theaetetus* anticipates at its end, the bifurcated investigations of the *Sophist* and the *Statesman* are set in place. Whereas philosophical and political knowledge are identical in the *Republic*, the examination of the nature of knowledge in the *Theaetetus*, on the contrary, is separated into distinct investigations into the knowledge (and its standards) of the *epistemon* and the *politikos*, thus recognizing each one in its own right. So, as opposed to the uncomfortable mid-position in which Socrates and Theodorus find themselves, the definitely affirmative middle that is opened up with the Eleatic Stranger's parricide of Parmenides yields a conception of discursive knowledge that in the subsequent dialogues is shown to depend on the interweaving of distinct forms, and an art that in the political domain of *doxa* is defined as one that combines or blends contrary virtues. Interweaving, blending, *symploke* are operations of, and in, the middle.

In the *Theaetetus*, by contrast, Socrates avers that if in the debate both parties—the Heracliteans and the Parmenideans—should prove to be unreasonable, thus preventing any decision in favor of one of them, and without him and Theodorus having made an original contribution, they would look like fools. But if Socrates finds himself in the middle, between the two extreme positions, is it not also because—notwithstanding his reluctance to engage with the one Parmenides—he does not simply identify with his doctrine that all there is is rest? However hypothetical the suggestion may be that the debate could result in a victory of the Protagorean doctrine, it nevertheless presupposes a vulnerability of the opposite doctrine, the Parmenidean one. Finally, the reference to finding oneself in the middle, between the two doctrines, signals that already for Socrates change is as much a dimension of reality as rest, and that, ultimately, it cannot be a question of choosing between the two, a position that itself announces the doctrine of the Stranger. But to undertake, at this moment, a rigorous examination of Parmenides' doctrine would also require subjecting it to what Socrates did in the case of Protagoras—that is, fortifying Parmenides' doctrine in as thorough a manner as possible, for it to appear not only in all its multifaceted complexity, but also in all its one-sided extremism. However, though he explicitly admits that Parmenides too needs to be examined, Socrates first postpones such an examination before then expressing a reluctance to carry it out.

In any event, Socrates tells Theodorus that he is "of the opinion that we must examine the others [the Heracliteans] first, toward whom we started out, the streamers. And if it's evident they're making sense, we'll drag ourselves off with them, and try to avoid the others, but if the arresters of the whole seem to be saying truer things, we'll flee over to them and away from those who set the immoveable things in motion" (181a4–b1). It follows clearly from these lines that Socrates recognizes the necessity of also examining Parmenides' extreme position.[60] So why, then, does he renege on this task when, after the final refutation of the Heraclitean doctrine, the time for examining Parmenides' doctrine has come? For the time being, let me only point out that, since Socrates (and Theodorus) find themselves in a tug-of-war between two radically opposite and one-sided positions, the examination of one is not possible without having the other constantly on one's mind. Furthermore, finding oneself positioned between two extremes, does one position not provide one with the tools to put the other into question? Indeed, the in-between position in which Socrates claims to find himself presupposes that, in spite of each theory's onesidedness, there is also some truth to each of them—in other words, that both change and rest are part of reality, and that both are required to make reality intelligible. It is therefore the case that Parmenides functions as a horizon or a fix with respect to which the examination of Protagoras can begin to take place.[61] In other words, Socrates' rebuttal of the Heraclitean philosophy of flux that forms the foundation of Protagoras' man-measure formula needs the Parmenidean doctrine in all its extremity to guide it in its examination. If Socrates proves unwilling to take on Parmenides after having refuted Heraclitus, is it not then because he does not wish to jeopardize his accomplishment by putting into question the tools that Parmenides provided to come to grips with the other extreme? Indeed, it needs pointing out that after having provided an explanation of why he does not continue with an examination of Parmenides, it is not only the case that Socrates returns to the guiding question of the dialogue—more precisely, to Theaetetus' claim that perception is knowledge—in order to refute it, but the specter of Parmenides hovers over the remaining parts of the dialogue. As Polansky observes, his "presence and absence is felt in the rest of the dialogue."[62] Let us also remind ourselves here of Socrates' observation to Theodorus that should their examination of the streamers and the arresters find "that there's no measure of sense in what both are saying, we'll be laughable, convinced that we're making sense though we're nobodies, and have repudiated in the scrutiny very ancient and all-wise men" (181b2–5). The result of proceeding to a rebuttal of Parmenides, whose help has been instrumental in the criticism directed against Heraclitus, might leave them completely empty-handed, and thus ridiculous. Or, is Socrates' reluctance to examine him to be attributed to the fact that he is not yet ready to fully work out the middle-position hinted at, deferring its full elaboration to another—that is, the Stranger in the *Sophist*? In other words, is the attachment to and strategic reliance on Parmenides an obstacle related to Socrates' inability to break with both traditions of Greek philosophical thought at once, and thus also with the unity that, notwithstanding the divide, they provided?

In any event, after having brought the examination of the flux theory to an end—as a result of which both Protagoras' conception of the man-measure and Theaetetus' conception of knowledge as perception prove themselves to be untenable—Theaetetus intervenes to remind Socrates of his promise to also "go through those who assert in turn that the all is at rest, as you just now proposed" (183d1–3). But Socrates does not comply with Theaetetus' demand, offering that "it's my impression [*doko*] that I'll not obey Theaetetus, at least about what he's urging" (183d12–e1). Let us remind ourselves that on several occasions (for example, 196d), Socrates urged Theaetetus to be more daring (*panta gar tolmeteon*), to have the nerve to make outrageous, if not shameless arguments regarding the Protagorean and Heraclitean statements. Is it not therefore all the more surprising that, when it comes to examining Parmenides, Socrates suddenly—and, given his former agreement, unexpectedly—retreats from his promise? To Theodorus' inquiry of why exactly he refuses to obey, he gives several answers. First, he says that "[a]though I'm ashamed [*aiskunomenos*] before Melissus and everyone else, who speak of the all as one at rest, lest our investigation be vulgar and common, I'm less ashamed [*aiskunomai*] before them than before Parmenides who is one. Parmenides appears to me at once, in the saying of Homer, 'as awesome to me as uncanny [*deinos*]' " (183e3–7). After the recollection that as a very young man he had met Parmenides, who at that moment was already very old—an encounter narrated in the dialogue *Parmenides*—Socrates adds that "he appeared to me to have some altogether grand and noble depth" (184a1–2). Even though Socrates, in his dealings with Protagoras, also acknowledges his respect for the latter as a philosopher by making him stronger than he was, it is a deep respect for Parmenides that holds Socrates back here from critically examining his thought. Let us note from the start that Parmenides is characterized, in terms of his own doctrine that Being is one, as the one "who is one." Parmenides' authority does not compare with any other. He is unique. His is the one authority that Socrates fears to dishonor and tarnish by engaging it. Parmenides appears to him at once as awesome and uncanny, that is, fearsome, and thus Socrates' refraining from examining him would have to be explained not only through his respect but also through a certain lack of courage to confront him. Even though throughout the dialogue Socrates constantly encourages Theaetetus to be bold and daring, he himself does not dare take on the uncanny or fearful authority of Parmenides' doctrine that Being is One. But it is not only fear that explains Socrates' reason for not challenging him. Another reason is that he is ashamed before Parmenides, in fact, as ashamed as can be. It is this shame (*aiskune*), this feeling of awe, that should interest us here.[63] The shame in question consists in the fear of *aiskuno*, that is, the fear of making the revered man, whom he holds in awe, look ugly, and dishonoring or tarnishing him through a speech that will inevitably be vulgar and common since he is not yet capable of an examination that, despite its criticism of Parmenides' awesome doctrine, would still be respectful of it.[64] But Socrates advances another, more pragmatic, so to speak, reason for refraining from an all-out examination of Parmenides' thought. Given the grandness and nobleness of the man he experienced, Socrates is not only afraid that he is not up to understanding what Parmenides said, and especially what he meant, but also that in turning to his doctrine the subject of the present dialogue about knowledge would remain unexamined due to the innumerable questions that Parmenides' thought would provoke. These questions would distract them from the subject of their inquiry, and if addressed adequately they would, by lengthening the speech, "wipe out the issue of knowledge" (184a12–13). In other words, a refutation of Parmenides' thought would be incomparably more arduous than in Protagoras' case, since the exhibition of his doctrine is so much more difficult than that of the latter, and Socrates admits that he is not up to it.

In conclusion, let me say that in spite of all these reasons for not engaging Parmenides directly, but continuing instead with the elaboration of knowledge—whose ultimate subject matter is what *is*—Socrates, by leaving in abeyance the prospect of also going through Parmenides, has formulated a task. It is the task of radically putting into question the other half of the Greek pre-Socratic take on philosophy. In the same way as the refutation of Protagoras, father of the statements at the heart of sophism, the refutation of Parmenides, father of the view that only Being is and that of it alone one can speak, is a parricide, and is accomplished in view of something new, as a result of which a new clarity will be achieved. It is a clarity that comes with the Stranger's discernment in the *Sophist* of the greatest kinds, the elementary building blocks of intelligible speech, which in turn represent the conditions for speaking clearly about what is. Parricide in Greece was considered the most heinous crime.[65] Even though both Protagoras and Parmenides are already dead when their doctrines are dismantled by Socrates and the Stranger, respectively, the complete refutations of the two authorities of Greek thought remain in a way comparable to such a crime. However, as we will see, the Stranger's innovative approach to a thought that all can share is not limited to the parricide of both figures. In addition to targeting the seemingly untouchable authorities of the Greek world, the crime is also one that concerns that world itself—more precisely, what is ethnic or native about the world. Only, this crime of parricide occurs in speech, in a speech that is dialogical and that draws everyone, however reluctant he or she may be to giving accounts, into itself.[66] It is a parricide that becomes inevitable when speech is to be able to elaborate on the conditions of intelligibility as such, conditions under which alone it is possible to speak to others in a way that is intelligible to all.

Chapter Two

The Sophist

At first glance, the reason for the inquiry in the *Theaetetus* into what knowledge is could seem to have been the mathematician Theodorus' expertise in only one kind of knowledge, and lack of expertise in others, not to mention his characterization of all talk other than mathematical talk as just "bare speeches" (165a2–3). But Socrates' question at the beginning of the dialogue, a question that undoubtedly also has an erotic connotation—namely, whether in contemporary Athens there are not some especially gifted young men—is indicative of still another motive. Even if these young men may "make geometry or something else of philosophy their concern" (143d3–4), Socrates' interest seems to be about a knowledge other than mathematics, a knowledge, I hazard to say, that probes the limits of mathematical knowledge. Although the devotion of the young men to geometry may also include *philosophia*, at this point in the dialogue, the term is not yet distinguished from geometry, or from any other disciplines taught at the Academy. The term does not yet designate the knowledge that Socrates may have in mind; it refers only to other liberal studies as they were taught in Plato's School. But by linking this exceptional knowledge to worthy young men, the knowledge to be inquired into hereafter becomes also linked to personality, that of especially gifted juveniles. Paul Friedländer can thus observe that "in the *Theaetetus*, the personality of the young man is the point of departure for the inquiry, leading to the question: What is knowledge?"[1] In distinction from a knowledge that is essentially technical and professional, such as that of Theodorus, Socrates' inquiry about highly talented youths in contemporary Athens shows that the knowledge he wants to examine is of a different kind than a *techne* or a profession. Instead, it is vocational, so to speak, a knowledge that causes the one who strives for it to be transformed by it, and, in the only way possible for human beings, to resemble a god—in short, it is philosophical knowledge.[2]

After having welcomed the Stranger introduced by Theodorus at the beginning of the *Sophist*, Socrates opens the conversation with a request to discern the genus of the philosopher by distinguishing him from the appearances under which he usually manifests himself in the cities—that is, from the sophist, the statesman, and the madman. With this question, Socrates sets the topic to be discussed throughout the dialogue before he himself falls silent.[3] It is to others, and in particular to a stranger, that he delegates the inquiry into a knowledge which, as we know from the previous dialogue, he does not claim to possess. However, it is worth noting how differently the respective examinations in the *Theaetetus* and the *Sophist* begin. If Socrates has chosen Theaetetus as an interlocutor because of his promising brilliance, the Stranger accepts the young Athenian simply on the basis of Socrates' recommendation.[4] In distinction from Socrates' familiarity with the young man at the outset of the dialogue (as the son of his friend), the Stranger accepts him as his interlocutor in the most neutral fashion, without inquiring into his character, without allusion to his physical traits, and with no hint of eroticism. By evoking Theaetetus' resemblance to Socrates, and thus his lack of all youthful charm, the dialogue also makes it clear from the beginning that the Stranger's speech, unlike that of Socrates' in the *Theaetetus*, is not intent on fighting for the young man's soul.[5] For the Socratic question regarding knowledge as such, a knowledge distinct from even the highest form of expertise that is mathematics, a promising partner was required, who, with the help of Socrates, was supposed to deliver a satisfying answer to the question. However, in order to avoid giving a *makros logos*, that is, a drawn-out speech, the Stranger only asks for an interlocutor who "submits to guidance easily and painlessly" (217d1–2) in an examination of the sophist, in the process of which the knowledge specific to the philosopher should also possibly emerge. This knowledge would characterize the thinking and discursive speaking of a person and thus define that person as a philosopher, but its exhibition is no longer dependent on a promising individual. Furthermore, this knowledge is brought to light by a stranger, who, in spite of his status as a decisive dramatis persona of the dialogue, seems to lack all personality.

But if, in the *Theaetetus*, the question of what knowledge is was intimately intertwined with a promising young person, it is not particularly surprising that in the two subsequent dialogues—the *Sophist* and the *Statesman*—the question becomes explicitly *what* or *who* the philosopher, the sophist, and the statesman are, in short, what kind of men they are, and what sort of knowledge defines them. With this shift in question, the theoretical concerns of the inquiry are now no longer intrinsically interlinked with individual personality, but rather with existence, that is, with specific figures in the *polis*, and thus with ethical and political concerns. It is certainly appropriate to recall here that "the hard and fast distinction between 'speculation' and 'practice,'" which is Aristotelean by origin, is foreign to the spirit of Plato.[6] Especially in his later dialogues, and to resist the sweeping abstractions and logical gymnastics of the schools, his own Academy included, Plato's aim is not only to constantly gain greater definiteness and fullness but also to secure the practical and individual application of universal truth. Lewis Campbell notes that "[c]ontemplation and action are not sundered."[7] In the examination of the knowledge to which the sophist lays claim, as well as that of the statesman, theoretical *and* practical concerns are intimately interwoven. Of course, this does not exclude the possibility that particular examinations may tend more in one direction than the other, but the complementary concern is never obscured or forgotten. Indeed, this is the case with the *Sophist* and the *Statesman*, and the preceding *Theaetetus* preprograms, as it were, the two examinations of the knowledge (or lack thereof, in the case of the sophist and the crowd of politicians) that constitutes both existences.

While it is far from clear whether the examination of knowledge in the *Theaetetus* has made the titular young man more sensitive to philosophical argumentation and thinking, it also remains undecided what knowledge is. But what has been learned is that, on the one hand, *logos*—that is, rational speech that also provides an account of what it advances—and, on the other hand, true opinion (*alethes doxa*)—that is, insightful judgment—are crucial to understanding what knowledge is. Undeniably, discursive speech with an account seems to be especially characteristic of the philosopher (of whom the sophist is a sham imitation), whereas true opinion is more the resort of the statesman whose task is distinct from that of the philosopher.[8] To preface the following reading of the *Sophist*, I point out that at a crucial juncture of their examination, the Stranger and Theaetetus arrive at the conclusion that for speech or discourse to be possible, concepts, rather than remaining totally isolated from one another, or combining entirely with one another, must be able to discriminately relate to one another in such a way that some can be combined with others according to certain rules, and others not. It is at this juncture that the Stranger asks Theaetetus whether, with this insight, they did not "fall unawares into the science of the free, and [whether it is not] probable that in looking for the sophist we've first found the philosopher?" (253c9–11). The knowledge of how to combine concepts, that is, "the science of the free" or "dialectical science," is the knowledge that defines the philosopher, a knowledge that, as its former qualification indicates, is "free" of authorities both in the theoretical and political spheres (253d1–3).[9] Even though the Stranger tells Theaetetus that they will "go on to consider [the philosopher] as well with greater clarity, if it's still our wish" (254b4–5), let me remark in passing that, at this point, Plato may still have considered writing a third dialogue devoted exclusively to the figure of the philosopher. But since, as some commentators have rightly noted—most recently, Fulcran Teisserenc—"philosophy reveals itself in transitive fashion through its movement of elucidation and determination of the objects to be cognized, and that are different from it," such as the sophist and the statesman, Plato may, after the completion of the *Sophist* and the *Statesman*, have decided that the question regarding the philosopher had been settled.[10]

So, if it is correct to say that the *Theaetetus*, without a definite determination of what knowledge is, nevertheless revealed two indispensable insights into its nature—one which concerns *logos*, and which, as is made explicit in the *Sophist*, belongs to the dialogue of the soul with itself, and another that belongs to true opinion, which I hold emerges from the coming together and intercourse of all the participants of a polity to be—then the respective objectives of the two following dialogues are set in place. Whereas on the one hand the prefix *dia* in *dianoia* and *dialogos*—the silent dialogue of the soul with itself—suggests "an intimate plurality" of the soul, its dividedness between itself and itself, which is constitutive of thinking and *logos*, on the other hand, the gap between all the citizens assembling in order to debate how to shape the polity has, I venture to say, the potential of engendering true opinion.[11] In short, with *logos* and true opinion proving to be essential to the nature of knowledge, a bifurcation emerges at the conclusion of the *Theaetetus* regarding how to proceed. With this, two new and distinct roads are opened up, and two new inquiries become possible.

The first of these inquiries has the primarily theoretical objective of distinguishing philosophical knowledge from its spurious counterfeit in sophistry as a *techne*, profession, or business. The purpose of this road of inquiry is to pin down the sophist frequently mistaken for the philosopher, by way of an uncompromising analysis which, as the Stranger's method of investigation demonstrates, proceeds in conformity with the strictest logical requirements regarding the use of concepts in rational speech. As we learn from the *Sophist*, these logical rules of examination are grounded on the specific ways in which "the greatest kinds," which form the intelligible building blocks of rational speech, can combine or not. The elaboration of this knowledge, which is the knowledge characteristic of the philosopher, and which sets him apart from all technically minded business, is the central theoretical accomplishment of the dialogue.

The second inquiry takes place in the *Statesman*. In this dialogue, justice is done to the recognition in the *Theaetetus* that "true opinion with an account" is different from knowledge as logical reasoning, that is, knowledge in an emphatic sense. However, true opinion is not therefore foreign to knowledge but rather has its true place in the practical domain. True opinion with an account is the counter-art, in the practical domain, to reason in the theoretical realm. In distinction from the way in which concepts interrelate and what sort of community they form, the *Statesman* is about the community of men within a *polis*. True opinion, if accompanied by an account, is the kind of "knowledge" that being together demands not only of all the members of a community, but especially of its head.

In the *Theaetetus*, knowledge is not defined in itself because the question about it is intimately connected with a promising young person, and there is no certainty that he will eventually make good on this promise.[12] Only history tells us that the young man was not only to become a famous mathematician (rather than a philosopher), but, as is evident from the dialogue's prologue, also a model citizen, who distinguished himself as a soldier during what appears to have been the battle before Corinth. This interconnection between knowledge and the knower must especially become an issue when the question turns to the specifically human forms of knowledge, or the pretenses thereof that are sophistry and statesmanship, not to speak of philosophizing—that is, forms of knowledge associated with three different forms of human existence. But since the present study is framed by an interest in the figure of the Stranger in Plato's trilogy, I wish also, from the beginning, to raise the question of whether there are any particular reasons why, when it comes to investigating these human forms of knowledge, Plato resorts to a stranger to conduct the investigation. Is there an implicit necessity that such an inquiry must call on a stranger? Could it be that such an investigation into the link between existence and knowledge (or the pretense thereof) requires a special courage that only a stranger could muster? Is there something new or fresh about this link, and about what will come to light through its investigation, that calls for an approach that only a stranger to ingrained presuppositions and habits of thought could possibly accomplish?

Since the Platonic dialogues frequently feature strangers, the prominent role that the Stranger enjoys in the *Sophist* does not, at first, appear to be something particularly new.[13] Even Theodorus, the mathematician who introduces the Stranger to Socrates in the opening lines of the dialogue, which takes place in Athens, is from Cyrene, and the sophist—the main topic of the dialogue—is one of those famous strangers who, without any affiliation with any city of origin, traveled in the fifth century BC from city to city to sell his "wisdom." In the *Apology*, Socrates, facing his judges during his appearance before a court whose language he claims not to have mastered, declares himself "a complete stranger [*atekhnos oun xenos*]."[14] Yet, all these strangers are identifiable, especially by their patronyms, and thus by their lineage. Even though in the *Laws* one finds oneself, as Henri Joly has noted, "among *strangers*,"[15] their names and origins allow their identification, except perhaps for the Athenian who is anonymous but who, since Cicero, is considered a proxy for Plato himself.[16] Apart from the Stranger in the *Sophist* and the *Statesman*, of whom we learn little to nothing, and who hence remains unidentifiable, the sole exception is, perhaps, the unknown bystander who, after Socrates' conversation with two sophists in *Euthydemus*, approaches Crito and defends philosophical thought from the sophists by emphasizing its political nature.[17] Nothing is known about him, and he vanishes quickly from the scene. But this participant does not compare to the Stranger in our dialogue. As Socrates points out to Crito, the opinions of such "frontiersmen between philosophy and politics," to which the unknown interlocutor belongs, only look well rather than being truly well, and are philosophically of little challenge compared to the eristics' negation of truth, which reveals difficulties that the philosopher cannot ignore.[18]

When, on the morning following the conversation reported in the *Theaetetus*, the protagonists meet again, all of them have clear profiles, and they form a rather homogeneous group in spite of oppositions such as old and young, mathematical and philosophical expertise, Athenians and foreigners, speaking and silent participants, and so forth. Furthermore, on the previous day, Theodorus had emphasized in some detail the physical resemblance between Socrates and Theaetetus, thus further cementing the homogeneity of the participants. It is to this group that Theodorus, originally from Cyrene and host of the Academy, introduces the Stranger, whom he apostrophizes as "*o xene*," and it is as such that he will be addressed throughout the two dialogues, as the Greek institution of hospitality would have required that he not be asked his name.[19] In itself, this is striking enough. Throughout the two dialogues he remains anonymous—more precisely, without a patronymic.[20]

From the masculine vocative "*o xene*" we take it that he is unmistakably a male and, since he refers to his interlocutor on several occasions as "my boy [*o pai*]," of a certain age. The question raised by Theodorus regarding the physical resemblance between Socrates and Theaetetus makes us aware that the Stranger does not resemble anyone in the group, and that he has no special physical features worth mentioning. He is not only without an identity but also without a "look" to himself by which he could be identified. That is, he is a stranger to the end.[21] Who exactly this stranger is is a major question, and since the novel manner of philosophizing that Plato proposes in our dialogue is tightly intertwined with him, the Stranger, even at the risk of some repetition—in the Introduction, for instance, I have already ventured a brief description of him—will require our full attention.

Undoubtedly, Theodorus introduces him as kin "from Elea," and, according to the current translations of the opening passage of the dialogue, "a comrade of the circle of Parmenides and Zeno" (216a3–4). Unlike the foreigner mentioned in the *Theaetetus* whose language we hear but do not understand, the Stranger, originating in Elea, speaks Greek and thus is not a barbarian.[22] He is thoroughly other, but not in the sense that he would speak in a non-Greek tongue and confront his hosts with a totally different way of life, such as that of the Persians, for example, whom the Greeks had recently defeated and did not wish to follow. Without exception, he is referred to as a *xenos* (a stranger), rather than *allodapos* (that is, "belonging to another people or land," in short, a foreigner).[23] But although the standard translation of *xenos* denotes a stranger, it can also refer to a foreigner, especially when coming from another Greek state. The stranger is a foreigner as well, as is evident from Socrates' question of "what those in that region [*ton ekei topon*, the distant place whence he comes] were accustomed to believe and name" with respect to the philosopher, the sophist, the statesman, and the madman (217a1–4).

As Theodorus adds in his opening address, the Stranger is also "a man very much a philosopher" (216a4–5). Although he is very much a philosopher, this qualification is not therefore a hint at the Stranger's profession that would allow for identification. He is also said to come from Elea, an Ionian colony on the Tyrrhenian coast of Southern Italy founded by expatriates from Phocaea—itself located on the eastern extreme of the Greek domain—after they had been threatened by the despotic empires of the Persians and found refuge on what from that moment on became the Western extreme of Magna Graecia. It is here, on the Western edge of the Greek domain, and after the first wave of Greek philosophy—the Ionian philosophy of nature, which originated on the West coast of Asia Minor, an area that had been colonized by refugees from the Greek mainland fleeing from the Dorians and other tribes—that the second wave of philosophical thought emerged.[24] Elea is the home of Parmenides and Zeno; it is thus "the authentic Ontopolis."[25] Yet, does Theodorus' announcement that the Stranger is a native of Elea and an associate of the Parmenidean school of philosophizing truly give us a more concrete sense of who the Stranger is? It has been observed that the first lines of the dialogue, in which Theodorus introduces the Stranger, are, philologically speaking, problematic. According to some high-quality manuscripts of the dialogue, rather than being referred to as "a comrade [*hetairos*] of the circle of Parmenides and Zeno," the Stranger is held to be "different [*heteros*] from them."[26] However one evaluates this reading, which had been prevalent up to and during the Renaissance, and which has the advantage of explaining why Plato has this stranger refute the philosophy of his own master, it requires one to wonder at least whether Theodorus' knowledge about the Stranger's origins permits one to unequivocally identify him as a member of a determined foreign community. Certainly, we learn later from the Stranger's own lips that he is familiar with Eleatic thought because "Parmenides the Great [. . .] beginning when we were boys and right through to the end protested" (237a5–6) the presupposition that Non-being could be. If, from boyhood on, Parmenides admonished him and others, like a father, does this not confirm beyond any doubt that the Stranger's home is in Elea? This is undoubtedly the case, and he is certainly familiar with Parmenides' thought, but this does not necessarily make him a strictly orthodox member of the Eleatic school. How could he be expected to demolish father Parmenides' doctrine if he were a member of his school? Is it not more likely that it is because he has ideas of his own that he can put those of his alleged "father" into question? Again, Elea is also a colony of expatriates and philosophers in exile. By being linked to such a location, the Stranger's physical origin inevitably remains somewhat uncertain. Besides this, his reference to Parmenides as a spiritual father from youth on who established what it is permissible to think, makes of Elea a spiritual rather than a physical home, especially since, as we will see, the Stranger uproots this affiliation and breaks with his Eleatic heritage, relegating it for its one-sidedness in relation to the past. He thus becomes other than himself if he had ever been a Parmenidean, other to such a degree as to no longer be able to be called a native of Elea. Notably, Elea is referred to, and certainly not fortuitously, as "that region," a region *over there*, a place far away, *ton ekei topon* (217a1).[27]

By introducing the Stranger as being from Elea by birth, Theodorus not only characterizes him by an alleged ethnicity, which for the Greeks made him immediately a stranger or foreigner, but also characterizes him as representing a specific philosophical school. Both the local name and that of the school—the Eleatic is the sobriquet by which he will be referred to by Plato commentators—make the Stranger a particular stranger, *the* Stranger, *o xene*. He is a unique stranger, one of his kind.[28] For the Greeks, as Émile Benveniste notes, "there is no 'stranger' as such; given the diversity of notions, the stranger is always a particular stranger, who carries a distinct status."[29] In what follows, I will thus speak of him as the Stranger. More importantly than the Stranger's ethnicity, landedness, or his belonging to a school, Plato's denomination of him, through Theodorus' introductory words, as a native of Elea and thus a stranger, may just be a way to highlight his individuality as a dramatis persona free of all partiality, whether ethnic or philosophical. Is it not this complete absence of native features that grants him a special standing, and a new kind of authority no longer rooted in tradition and nativeness?

But what about Theodorus' characterization of the Stranger as "a man very much a philosopher"? At least two things need to be mentioned here. Theodorus, the mathematician, was a former friend of Protagoras. In search of real truth, however, he deserted the sophist's art of speech and empty dialectic for mathematical knowledge, that is, the solid knowledge of immutable numbers and mathematical ratios. It follows that Theodorus, and by implication his student Theaetetus, who will be the Stranger's interlocutor in the dialogue, does not yet know what a true philosopher is or what his knowledge consists of.[30] Indeed, at the beginning of the inquiry into the sophist, whom many confuse with the philosopher—the philosopher being one of the disguises in which the sophist appears in the cities—nothing has yet been established with respect to the nature of the philosopher himself, or with respect to the knowledge particular to him. In short, Theodorus' characterization of the Stranger as a philosophical man does not make him any more concrete. If the Stranger's task is to elaborate on what distinguishes a philosopher from a sophist and a statesman, then, as a philosopher (though we do not yet know who or what a philosopher *is*), he must do this primarily through a process of discursive praxis, making himself known as a philosopher only in a transitive fashion rather than by identifying himself as one. Since we do not yet know what a philosopher is, the Stranger cannot arrogate to himself that designation or title. Only through his discursive praxis can he possibly reveal himself as a philosopher. As Teisserenc observes, "The signification of the Stranger's anonymity becomes evident here: his nature as a philosopher is, in an essential fashion, involved in the philosophy he puts to work. To name him by a proper name, by calling him a philosopher, would consist in giving him an identity that would be anterior to the dialectic, and which would be independent of the latter."[31]

Now if, in distinction from all the other participants of the dialogue, including those who, like the young Socrates, remain silent throughout, we are not told anything about the *xenos* himself, is it not precisely because Plato purposely wants him to remain a stranger, a Stranger with a capital S, if you will, and nothing but a stranger?[32] Rather than being accidental, the foreignness of the Stranger may occupy a decisive role in the dialogue; furthermore, its role is not only limited to having a significant dramatic effect but is, in fact, of theoretical importance. Finally, if it does not make historical sense to ask *who* the Stranger is, it is also important to avoid the temptation to which many commentators succumb, namely, to account for the Stranger by construing him as an extension of Socrates, or simply as a double of Plato.[33] Of the same order of this temptation is the explication Gilbert Ryle has advanced for the substitution of Socrates by a stranger: namely, that after his return from Sicily, Plato had an incapacitating illness that no longer allowed him to be the mouthpiece for Socrates—a role he had so far regularly occupied—on the occasion of the reading performances of the trilogy.[34] All of these readings avoid the question of the Stranger himself, and what it ultimately means for the dialogue to feature a stranger as such, without a patronymic, without a name to begin with. In other words, all of these accounts avoid the question of the theoretical (and practical) significance of the Stranger *qua* stranger in the late dialogues. Rather than *who* a stranger is, the question that philosophy raises for the first time in the *Sophist*, and which, as I submit, is intimately interwoven with philosophy itself, is *what* a stranger is. In any event, according to Jean-François Mattéi, "[n]ever at his place, always ready to leave, *the Stranger is exiled*. We guess that he cannot yet return to the country that is its own."[35] Having no patronymic, no identity, and no home, does the Stranger of the *Sophist* not have an eerie resemblance to the chorus's characterization in *Antigone* of the human being as the most uncanny (*to deinotaton*) of all beings?[36] The Stranger's uncanniness is that he does not have a name, a look, or a definable origin but is instead just a stranger.

However that may be, let us ask what a *xenos* is to begin with. According to Liddell and Scott, the term means, first, "a guest-friend, applied to persons and states bound by a treaty, or tie of hospitality," and only secondarily does it apply to strangers, wanderers, refugees, or foreigners.[37] As indicated by its further meaning of "a hireling," especially as a "mercenary soldier," the contractual connotation makes it impossible to translate the term simply as "guest," as is conventionally done. A guest, or guest-friend, does not necessarily have to be a foreigner, but can be a member of one's own community whom one receives in one's home; however, the Greek notion of the *xenos* does require this guest to be a foreigner, but again not just anyone who happens to show up at one's door. As Émile Benveniste avers, the Greek notion of the foreigner concerns "[s]omeone born elsewhere, provided that he has conventional links, enjoys some specific rights, which cannot be granted even to citizens of the country."[38] The *xenos* is more than just a guest; one has an obligation to host him, and the foreigner as a *xenos* has, in turn, an obligation to reciprocate for the welcome he receives. In other words, he is not just any foreigner in general toward whom one would have a moral obligation, but as Benveniste has shown, he is a foreigner determined by an institution—*xenia*—the institution of hospitality over which a god, the protector of foreigners, presides. Indeed, as we will see, in his response to Theodorus' announcement that he brought with him a stranger, Socrates evokes the possibility that, rather than a stranger, Theodorus might have brought a god, or that, according to Homer, the Stranger might be accompanied by one. This god is *Zeus Xenios*.

In Book V of the *Laws*, while discussing one's obligations toward foreigners, Plato quite explicitly states that, compared to sins against fellow citizens, offenses against aliens "more directly draw down the vengeance of God. For the alien, being without friends or kinsmen, has the greatest claim on pity, human and divine. Whence he that is able to exact the vengeance is all the readier to come to his help, and none is so able as the god or spirit who protects the alien as minister of Zeus Xenios."[39] The institution of *xenia* does not only determine the host's obligations toward the foreigner, that is, the alien's rights, but also, in turn, the foreigner's obligations with respect to his or her host. In addition, *xenia* as an institution also comes with a time limit, foreigners in ancient Greece enjoying a welcome as a guest in general only for three days, after which he or she is supposed to leave. The notion of the foreigner in Greece has thus to be understood within the contractual framework of an institution, which comprehends precise obligations of all parties involved.[40] To translate the term *xenos* as "stranger" certainly captures the foreignness of this guest, but does not render the obligations that one has with respect to him as a guest, nor the guest's obligation of mutual reciprocity. What follows from this is that a stranger *qua* stranger is always someone to whom one has an obligation, and that he or she does not first have to be invited to become a guest. Thanks to the institution, he is "by nature," as it were, already invited from the beginning.

At this juncture, I would like to broach, however briefly, and in a preliminary fashion, Plato's stakes with reference to the *xenos*, apart from the doctrine that will eventually be laid out. I am concerned here with Plato's stakes in giving a prominent voice to a stranger in the *Sophist*, and subsequently in the *Statesman*, the stakes, in other words, of giving a stranger, rather than a native, the role of saving or uprooting, and indeed founding, philosophy anew. Let us remind ourselves that after Theodorus' introduction of the Stranger, Socrates, in an explicit reference to Book 17 of Homer's *Odyssey*, wonders whether Theodorus might not have brought a god instead of an ordinary guest to the meeting.[41] More precisely, Socrates asks Theodorus whether it might have escaped him that the guest he has brought, if not himself a god, might be accompanied by one. Socrates wonders,

> not only do different gods accompany all those human beings who share in a just shame [*dikaias*], but [. . .] also, in particular, the god of strangers proves not least to be their companion and looks down on the acts of outrage and lawabidingness of human beings? So perhaps your stranger who attends you might also be one of the Mightier, come to look us over and refute us who are poor in speeches, and is a kind of refutative god [*theos on tis elenktikos*]. (216a8–b7)

With the suggestion that, in spite of his appearance, the Stranger might indeed be accompanied by a god, if not himself be a god, Socrates not only introduces one of the major themes of the dialogue—the relation between original and copy—but also, and immediately, raises the status of the Stranger to that of someone who might have an extraordinary power of cross-examination, giving accounts, or reasoning that surpasses that of the participants, Socrates himself included.[42] In other words, Socrates and the other participants in the dialogue express their welcome to a stranger, who has come to Athens from abroad like a god of refutation to expose their weakness in philosophical discourse and to put into question some of that discourse's underlying, self-evident, and hitherto unquestioned beliefs.[43] Even though Theodorus seems to provide a more down-to-earth estimate of what the Stranger is when he replies that he is of a more measured mind and, in his words, "is in no way a god; he is, however, divine"

(216b10–c1) as all philosophers are, he also reveals his lack of knowledge of what a philosopher is. By lumping together both the philosopher's art of cross-examination—elenctic art—that Socrates evokes and, as becomes clear later in the dialogue, the sophists' art of controversy—eristics—as bare, empty speech compared to the precise and technical knowledge that he has of mathematics, geometry, and astronomy, Theodorus confirms that, in his eyes, philosophical inquiry has nothing specific about it.[44] For this very reason, Socrates' statement crediting the Stanger with an unheard-of power of cross-examination, giving accounts, or reasoning that surpasses that of the participants, himself included, remains uncontested. Socrates and the dialogue's other participants thus express their welcome to a stranger who, resembling a god of refutation, has come to Athens from abroad, that is, from a place as remote as Elea, to look them over and expose their poorness in philosophical argumentation. At this point, the reader does not yet know what the Stranger will take issue with, or how radical his interrogation of the whole of Greek philosophizing hereto will be. But we should already take note of the unheard-of fact that, here within Greek philosophical thought, a stranger is greeted and invited to radically put into question or refute Greek philosophical reasoning, including Socratic reasoning and its method of examination.

However, before continuing, I wish to address one possible objection—namely, that the Stranger is not really a stranger because he speaks Greek. Without the Greek language, however, no conversation would have been possible between him and his Greek hosts who generally, as has been well established, spoke exclusively Greek and did not seek to master foreign languages.[45] Now, it is certainly true that the Stranger comes from Great Greece, even though Elea is located at its Western edge. Therefore, some might hold that he is not a "true" stranger. He is, decidedly, not a barbarian. But let us bear in mind that, for the Greeks, any citizen from any other *polis* in Greece—who would still, therefore, be a hellenophone—was by definition a *xenos*, a foreigner. Undoubtedly, without distinction, all non-Greek speakers were referred to as barbarians.[46] This onomatopoetic term, although it does indeed designate all non-Greek foreigners, is not necessarily a denigrating term, suggesting, as it does today, primitivism. Yet, in the context of ancient Greece, when the term is used in relation to highly developed civilizations such as Egypt or Persia, who certainly possess an onomastic language and thus *speak*, it tends to mean that they do not therefore already live in a culture of *logos*, in a world of public speech and exchange, as the Greeks effectively did.[47] Indeed, in this context it is important to point out that what, according to Herodotus's *The Histories*, makes the Scythians barbarians is not simply certain customs they hold, such as drinking milk and undiluted wine, but the fact that, in spite of being nomads, they lived under the rule of a king, in other words, a despot.[48] Anyone living under any royal power or theocratic authority was by definition a barbarian, because this excluded speaking with others in public. More important in the present context, however, is the fact that, in the *Statesman*—though not in the *Sophist*—the Stranger (and thus also Plato) objects to dividing the whole class of human beings into Greeks and barbarians, thereby contesting the distinction between intra-Greek strangers and outside barbarians, between strangers and those who are altogether other.[49] In any event, the fact that the Stranger speaks Greek does not make him any less of a stranger in Athens. Indeed, even though he is not a barbarian, and thus does not develop and teach a new philosophy by way of a completely unintelligible gibberish, as might be the case with an entirely foreign foreigner (if such a thing were conceivable), the fact that he is a Greek foreigner confronts his Greek hosts with a difference within their own idiom. I am not referring here to intra-Greek dialects. Even though he speaks Greek, his is a language of the other, and consequently he challenges his Greek hosts to open themselves to otherness or, more precisely, to open themselves to philosophy as a kind of thought, as we will see, that will reveal itself to be the thought *of* the stranger.

I return to the Stranger's alleged origin. Rather than the Stranger himself, it is Theodorus who identifies him as a native of Elea and "a comrade of the circle of Parmenides and Zeno" (216a3–4). Although the Stranger alludes to Parmenides as his father later in the dialogue, and as Parmenides the Great who had instructed him and others from childhood on, the doctrine he develops in the dialogue presupposes an unsparing critique of Parmenidean thought. Since I am primarily interested in understanding the doctrine of the Stranger, I am concerned more with how he himself presents Parmenides than with inquiring into whether or not he treats the historical Parmenides fairly. I even wonder whether the Stranger, when noting that he and Theaetetus may have "disobeyed Parmenides to a further extent than his prohibition" (258c7–8) of inquiring into Non-being by establishing the species under which Non-being is to be subsumed—namely, the Different—he himself does not acknowledge that the Parmenides whom he demolishes is not simply the author of the poem attributed to him. Hence, I forgo a systematic comparaison of Parmenides' poem with the Stranger's characterization of him in the *Sophist*. However legitimate and necessary such an exercise may be, for my purposes here I can set Parmenides' poem aside and restrict myself to the way the Stranger reconceptualizes the latter's argument. It is certainly true that the doctrine demolished by the Stranger cannot simply be identified with the historical Parmenides' thought, nor with that of any particular Eleatic school, but the dialogue leaves no doubt that the target of the Stranger's refutation is the venerated Greek philosopher Parmenides. Notwithstanding the possibility that Plato, when stylizing the doctrine of Parmenides, may have had in mind the disciples of Euclides of Megara, who were proponents of a logic based on an extreme Eleatic doctrine, the literality of the dialogue demands us to respect that the target is Parmenides. Furthermore, in the same breath, the doctrine demands that we take Elea to be the home of philosophy, the Ontopolis par excellence. Sylvain Delcomminette suggests that "perhaps we might say that Elea stands, not specifically for Eleatic philosophy, but for philosophy *in general*" and that, as a result, his origins in "Elea" would indicate that "the Stranger's true home is philosophy."[50] What we have advanced regarding the spiritual fatherhood that Parmenides exercised on the Stranger as a young boy may support such a conclusion. However, Delcomminette's suggestion leaves open the question of what kind of "philosophy" could be the home of someone who not only lacks an identifying patronymic but who will also be led to reject the spiritual heritage of Parmenides in its entirety. Indeed, as we will see, the development of the Stranger's doctrine in the *Sophist* is based on a radical rejection of all previous philosophical schools, including the Eleatic school. By repudiating the views of all his predecessors, Plato indeed suggests that, in Stanly Rosen's words, "[p]rior to the Eleatic Stranger, *there have been no genuine philosophers, but only fantasms of philosophers*"[51]—and, by extension, no philosophy! If "Elea," as the name of the Stranger's home, thus stands for philosophy in general, it is in a sense of an unheard-of kind of philosophy whose outlines will be produced transitively through the nameless Stranger's dialectical examination of the figures of the sophist and the statesman; it will be a nameless philosophy, the philosophy of the nameless Stranger, and, by the same token, Elea would be a home without any local, native, or ethnic connotations.[52]

In what follows, I intend to bring home the point that the Stranger's philosophical doctrine is (genuine) philosophy, *for the first time*. And, furthermore, I will argue that it is philosophy precisely because it is elaborated by an unaffiliated stranger, by one who is not only a foreigner in Athens but who is also estranged from any home, in short, by a subject no longer native, earthborn, or autochthonous. This late dialogue by Plato not only centers on the Stranger, it is a dialogue that develops what Henri Joly refers to as Plato's "*philosophy of the stranger*," a philosophy in which Plato breaks with what is commonly regarded as having been the hallmark of his thought until then, the thought of identity.[53] Needless to say, if at the end of the *Sophist* the philosophy that the Stranger proposes does not yet appear to have satisfactorily resolved all the questions that triggered it, it is, on the one hand, because what the Stranger develops is "only" a fundamental sketch of such a philosophy. Hans-Georg Gadamer remarks that what happens in this dialogue cannot be "transformed into conclusive argumentation."[54] The doctrine of the Stranger is only like a scaffold to prepare Theaetetus for the philosophical task of thinking Non-being—that is, Difference or Otherness—and not yet a completed and inherently coherent doctrine. The dialogue contains, Gadamer writes, "only faint and cautious steps, which the Eleatic asks of his young partner, in order to bring him onto the way to the concept."[55] On the other hand, as may become obvious at a later point, the fundamental precondition of the novel way of philosophizing that is sketched out in the dialogue might also be of such a nature as to complicate all possible definite closure of philosophical thought.

Before Plato calls on the Stranger to speak, Socrates, still in conversation with Theodorus about the guest he has brought with him, says that philosophers are certainly as difficult to discern as gods are, since, abetted by "the ignorance of everyone else, these men—those who not in a fabricated way but in their being are philosophers—certainly show up in all sorts of apparitions" (216c4–6). Sometimes they appear in the disguises of the statesman, the sophist, and even the madman, and therefore Socrates would like to know what the Stranger's Eleatic associates think about these designations, in particular, whether they conceive of them as names for one referent or as names for three different figures.[56] With this question, the overall concern of the dialogue is announced: to mark off clearly what the sophist and the philosopher are. In the subsequent dialogue on the *Statesman*, the Stranger will do the same for the titular figure, and the never-written dialogue on the philosopher, if Plato ever considered writing it, would possibly have distinguished the philosopher from the madman.[57] Now since, as demonstrated by the six successive *diaereses* or divisions with which the Stranger proceeds in the first part of the dialogue, the sophist is a master of disguising himself, eluding all attempts to pin him down by a definition, the question of *what* the sophist *is* and what distinguishes him from the philosopher—that is, what he *is not*—implies from the start the question of what Being and Non-being are.[58] The task that the Stranger faces when seeking to pin down the sophist requires nothing less than an

interrogation of the reflections on Being and Non-being that have dominated Greek philosophy from Ionian physiologism to, in particular, the Eleatic doctrine of Being. For, indeed, the sophist's power of infinite disguises, by means of which he eludes being captured by a definition of his essence, makes it necessary to interrogate the Parmenidean doctrine according to which one can say only of Being that it is, whereas Non-being, because it is not, cannot be said without contradicting oneself. In short, in order to hunt down the sophist and to establish his existence, the Stranger will in fact have to become the refuting god that Socrates invoked at the beginning of the dialogue and, thus, also the re-founder of philosophy—more precisely, the founder of a novel way of philosophizing, if not even the founder of the first genuine form of philosophy in Greece.

Let us remind ourselves that by welcoming a foreigner to their group, the interlocutors have, in conformity with the institution of hospitality, obligated the invitee to reciprocate. To Socrates' demand to learn what the Eleatics are accustomed to believe about the philosopher, the sophist, the statesman, and the altogether mad, the Stranger shows himself obligated to gratify Socrates and all others present by agreeing to investigate the subject matter. But by having stated that the Stranger may possibly be a refuting god, Socrates and the others have also implicitly invited the Stranger to refute all the principles of the different trends in contemporary Greek thought that subtend its dominant doctrines and opinions. For what I wish to highlight in my reading of the *Sophist*, and later of the *Statesman*, it is of capital importance to realize what, indeed, is being asked here of the Stranger: something no native can possibly perform, something that only he can do because of the contract of hospitality that gives him rights that the native cannot have. What Plato thus has a stranger perform, as we will see, is the unheard-of task of a radical examination and confutation of the entire history of Greek philosophical thought. The task expected of the Stranger, who is bound to reciprocate with a gift to his Athenian hosts, is all the more unique, as this gift is nothing less than a gift of parricide regarding at least one of the fathers—and thus one of the most foundational figures—of Greek thought, a gift that Plato, through the voice of Socrates, invites him to make. The explicit gratitude expressed later in the *Statesman* by Socrates and Theodorus for the Stranger's accomplishment, especially with respect to the sophist, which was clearly not possible without a parricide of a leading figure in pre-Socratic thought, is therefore all the more significant. As if that were not enough, Theodorus begs him at the beginning of the *Statesman* not to "weary of gratifying us" one more time (257b8).

At this point, some clarifications may be warranted, since many Plato scholars will certainly balk from the start at my claim that, in the *Sophist*, a wholesale rejection of Greek philosophy takes place and clears the ground for a new beginning for philosophy in Greek thought. To argue that with the trilogy a novel conception of philosophizing occurs is in no way to suggest that it is reinvented from scratch: it is not created ex nihilo, but in conversation with key figures from an inherited and venerable past. The new philosophy I am speaking of is articulated in intimate interrelation with earlier positions on Being, and thus involves itself with a living tradition. While breaking with this tradition, the new philosophy also seeks its continuity.

In Plato scholarship, as is well known, the status of his works, the dates of their composition, and their authenticity have been objects of considerable controversy, dominated by the question of the unity of his work. Thus, to claim that, in the later dialogues, the Stranger effects a break with all previous philosophical currents and invents philosophy anew seems to put the unity of Plato's work into question. In this chapter I take seriously Plato's recourse to a stranger to inaugurate this philosophical revolution, and I explore what the necessities and implications of this dramatic move are. However, this does not, on another level of reflection, prevent me from agreeing with A. E. Taylor that the Eleatic "is a transparent disguise for Plato himself," and that "the real difference between the 'early' and the 'late' dialogues is simply that Plato's center of interest, as we may call it, has shifted."[59] The Stranger can be viewed as the dramatic staging of the shift in Plato's thought, but as I will argue, the Stranger's role in the dialogues in question exceeds this function. In any event, what takes place in the trilogy in particular is not incompatible with Plato's earlier positions, and does not formally contradict them or imply any formal criticism by Plato himself upon his earlier insights. Undoubtedly, if, on the basis of Aristotle's reading of Plato and the subsequent Platonist interpretation of Plato, it is assumed that there is something like a definite theory of ideas in his work that gives it unity, then, of course, the doctrine of the "greatest kinds," with its conception of the ideas as elements of speech, may be taken as inconsistent with the theory of ideas and may be considered as an act of infanticide.

Whereas the difference between the earlier and the later dialogues has led some to contest the authenticity of the latter—with Joseph Socher, for one, holding that the *Sophist* had to be written by a Megarian, since in this dialogue Plato's doctrine is impugned, and thus directed against Plato himself—others, like Wincenty Lutosławski, have argued that "with the substitution of categories for ideas, of the individual soul for the supercelestial space, of analysis and synthesis for poetical vision, of activity and passivity for immutable identity, of critical cautiousness for poetical eloquence," a "new development" occurs in Plato work. It is, Lutosławski adds, "a momentous step in the history of human thought and would have required another thinker than the author of the *Republic* and *Phaedrus*, were he not of such an immense intellectual power and had he not lived so long as to initiate a new philosophical movement after the age of fifty."[60] Yet, if the new development in question concerns above all Plato's theory of the ideas—and in the continuing controversy about his late works this is, indeed, one of the major issues—and if, by replacing the ideas by "categories," a term never used by Plato himself but that emerged later, and in an entirely different domain of representation, something like a turn occurs, away from ideas understood as intuitable transcendental intelligibles in some *topos ouranios* and toward their comprehension as supposedly logical functions, seemingly closer to the Aristotelean concern with the categories, many critics fear that this would put the unity of Plato's work into question.[61]

Apart from some brief remarks on the novel concept of ideas that the Stranger introduces with his elaboration on the "greatest kinds," and their difference from the however convenient term "categories," I do not intend hereafter to expand in any detail on the notion of the idea in the *Sophist*.[62] Yet, since in this chapter I stress the novelty of what the Stranger accomplishes in the two dialogues in which he speaks—developments that, as we have seen, are prepared by Socrates' examination of Protagoras, and in particular by the reflection on otherness in the *Theaetetus*—it should be evident that I sympathize with those commentators who argue that Plato develops something new with the trilogy, in a way reinventing philosophy, if not even inventing it as if for the first time. As Taylor remarks, "the Plato of the *Sophistes* is a man who has made a great discovery," a discovery that explains the "new *tonality*" in all his later works.[63] As opposed to the earlier dialogues, which are rather devoid of technical terminology, beginning with the *Theaetetus* an opposite trend occurs, in the direction of an "incipient terminology" of philosophy, a "notion of a philosophic vocabulary" which, in Lewis Campbell's words, "are fresh from the mint; they retain the gloss of novelty, and the hues of life."[64] In addition, as Campbell's impressive account demonstrates, the differences between the earlier and later dialogues are considerable, both stylistically and regarding the specifics of diction.[65] But a number of new themes also emerge in the later dialogues. Their focus is no longer on what constitutes virtue, justice, the good, knowledge, and so forth, in themselves. Instead, they assume a plurality of kinds of knowledge, such as the knowledge the sophist pretends to have, the kind of knowledge that makes the statesman a statesman, and that which makes the philosopher a philosopher.[66] The seemingly inconclusive outcome regarding the nature of knowledge in the *Theaetetus* is, perhaps, also the beginning of a new understanding, much stricter than before, of how one arrives at definitions. In this context, I draw attention to the new definition of the sophist in the homonymous dialogue. In spite of the vehement critique aimed at the sophists in the *Gorgias* or *Protagoras*, "it is never even remotely suggested that they were conscious charlatans, and still less that they had elaborated an *art* of imposture," as Plato will argue in the *Sophist*.[67] Even though no dialogue about the philosopher exists, does not the madman (*pantapasin ekontes manikos*), the "altogether crazy" (216d3), with whom the many confuse the philosopher, provide a new way of producing a stricter definition than before of the knowledge that the philosopher has? About to take on Parmenides, and thus to make the indispensable step constitutive of properly philosophical thought, the Stranger wonders whether he is not completely crazy (*mantikos*). Indeed, besides having to be a dialectician, is not a strict definition of the philosopher, which now also includes the philosophical courage of daring to examine all authority, whether that of the many or even of only one of Greece's most venerated thinkers, something that gives him the look of a madman? Is Theaetetus, beginning with Socrates in the *Theaetetus*, and later with the Stranger in the *Sophist*, not repeatedly urged to demonstrate such philosophical courage that, in the eyes of the many, is insane?[68] Finally, to conclude this digression, I wish to point to the introduction in the *Sophist* of the novel problematic of the interconnection or *koinonia* of the ideas. Undoubtedly, in the same way as in the *Phaedo* and the *Republic*, the philosopher's task still consists in discerning ideas, but no longer in an intellectual region entirely separate from that of the concrete world and speech; instead, ideas are intrinsically intertwined with the world. It is in this context that the problem of the interconnectedness of the ideas arises. Their very interconnectedness breaks with Plato's earlier conception of the ideas, in which all mixture between them was avoided so as to stress and maintain their purity.[69] But what is of cardinal importance regarding this problematic, to which I will return in due time, is not only the complex interconnectedness of the "greatest kinds," but that their multiplicity, as Monique Dixsaut puts it, is "emancipated," as it were. Indeed, as the five interrelated *eide* or *koina* show, the Stranger exhibits a multiplicity that is not the effect of a division, but that is instead a "primary multiplicity which does not *derive* from a unity, and which ultimately is not *reducible* to it."

This, Dixsaut writes, "confers upon Platonic dialectics its freedom: it has not to submit to the unity of a unique, and therefore unifying, principle."[70]

To proceed, the Stranger's doctrine, which derives from a refutation and, as will be argued, a transformation of Parmenides' conception of Being, has in a way been prepared in Plato's later dialogues, particularly in the *Parmenides* and *Theaetetus*. By holding that only Being is and can be spoken of, whereas Non-being is unutterable and irrational, Parmenides limited intelligibility to Being alone. In the wake of Socrates' examination of Protagoras' thesis in the *Theaetetus* that there is only changeableness, and that the particularity of phenomena can be expressed only by a language from which all universalia have been expulsed, the Stranger now takes issue with the opposite claim, which reduces philosophical discourse to the saying of the immutable, the One, or Being. For Parmenides, the Absolute alone is intelligible, and of the particular one cannot speak. Undoubtedly, for the Stranger to thoroughly transform Parmenides' thought by expanding intelligibility to Non-being and in the same breath developing, as I claim, a new philosophy—if not, even, philosophy for the first time—Plato's refinement in the *Parmenides* of Parmenides' ontology and discursive account of Being has been instrumental. There is no denying that the expansion of intelligibility to Non-being in the *Sophist* occurs against the backdrop of the form of propositional thinking required by the thinking of Being itself that, in the *Parmenides*, improves upon what Parmenides' fragments suggest.[71] Yet, notwithstanding these antecedents, I dare to claim that philosophy emerges here for the first time, not least because, in the dialogue, a stranger is charged with the task not only of developing, in systematic coherence, the elements of a new doctrine, parts of which had already been laid out in earlier dialogues, but also of enacting the break with certain previous stances of Platonic metaphysics, most notably and consequentially Plato's elaborations on the ideas. In the guise of the Stranger, Plato commits here not a kind of infanticide regarding his earlier conception of the ideas, but recasts the ideas entirely in the direction of the minimal universal building blocks of intelligible speech. In my view, the eminent role assigned to the Stranger in the *Sophist* is not accidental or philosophically trivial; on the contrary, it bears on the argument itself, and thus, the consequences that this has for philosophical thought itself need to be drawn. In other words, I wish to propose that the development of philosophy—as opposed to what in the *Sophist* and *Statesman* are called tales of sages or wise men—requires a radical break with everything merely local, and must occur in a discursive form that has shed local colors; furthermore, I argue that only a foreigner can be up to such a task. From the perspective of the native, a philosophy that radically questions the authority conferred by the soil or the earth is inevitably seen as the philosophy of a foreigner, even if the latter thoroughly displaces the relation of self and other.

At first glance, the extraordinary weight of the fact that Plato entrusts a stranger with the development of a philosophy of Non-being—a philosophy, as we will later see, in which otherness plays a cardinal role—must be taken to suggest that the new philosophy is one that has not grown on Greek soil and that thus has to be developed in tandem with a radical questioning of nativeness, ethnicity, and autochthony. Even if this new philosophy has its antecedents in previous developments in Plato's thought, the dramatic effect that results from allowing a stranger to develop it is that its novelty stems precisely from its foreign origin. Now, the statement that philosophy is philosophy only because it is elaborated by a stranger does not mean that it is philosophy just because some stranger happened to develop it; rather, philosophy is philosophy because there is an intrinsic relation between philosophy and foreignness, alterity, and otherness. In its critical examination of autochthony and its simultaneous empowerment of a stranger, the *Sophist* does not, of course, advocate a simple inversion of the positions of the native and the foreign, or imply that philosophy would be philosophy only at the expense of all nativeness. Rather, philosophy is philosophy only on the condition that its starting point is not first the native self who then reaches out and opens itself to others, or to the foreign. This means that philosophy is philosophy only if, from the start, it is of such a nature that any concern with the self is predicated on, and framed by, a relation to otherness. This requires an opening that displaces the initial privilege of the self without, however, simply replacing it with the other. If it is a stranger who Plato burdens with this task, it is not simply for dramatic effect. The empowerment of the stranger is called for by a philosophy that extends intelligibility, or *logos*, to Non-being as understood in the Stranger's doctrine, and whose "center" is constituted by the thought of the other (*heteron*).

Before engaging Parmenides directly, several attempts are made by the Stranger and Theaetetus to track down the genre, look, or aspect of the sophist by way of the characteristically Socratic method of division: first, as a hunter of rich young men for cash payment; second, as a wholesale or, third, retail peddler, mostly in secondhand knowledge concerning virtue but of which he is at times also, fourth, the manufacturer; fifth, as an eristic mercenary, that is, one who teaches how to dispute concerning good and evil, for gain; and sixth, as a philosopher-like cleanser of souls. However, each attempt fails (or rather, falls short), either because the art of the many-sided animal that is the sophist is much more complex than the individual genres by way of which the Stranger and Theaetetus seek to define him, or because (as in the case of the sixth division) the genre is still too vague. Further, by pretending to master multiple forms of expertise, the multifaceted animal called "sophist" seems to lack a center in which all these forms of skill converge. Having so far only produced a number of defining names for one referent, which should have only one name that fits his character and his art, the Stranger and Theaetetus make a final attempt by returning to, and expanding on, the fifth definition and analyzing him under his look as a debater and a teacher of controversy (*antilogistikon*) about everything; this, as they hold, is what reveals him most of all. However, if this "universal" art presupposes a knowledge of all subject matters, the sophist is necessarily a fake, as has already been said, since it is impossible for any human to be omniscient. But whence, then, comes the wondrous power of sophistry by which the young, in particular, are seduced? As the Stranger explains, this power originates in the sophist's seemingly demiurgic art of mimicking an apparent knowledge in all subjects. Indeed, like a painter he produces replicas, but in speech, "spoken images of everything" that from a distance look like the real things to the inexperienced and thus give them the illusion that, although they are only "homonymous imitations of 'the things which are,'" "seem to be truly said and, in addition, the speaker to be the wisest of all in everything" (234b7–c8).

According to the thus refined fifth definition, the sophist now appears "as a kind of enchanter and imitator," belonging to "the genus of conjurors [*thaumatopoion*]" (235a8–b6), insofar as he knows how to produce a deceptive semblance of universal knowledge. With this, the genre in which the Stranger seeks to locate and thus arrest the sophist through a final division is coming into view. Yet, in order to determine the exact place that the sophist occupies within mimetic art, the Stranger must divide mimetic art into two forms: likeness-making—that is, the making of true images (*icons*)—and semblance- or apparition-making (*phantasms*)—that is, the art of making images that simulate, but are not, faithful copies.[72] Since no image *is* what it represents, the distinction is one between image-making that acknowledges this difference, and one that does not, so pretending, on the contrary, to *be* what it only represents. As copies, both a true image and an image of mere semblance imply Non-being (since they are not the thing represented), but by offering the image as the thing itself, the phantasm effaces the difference and makes it appear as being. The art of the sophist consists precisely in making what is not seem to be by giving being to what is not. This discovery confronts the Stranger and Theaetetus with a genuine difficulty, since it presupposes that the sophist is at home in an art of discursive image-making that makes what is not seem to be. If the Stranger and his interlocutor are at a loss regarding the kind of image-making to which the sophist's speech belongs, it is because, given what they take Non-being to mean, it appears impossible to them to establish discursively such a branch in the art of image-making, one that makes distorted, illusive, deceptive, and ultimately false images of what is, one that in the same process endows that which is not with a reality of its own. Such an art, and by extension its practitioner, implies that what is not has being. If we are here at a decisive crossroads in the dialogue, it is because the new look that could be used to pin down the sophist requires the daunting task of demonstrating that Non-being has reality and that it pervades Being as much as the discourse on it. Such an assumption, however, without which the sophist cannot be arrested once and for all, runs up against the whole of the reflections on Being that have dominated Greek thought from Ionian physiologism to, in particular, the Eleatic doctrine of Being. In other words, this assumption runs counter to the doctrine of "father Parmenides," as the Stranger will soon call him, according to whom one can say solely of Being that it is, whereas Non-being, because it is not, cannot be said without contradicting oneself, since to speak of it is inevitably to consider it as something that has Being. In short, in order to hunt down the sophist and to establish him as a maker of distorted images and falsehoods, the Stranger will in fact have to put Parmenides' assertion to the test and become not only the refuting god that Socrates called him at the opening of the dialogue, but thereby, I hold, also the founder of a novel way of philosophizing, if not even the founder of the first genuine form of philosophy. Undoubtedly, commentators of the *Sophist* have not been blind to the fact that the refutation of the Parmenidean conception of Being and Non-being, as well as the doctrine taught by the Stranger, represents a breakthrough in Plato's thought. Hegel's laudatory account of the dialogue in *Lectures on the History of Philosophy* is just one example.[73] But what has not drawn the attention of these commentators is the fact that this doctrine is taught by a stranger and that, especially in a Platonic dialogue, this is not without implications for the theory itself. Without taking into account the narrative and dramatic nature of the context in which the Stranger's doctrine is developed, it is not possible to gauge its full originality.

But let me return to the impasse, perplexity, or aporia in which the Stranger and Theaetetus find themselves after having distinguished between an art of making faithful copies and an art that simulates doing so, the latter of which implies that the Non-being and falsehood of the unfaithful copies must in some sense exist, that is, must have Being. As the Stranger remarks, to affirm that Non-being has Being is an audacity when considering "Parmenides the Great" and his contention that only Being is and that Non-being, because it is not, is "unthinkable, unsayable, unutterable, and unspeakable" (238c12). Non-being cannot be something, because to take it for something is already to confer Being on it; as a concept it is *alogon*, a non- or un-concept—in short, unspeakable. In other words, without first resolving the question of how one can speak of Non-being without being hemmed in by contradiction, it is impossible for the Stranger and Theaetetus to pursue the effort that they have begun in the final *diairesis* to surround the sophist. If the Stranger interrupts the characteristically Socratic method of division—that is, the first outline within Greek thought of a method for thinking and cognition—with the lengthy ontological investigation into the relation of Being and Non-being that constitutes the central part of the dialogue, before subsequently resuming the division, this also amounts, of course, to a sort of refutation, or at least a recasting, of the Socratic method of philosophical investigation itself.[74]

While invoking "Parmenides the Great," the Stranger addresses Theaetetus as "my boy [*o pai*]," and tells him that, "beginning when we were boys and right through to the end," "Father Parmenides"—as he is referred to later in the dialogue—would testify stoutly and speak repeatedly of the impossibility that the things that *are not*, *are*, and would warn that one should keep away from this line of inquiry (237a5–9). Consequently, the Stranger's ontological investigation is clearly directed at the young Theaetetus (as well as Young Socrates, who is quietly listening). As a student of Theodorus, but at the same time as someone whose extraordinary gifts may predispose him to a kind of knowledge other than that of his teacher, the Stranger's intention is also to wean Theaetetus away from the mathematical approach to knowledge and toward a new, unheard-of philosophical path of inquiry distinct from all previous paths, the Socratic path included. Indeed, Theaetetus agrees to the Stranger's proposal to challenge the statement that Non-being is not, which still prevents them from cornering the sophist, telling him to "go and consider it on your own and then lead me too along this way [*kata tauten ton hodon*]," the way explicitly prohibited by father Parmenides (237b6–7).[75]

The Stranger admits later in the dialogue that when he was younger, he believed that he understood precisely what was meant by the expression "that which is not." Now, by contrast, he muses, "we are in the perplexity about it" (243b10–12). The notion of Being, after subsequent examination, proves to be as full of perplexities, if not even more so, than that of Non-being. Given this, it will be necessary in what follows to highlight the presumably irrational nature of Non-being on the basis of which Parmenides forbade his disciples to even consider it, directing them instead to exclusively pursue the only possible road, that of Being. But the Stranger's exposition of Parmenides' interdict against speaking of Non-being seems, paradoxically at first, to amount to a full vindication of Parmenides' testimony and to an admission that it is impossible to refute it by holding that, in some way, Non-being is. As we have seen, however, the latter is an assumption without which the sophist cannot be nailed down. Yet, the purpose of this exposition is also to bring out the enormous difficulties that anyone would face when challenging the prohibition in question, thus highlighting the courage it takes to do so. Since Parmenides declared Non-being to be "unthinkable, unsayable, unutterable, and unspeakable," "whenever someone tries to refute it, he himself is compelled to contradict himself about it," because in doing so one must speak of Non-being as "something," that is, as something that as such necessarily has being (238c12–d8). The chief difficulty, according to the Stranger, is that it is strictly impossible to attribute anything that exists—above all, number, that is, unity or plurality—to Non-being, because doing so is precisely to endow it with beingness. The risk, then, is that by pronouncing Non-being, one is not speaking at all (237e4–7), since one speaks about nothing. As a result, it is impossible to say in any way that Non-being is, or what it is, because this would make it a form of Being, and one thus contradicts oneself. However, even before he interrupts the seventh division for the central ontological digression, it is also made clear that the Stranger's seeming vindication of the Parmenidean prohibition has already set into motion a countermovement to the doctrine. Indeed, if it is strictly impossible to think and speak of Non-being, "the proof of Parmenides, as expounded here by his Eleatic disciple, is caught [itself] in a contradiction," in that such proof is not possible without one speaking of it as something—that is, by definition, something that is "a" being.[76] Indeed, Parmenides' proof is self-contradictory because it is not possible without assuming that, at least in some way, Non-being is. The perplexity of the Parmenidean concept of Non-being thus consists of the fact that it is unthinkable because nothing can be predicated of it without making it into something that is. Even to say that it is not is to speak about it as if it had Being, and in doing so one falls short of what Non-being is in itself, or in truth. As we will see, this countermovement, which subtends the Stranger's exhibition of the inner perplexity of Non-being, ushers in a novel way of thinking Non-being as no longer the opposite of what will soon be shown to be the equally perplexing notion of Being.

In any event, as Plato makes clear—particularly in the context of the seventh attempt to define the sophist as a deceptive image-maker—the sophist borrows his tools from the Parmenidean workshop.[77] The sophist's denial that there are false images, in order not to be pinned down, draws unmistakably on the declaration that Non-being does not exist and that one can speak only of what is. On the grounds of Parmenides' doctrine, it is thus simply impossible for the sophist to make false statements. Hence the Stranger's wish to "even slightly [. . .] pull ourselves away from so mighty a speech" as that of the sophist (241c9–10)—"mighty" because calling on Parmenides' authority—so as to able to engage the thesis of father Parmenides in a direct manner. Without establishing that, in a way, " 'that which is not' is in some respect, and again, in turn 'that which is' is not in some point" (241d7–8), it is impossible not only to track the sophist but, especially since he draws his resources from the philosopher, to establish also what distinguishes the philosopher from the sophist, his phantasm.

Before explicitly delving into the controversy over Being and Non-being, the Stranger presses Theaetetus not to take him "to be, as it were, a kind of parricide [*hoion patraloian*]" (241d3). In response to Theaetetus' exclamation of surprise at this request, the Stranger explains: "It will be necessary for us, in defending ourselves, to put the speech of our father Parmenides to the torture and force it to say that 'that which is not' is in some respect, and again, in turn, 'that which is' is not in some point" (241d5–8). Let us remind ourselves that in the *Theaetetus*, Protagoras had also been called the "father" of a doctrine, in his case a doctrine holding that what in each case appears to oneself in perception—that is, what for Parmenides is only of the order of illusion—also *is* for oneself. Now, the epithet "father" is attributed to Parmenides, who stands for the doctrine according to which only Being is, and the constantly changeable manifestations of appearances are of the order of Non-being. If Protagoras deserved to be named a "father," it was, as I suggested, because he is the author of a geneticist theory of becoming—more precisely, of infinite engendering at the exclusion of all permanence or rest. By contrast, Parmenides is, as Dixsaut remarks, referred to by the Stranger as "the 'father,' because in order to speak of Being he dismisses all forms of engenderment."[78] I leave open the question of whether these two fathers of Greek thought, Protagoras and Parmenides, are thus construed, respectively, one as promoting a fertility of illusory appearances, and the other a sterility of the One or of Being. Now, of course, the appellation "father" makes sense only within the framework or institution of the family. This issue is especially important here, since in the *Sophist* a stranger is welcomed into the family, as it were, of the discussants. Furthermore, although he has been invited to refute the authority of Parmenides, this stranger has, paradoxically, to defend himself as not being a parricide. As Jacques Derrida observes, "a foreigner can be a parricide only when he is in some sense within the family," that is, only when he is something like "*a foreign son*."[79] The Stranger's remarks, that from childhood on Parmenides was a father to him, but that, now in order to be able to defend himself against the sophist, he and Theaetetus have "to put the speech of our father Parmenides [*ton tou patros Parmenidou logon*] to the torture [*basanizein*] and force it to say that 'that which is not' is in some respect, and again, in turn, 'that which is' is not in some point" (241d5–8), suggest that the foreigner belongs to the philosophical household formed by the discussants. Yet he is also a foreigner to his Athenian hosts who have invited him into their midst. At this point, it may be warranted to recall with Benveniste that the institution of *xenia*, which offers a foreigner hospitality in another land and secures the reciprocity of the guest, thus allowing for alliances and exchanges between societies, is predicated on "the idea that the stranger is of necessity an enemy and correlatively that the enemy is necessarily a stranger. It is always because a man born elsewhere is *a priori* an enemy that a mutual bond is necessary to establish between him and the EGO relations of hospitality, which would be inconceivable within the community itself."[80] If the Stranger did indeed belong to the (spiritual) family of the Eleatic, his demolition of father Parmenides could be viewed as a parricide, but as a guest-friend in Athens—thus, an enemy hosted and committed to reciprocity—he must vigorously deny that his critique is anything like a parricide. His request to Theaetetus not to consider his refutation something like a parricide is therefore not simply a denial in a Freudian sense: it is a nod toward the hosts, who cannot not suspect him of violence against them, implying that even in his role as a refuting god he will be faithful to the contractual expectations by recognizing the greatness of the figure he will dismantle. Does this mean that, in truth, no parricide occurs here? Or, is the Stranger's denegation to be understood as meaning that "precisely therefore he will commit a parricide, and at the same time not?"[81]

At this point, a closer look at the Stranger's proposal to question Parmenides' interdiction becomes inevitable. Let us remind ourselves again that the critique of Parmenides' mighty speech is required by the fact that the sophist hides behind what it asserts, namely, that one cannot speak of Non-being, and thus there is no deception and no falsity to his speeches. To twist ourselves free from the force of the sophist's self-vindication, we must, the Stranger avers, put "the speech of our father Parmenides to the torture [*basanizein*]," that is, inspect it closely, and put it to the test. But even though one can, in doing so, free oneself only slightly from the grip of so powerful an argument, the violence involved is considerable, as the reference to torture implies. And for this reason, justifiably, the refutation has all the looks of a parricide. In any event, the Stranger admits that "a kind of reluctance" kept him so far from "set[ting] upon the paternal speech [*patrikoi logoi*]" (242a1–3), and that if, under the pressure to corner the sophist, he now finally musters the nerve to begin "a speech fraught with danger," he is also afraid of looking crazy (*manikos*) (242a11–b6). The audacity required to take on a thesis as authoritative as that of Parmenides might be taken as a sign of sheer madness.[82] According to the Stranger, father Parmenides admonished him from early childhood on not to follow the road of Non-being. The way he now proposes Theaetetus to take is precisely the one way prohibited by the Eleatic. Now, to justify taking this road in defiance of Parmenides' verdict, it is not only necessary to take on Parmenides alone, but, in the Stranger's words, "everyone else who has ever started out to make a determination of the things which are, how many they are and of what sort." What makes the task of refuting Parmenides so huge is that it cannot be undertaken without confronting the entire history of all the fathers of "philosophical" thought, who are accused of having discoursed to us in rather offhand fashion (*eukolos*) (242c4–7).

Several remarks are warranted here. The Stranger's turn away from the sophist is a turn away from the question of Non-Being and toward that of Being, and thus prepares the exhibition of the latter notion's perplexity. From the start, the Stranger's words also make it clear that the path he takes for a refutation of Parmenides is one by which Parmenides is placed into a whole line of other fathers, thus already putting into question or relativizing the authority of him whom Socrates in the *Theaetetus* still characterized as the One. Parmenides the One, therefore, is only one among others. Moreover, these manifold fathers no longer admonish children, but grownups, and the way they are said to speak to them, as the Stranger says, "appears to me to narrate to us, as if we were children, a kind of myth" (242c9–10). The parricide of father Parmenides first amounts, then, to what the Stranger defines as an act of disobedience of his prohibition (258c7–8), but also to a disobedience that ultimately goes further than simply disregarding the prohibition. It is a disobedience to the extent that it puts into question not only the prohibition of going down the road of Non-being but, by associating Parmenides with the whole of the thinkers that in an offhand fashion treat everyone else like minors, telling them tales regarding what is, furthermore not only questions the uniqueness of his authority but also the way that he and others like him speak. If the Stranger is thus afraid of looking crazy in going this new way, it is because it is the way of the philosopher, a way that, by questioning the paternalist structure of all previous "philosophy," also seeks to emancipate philosophy from the institution and social structure of the family.

Still, notwithstanding these observations, by refuting father Parmenides the Stranger's filial piety is not at issue. Even if the separation of the philosopher from the sophist requires what Theodor Gomperz called "a liberation from the fetters of Eleatism," the Stranger's association with Elea is indicative of his commitment to accomplishing this in conformity with exigencies regarding thinking that are essential and inescapable for philosophical thought, and which, as is evident from the *Parmenides*, are associated with the latter's name.[83] Granted that the Parmenides from the homonymous dialogue is Plato's construction, a Parmenides "who has become a dialectician," and is therefore also distinct from the historical Parmenides as well as the one who will be refuted in the *Sophist*, I hold nevertheless that it is in the spirit of Parmenides' exigencies of rigor that the Eleatic Stranger takes on "his father."[84] But before proceeding further, let us remind ourselves that the Stranger's questioning of the Parmenidean doctrine of Being and Non-being is necessary not merely in order to be able to make the final division and to surround the sophist but, more generally, in order to defend philosophical thought from the empty sophistic eristics that draws its tools from Parmenides himself.

So far, the sophist has eluded the seventh definition, in which the Stranger reworked the fifth attempt to nail him down as a semblance-maker who confers Being to what is not. The sophist has resisted capture by refusing to acknowledge Non-being (in the shape of falsehood) on the basis of Parmenides' claim that one can speak of only that which is, and not of that which is not, the implication being that what he offers in speech cannot possibly be false but, by definition, is true. Without a parricide, then, aimed at Parmenides' doctrine of Non-being, it is impossible to demonstrate the existence of false discourses and opinions and, by extension, of images that claim to be what they imitate. One could go so far as to say that the parricide is needed to even defend Parmenides from himself—not only from unintentionally providing the sophist with a justification of his trade but also from a sophistic temptation within philosophical thought itself. More pointedly, in other words, because of the concurrence of Parmenides and the sophist regarding Non-being, the parricide is the condition of possibility for something like philosophical thought itself. Now, as some commentators have argued, the refutation of Parmenides, rather than being a parricide, might strictly speaking be only a radical transformation of his conception of Being and Non-being intent on overcoming the Eleatic sterility of these concepts through what would be philosophy in a rigorous sense. Indeed, Parmenides' stringent requirements for any philosophical investigation whatsoever in the homonymous dialogue, which to a large extent orient the Stranger's examination of Being and Non-being, is a case in point.[85] But these very requirements for any philosophical inquiry, according to which one must undergo thorough training before daring to embark on any philosophical investigation—a training to which, as Socrates observes, there is no end (*amechanon*, 136c7)—and of which Parmenides agrees to give an illustration in the dialogue, are also stringent to the extent that they cannot be "experienced" except as violent.[86] Even though Parmenides himself complies with these rigorous rules of philosophical thinking, his doctrine of Being and Non-being cannot but submit to a violent revolution when tested by the Stranger against these standards. Stanley Rosen argues that, in his debate with Parmenides, "[t]he Stranger rules out a form of pure nothingness," that is, Non-being as the radical opposite of Being. This is no doubt the case, but does this in any way allow the conclusion that "in this important sense, he commits no parricide with respect to Parmenides"?[87] To construe Non-being as Otherness, as does the Stranger, is an affront as significant as understanding it as pure nothingness which could in no way combine with Being. But, I ask, is the explicit evocation of a "parricide" in the *Sophist* not also testimony to the powerful esteem in which the Eleatic philosopher was held in Greek thought, and as a result of which any question posed to his authority would inevitably be met with the suspicion of parricide? With the Stranger's reference to Parmenides as a father—a title of unquestioned authority enjoyed by the paternal figure in Greece until it started to be challenged by sophist enlightenment in Athens at the end of the fifth century, about the same time that the dialogue on the sophist supposedly occurred—his struggle against the latter's doctrine, even if limited to only a transformation, cannot escape the looks of a literal parricide.[88] The Stranger's radical scrutiny of the tales about the Oneness of Being is testimony to a special kind of violence that cannot be overlooked. It is a violence, first and foremost, because the refutation is the work of a foreigner, one who by definition is bellicose, and second, because of the violence specific to philosophy as such. For these reasons, the Stranger's refutation of Parmenides is faithfully alluded to as a parricide throughout most of Plato scholarship, even though it may not be one in a straightforward way.[89]

Before looking more closely at this "parricide" itself, let me pause here for a moment to reconsider the fact that, in the *Sophist*, Plato not only proceeds to a radical uprooting of all Greek thought hitherto, and in particular the thought of one of its most important founding fathers, but also entrusts a stranger with this task. Greek thought thus welcomes a new foundation for itself that has not grown on its own soil, and that it adopts from abroad, as it were.[90] In other words, it allows *within itself* a violence directed at everything native in philosophical thought, and at the narrative or mythic form through which it first manifested itself in Greece. The extraordinary event of allowing and condoning the parricide of a—or *the*—founding father by a stranger is further highlighted by Hannah Arendt, who notes that such a thing could never have occurred with the Romans, who "felt they needed founding fathers and authoritative examples in matters of thought and ideas as well, and accepted the great 'ancestors' in Greece as their authorities for theory, philosophy, and poetry."[91] I would add that such a thing could not have happened elsewhere at all. Indeed, it is something specifically Greek, if not what sets philosophy, as something Greek, apart from all other forms of inquiry or thought.[92] As we will see in a moment, what is at stake in the Stranger's parricide is the opening to a new way of thinking, one that not only occurs in Greece in a mode suggesting that it comes from the outside, and is thus not native or autochthonous, but that also inscribes within itself, on a most elementary level, a fundamental and irreducible relation to what is Other.

In his first account of the notion of Non-being, the Stranger seemed to vindicate Parmenides' claim that Non-being is unsayable and unutterable. But after requesting that Theaetetus not take him for a parricide, he finally musters the courage "to set upon the paternal speech" (242a2), intent on rejecting it. However, wondering "what kind of beginning would one make" in such "a speech fraught with danger" (242b6–7), he finally decides to begin by examining, from the beginning, the stories (*mythoi*) that Greek philosophy—starting with the Ionian philosophy of nature and, especially, later Eleatic philosophy—tells about Being's numerical nature (namely, that it is one, two, or three), and which since then seem to be taken for granted.

Putting the question of Non-being aside for the moment, he thus brings Being to the center of the examination.[93] By observing the way in which Parmenides and all of his predecessors have spoken about Being as "a kind of myth" (242c10), the Stranger emphasizes, first of all, the merely local and native setting of these thinkers' speeches. But each of them also tells a story of his own without caring "whether we're following them as they speak or we fall behind, but they severally get on with their own thing" (243a9–b2). In other words, what these thinkers say about Being is not only of the order of a fable, but their saying is also idiosyncratic and completely disregardful of its intelligibility to others.

First, the Stranger begins his overview by distinguishing several groups among those storytellers according to whom Being is either numerically one, two, or three, or a combination of these views. Let us note that the Stranger's inquiry into these views regarding what is comes about not only in order to fathom what precisely is meant by Being in each case, but also—since Being, as Aristotle will later say, is thus said in several ways (*pollakos legomenon*)—to prompt the need for establishing what Being is in itself, or as Paul Natorp puts it, "according to its concept alone (*alethos hen*)."[94] Furthermore, the Stranger accuses the storytellers in question of not only casual but also obscure language, and a lack of concern for ordinary people. In other words, this group of early storytellers formulated its views about Being with no concern for intelligibility, with no concern for *logos*, rational speech, and the exigency of accountability that comes with it. Let me emphasize right away that the Stranger's examination of these stories consists in calling its tellers back to the need for universal intelligibility, and that, even though he is a stranger, he confronts these Greek stories not with other exotic stories about Being from lands far away, but, paradoxically, with what will be understood after him as the rules of rational speech or Greek *logos*. The whole thrust of the resulting cross-examination of, in principle, all the philosophers hitherto is to force them to account for what they are saying about Being, something that may have seemed perfectly evident at first, but might in fact be just as confusing as the speeches about Non-being.

In explicating the Stranger's discussion of the storytellers' doctrines that elaborate on Being and beings in a numerical fashion, a discussion which in fact amounts to a first doxography or history of philosophy, but whose outcome here is to shelve all of Greek thought hitherto, I limit myself to what the Stranger labels as "our Eleatic tribe [*ethnos*], which had its beginning from Xenophanes and still earlier, on the grounds that all the things so-called are one, [and] proceeds in this way with its own myths"

(242d6–8).⁹⁵ As was the case with those who claim that Being is two or three, the Stranger and Theaetetus ask what in the world those who speak of Being think they are saying when they state that Being is One without first having examined the concept of Being itself. In the fictional cross-examination that follows, in which Parmenides and his disciples are drawn into the sphere of *logos*, that is, rational and accountable argumentation, they are forced, in the same way as the other earlier thinkers of Being, to admit the opposite of what they claim—in their case, that the Being they hold to be One is in fact more than one. In sum, if the proponents of Being as One assert that the All is Being, then Being, which is one and the same thing, has two names. Furthermore, since by definition a name names something separate from it, Being, rather than being One, is two, and thus is not identical to itself. Since the Parmenideans also hold that the All is the Whole, and a whole is by definition made up of parts, Being as a whole would be of many parts, yet as One it must be completely without parts. As a Whole, then, Being would again be more than One. Once Parmenides is thus drawn to argue for his thesis in a "common" language and in an exchange with an interlocutor who puts his assertions to the test, the doctrine of Being on the basis of which he rejected the thought of Non-being reveals itself as anything but self-evident. The examination of Being whose logic already drove Socrates' refutation, in the preceding dialogue, of the different solutions to the question of what knowledge is brings to light in measureless perplexity the countless difficulties involved in each solution. Each of the Parmenidean determinations of Being, the One, and the Whole, "turns out to fall short of itself [*endees to on heautou xumbainei*]" (245c3–4) and, as a result, "Being" reveals itself to be just as problematic as Parmenides' conception of Non-being—unthinkable, that is.

Next, the Stranger turns to another group of earlier thinkers about Being who are less precise than the first group in that they do not seek to count Being and beings. But what they mean by Being is just as hard to understand and, in turn, involves aporias, although of a different kind. I am referring to what the Stranger, drawing on a popular myth about the struggle between the Olympian gods and a savage race of sons of the Earth (*Ge*), who sought to storm mount Olympus and dethrone the gods, characterizes as the *gigantomachía tes ousías*, that is, the battle of gods and giants about beinghood. This "tremendous" struggle, as the Stranger calls it, opposes the earthborn giants to those "way up high." The former violently "drag everything to earth out of the sky and the invisible, and simply (artlessly) get their hands on rocks and oaks," insisting that only that has being which can be grasped with both hands, thus "defining body and being as the same," and the latter, "somewhere from an invisible position," and seemingly more gentle than the giants, defend themselves very cautiously, by "forc[ing] the simply true being to be some kinds of intelligible and bodiless species" (246a7–b10).[96] But they, too, violently "smash" the bodies of their opponents and what they call truth "up into little bits in their speeches" (246b11–c1).[97] Although the positions of both the Chtonians and Ouranians, or the materialists and the friends of ideas, will be put into question in a staged conversation with their proponents, I wish to emphasize first that the debate with those "who are sown and autochthonous" (247c6–7)—that is, the giants or the earth-born, who feel no shame at rejecting the difference between corporeal reality and invisible idealities—concerns a mode of thinking that considers itself native, sprung from the soil, and that therefore totally despises the other side that contends that something "is, though it's without body" (246b3). The disregard for difference, which is characteristic of this brand of thinking, is particularly rigid and violent as well, in that it is "unwilling to hear anything else" (246b4). Thus, as the Stranger acknowledges, it is "perhaps [. . .] pretty nearly impossible" to deal with (246c11). And, on the other hand, even though the friends of the forms are, in the Stranger's words, "tamer" (246c9–10), they are violent in their own way, and this camp of philosophical predecessors, who share with the materialists a similar rigidity, must thus also be taken to task. The friends of forms are just as unyielding in their opposition to contrary views as the materialists. The Stranger's critique of the dogmatic one-sidedness of both, and their judgment that the position opposing theirs is insignificant, immaterial, and of no worth, anticipates his account later in the dialogue of the category of opposition. According to this account, intelligibility requires recognizing that what is seemingly the opposite of one's own stance is just as valid, and thus has being in the same way as one's own position. But at this moment, and for several reasons, I stress in particular the Stranger's depiction of the giants. Autochthony as a concept of beginnings implies the origination of a people from the earth itself. Whereas the presence of a people in the land as a result of migration suggests the violent conquest of the land, autochthony is often believed to represent an origin free of violence. However, according to the Stranger, the autochthonous giants are anything but peaceful. Indeed, in the *Sophist* we behold Plato's perhaps most radical indictment of autochthony as violently blind to difference and otherness, and thus, as we will see, to *logos* as rational speech and the community such speech presupposes.

The two camps in question have forever been at war over corporeality versus incorporeality, a war that consequently cannot, in principle, be settled by argument.⁹⁸ So, the question is how to "get piecemeal from both of this pair of genera a speech on behalf of the being they set down for themselves" (246c6–7). The difficulty is especially severe in the case of the earthborn since they even refuse to consider or listen to the position of their adversaries. In the ensuing fictional debate, the Stranger, recognizing it is not possible "to make them better in deed," proposes to "make them so in speech" by asking them to answer "in a more lawful way than they now do" (246d3–6). In the fictional debate in question, as Paul Friedländer remarks, this is accomplished by "lending them our words and arguments."⁹⁹ By providing them with words to articulate their rigid positions, they are tricked into abandoning, however unknowingly, their stubborn refusal to acknowledge difference and otherness. By agreeing to enter speech, they have already, in principle, made several concessions. Rather than rehearsing the ensuing conversation, in which Theaetetus plays the role of the materialists, let me draw attention, in the original Greek text, to Plato's submission that by entering speech and having made some concession regarding the reality of such invisible things as are the soul or justice, the earthborn have already become reformed, or "better." In this passage, he uses the term *andres*, from *aner*, a man (as opposed to a woman) who is a member of a city, a free man, in short, also sometimes translated as "citizen-soldier" (247c5–6). In other words, by consenting to enter language, the aboriginal earth-born warriors and genuinely fierce materialists have in a way, unknowingly to themselves, become members of the *polis*. By refuting themselves in the very process in which they enter language, they have given up their nativeness and have, however reluctantly (and minimally), entered dialogic and agonistic communal life.¹⁰⁰

Undoubtedly, the friends of forms, who hold that only incorporeal things have reality or true being and that everything of the order of the corporeal is only "a kind of sweeping becoming," already participate in speech in that they defend themselves against the materialists by means of "some kinds of intelligible and bodiless species" (246b10–c2) that they force upon their opponents, thus breaking up and shattering to pieces what the latter claim to be bodies. But the friends of the forms are not only as rigid as their opponents, they are equally as dismissive of difference.¹⁰¹ To the extent that they do not acknowledge that any opinion, however different it may be, partakes in the *logos* precisely insofar as it is different or other, they do not practice rational speech. For this reason, they too must be made somewhat "better." The Stranger accomplishes this by engaging them in an argument in which they are no longer able to uphold their adamant opposition of Being and becoming, and are compelled to admit that Being, which they posited as immutable, combines with Motion, meaning that Motion and Becoming are thus also real. But this in no way implies that the Heraclitean position, according to which flux is real, would be an alternative to their initial position. On the contrary, at this juncture of the dialogue the Stranger states that, for the philosopher, only one course is open in the face of doctrines that either claim that Being is motionless, or by contrast that Change is Being, namely, to want it both ways, like children do. The philosopher, "in accordance with the prayer of children, [must] say that all that is motionless and in a state of motion are both together 'that which is' and the all" (249d1–4). In distinction from the two camps of earlier philosophies discussed, both of which cling to one-sided conceptions of Being, the reference to a child's desire to want it both ways announces a new way of philosophizing. Genuine philosophy arises from a confrontation between incompatible alternatives which, therefore, are impossible to hold simultaneously; genuine philosophy consists in the effort to find a way out of this impossibility. Consequently, philosophy originates from the insight that there is a fundamental link between the seemingly exclusive positions, first and foremost, regarding Being and what is at first glance incompatible with it, what differs from it, its other—namely, Non-being.

The Stranger's suggestion that philosophy arises only as an answer to an unmanageable impasse is further highlighted when he draws Theaetetus' attention to the fact that only now are they on the verge of recognizing the perplexity (*aporia tes skepseos*) that belongs to the inquiry into Being (249d9–10). As revealed in the debate with the formalists or friends of ideas, Being is both Movement and Rest. But what does "to be" mean when it is said of both Movement and Rest? By claiming that both Motion and Rest, which are opposites, have being, Being is necessarily posited as a third thing distinct from them. As a third thing, however, Being is neither Motion nor Rest. Yet, if Being is not Movement it must be at Rest, and if it is not at Rest it must logically be in Movement. It follows that Being cannot be at the same time in Movement and at Rest. Considering the extreme perplexity in which they already found themselves when they sought to say what Non-being is, the Stranger and Theaetetus agree "that it's no more readily available to say about 'that which is' whatever it is than about 'that which is not'" (245e12–246a1). In fact, the impasse into which they have now run while examining Being may be even greater.

Throughout the *diaireses* intent on capturing the sophist, both protagonists have repeatedly encountered aporias, which forced them to start anew. But after the failure to say what Non-being is, the aporia that emerges when they seek to determine Being marks an even greater failure, one that leads to the most crucial transition in the entire dialogue. Indeed, the difficulty they face is that, with the impossibility of saying what is to be understood by Being, determining the nature of Non-being is out of the question, and no progress can be made in nailing down the sophist. The Stranger and Theaetetus now confront the double impossibility of thinking both Being and Non-being. They are stuck in an aporia between two unsolvable issues that affect thinking and speaking themselves. And yet, as the Stranger remarks, "inasmuch as 'that which is' and 'that which is not' have equally partaken of perplexity, there's now the expectation that from now on, just as the other of them comes to light, whether more dimly or more clearly, so too the other comes to light. And if, in turn, we're incapable of seeing either of them, then we'll push the speech at least—whatever be the most decent way we can muster—in this way simultaneously through them both" (250e6–251a4). If the aporia in which they find themselves at this point is the most crucial aporia in the dialogue, it is because the very enterprise of forcing a way through this impasse is what will thereafter define philosophical thought. By opening a passageway as fitting as possible between Being and Non-being, whose aporetic nature results from a misunderstanding of the nature of Being by the entire tradition in whose wake Non-being had to be conceived as the opposite of Being, the Stranger presents himself as the "first" philosopher or as a new kind, if not an other kind, of philosopher.[102] The new philosophy that arises with the parricide of father Parmenides is one in which Non-being, rather than denoting the opposite of Being—namely, that which absolutely is not—names that which is other than Being. Differently worded, it is a philosophy in that it abolishes the absoluteness of the distinction between Being and Non-being, an abolishment under which alone the possibility of difference and otherness can emerge. Understood as Other, that which is not is "scattered and distributed across all 'the things which are' " (260b10–11). As the Stranger observes, about each thing "there are many things which are [. . .] and many which are not," in other words, things which are Other (263b14–15). However, the many things that are not, and are thus Other, are infinite in number (256e9). Furthermore, what is Other is doubly so: it also comprises Otherness that *is* not (*hetera ton onton*, 263b7), which does not participate in Beingness, and is therefore possible falsehood.[103] With this, the possibility becomes manifest of successfully demonstrating that Non-Being, in a way, is, and thus also that falsehood is something real.

The core of the Stranger's new philosophy is his doctrine of "the greatest kinds" (*megista gene*) which, in my reading, are the elementary building blocks of all intelligible forms, and which he develops throughout the digression that interrupts the final *diairesis* attempting to define the sophist. Implicitly, the doctrine of the greatest kinds has already informed much of the Stranger's argumentation so far, and can be considered as the explicit formalization of the "categories" by which it proceeded. "Kinds," in the expression "the greatest kinds," translates either *gene*, *eide*, or *ideai*, which Plato here uses interchangeably and which, in addition to "kinds," are also commonly translated as "forms" or "looks." "Greatest" means the most important, because the most comprehensive and, thus, the most universal ones. Therefore, for essential reasons, the greatest kinds are the most frequent in the *logoi* about what is. But before I say more about them and the community (*koinonia*) in which they relate to one another, without which no form can be what it is, we must first follow the Stranger and Theaetetus through the various steps toward finding a fitting way out of the aporia that they just encountered.

The Stranger begins by asking how it is possible that one and the same thing can be called by several names. More precisely, as shown by the example of the human being that he summons for the occasion, he wonders about the difference between the human being itself (*auto*) and all the *other* things (*ta alla*) that we say of him while, in the same breath, we speak of him himself (251a9–b4).[104] From an Aristotelean perspective, and especially from a modern perspective, Plato seems to raise here the question of the possibility of predication. Even though that which might be taken to correspond to judgment is, in the *Sophist*, accounted for by a grammatical combination of nouns and verbs, the assumption that Plato lays here the groundwork of a theory of predication is itself based on an interpretation of *logos* or speech as logical statement, that is, primarily as judgment.[105] In particular, this interpretation dominates the neo-Kantian readings of Plato. But the question the Stranger raises at this point concerns only the *other* names by which one can speak about a thing whose actual name, strictly speaking, designates it. How are these manifold names interlinked in our speeches? How do they participate (*metexeton*) in one another, rather than stand in a logical relation of identification by way of a copula, and share (*xummixis*) in the quality of one another so as to form a discursive community (*koinoniai pathematos heteron thateron*) (252b1–12)?[106] This question, broached at first with respect to names, prepares the ground for the decisive passage, by way of a mediation about the alphabetical letters, to the question of the genera or intelligibilia constitutive of the identity of forms. In all cases, the question is how something itself (in the case of the *gene*, sameness) can interlink in speech with *other* things (specifically with otherness, in the case of the *eide*). On the basis of the insight that, in speaking, even those who do not admit any interlinkage between something named and other names cannot but by their own speech contradict themselves (252c2–8), the question regarding the names, the letters, and the genera, dismantles the sophist's hegemony over what in the preceding chapter I have called "elseness," that is, unspecified "otherness" or the universalization of difference *simpliciter*. In other words, with his question regarding the interconnection of names in speech, the Stranger is about to break with the naturalist-indebted conception of otherness as *allos* in pre-Platonic thought and replace it with a discursive conception of otherness in the sense of *heteros* which, as we will see, does not simply disregard "elseness" but, on the contrary, puts it into its legitimate place.

In any event, the question about the One and the Many serves to prepare a new level of reflection in which the problem of Being as it has been discussed so far—either as one (Being), two (Rest and Change), or three (different from both Rest and Change)—is connected to the problem of the possibility of discourse, that is, rational speech or *logos*. In short, the problem of Being is connected to the possibility of attributing the Many (the other names like, for example, Rest and Change) to the One, to Being, which thus can be said differently. Addressing all those who have ever spoken about Being, the Stranger asks whether Being, Motion, and Rest can all partake of one another, whether there is no combination at all between them, or whether only some of them, but not others, can form a community. As the concern with speech and speaking about Being makes manifest, Being, Motion, and Rest are here neither predicates nor simply names but, rather, as will become clear soon, minimal intelligible forms of speech, that is, the "kinds" or "looks" evoked by the "greatest kinds." A lack of "any capacity for sharing with anything [*medemian dunamin echein koinonias eis meden*] in any respect" (251e9) would amount to overthrowing all discourse on Being, that is, all ontologies, and more generally to suppressing all *logos*, all speaking whatsoever, whereas total combination would mean the total dissolution of difference.[107] Thus, only one alternative is left: some forms mingle, and others do not.

Being, Motion, and Rest are already understood here as forms, kinds, or looks. As such, some can combine with one another, while others cannot, and it is this possibility that allows for *logos* or rational speech about what is. This means that, according to the Stranger, they and their formal combinations are the elementary formal building blocks of speech. Without them, no discourse could possibly guarantee that it was discoursing about a recognizable something distinct from a recognizable something else. These minimal forms warrant the identity, for example, of what in earlier dialogues Plato had called the idea of justice, or any other idea in the earlier Platonic sense, thus making sure that the speech about it remains unwaveringly focused. Indeed, with the Stranger's theory of the "greatest kinds," Plato sketches out, as it were, a doctrine of "categories" *avant la lettre*. Even though, for reasons of convenience, I will continue to use the term "categories" when speaking of these discursive intelligibilia whose intelligibility, as the Stranger makes clear, rests on their interrelation or mixing together (*summeixis*), caution is nonetheless warranted.[108] For, indeed, Plato never uses the term for these genera generalissima. Furthermore, their intelligibility also has a broader, if not indeed more general thrust for what he understands by knowledge than the role that, beginning with Aristotle, the categories, as the fundamental ways of logical combination—that is, of judgmental forms or forms of predication—have enjoyed in the epistemological conception of knowledge.[109]

The expression "the greatest kinds" suggests there are more kinds than the total five that the Stranger selects for his discussion and, further, that even those that are said to be the greatest, those most frequently used in speech, and which therefore enjoy a generality of the highest nature, might also be more numerous. Indeed, the Stranger never gives an exact number of the pure forms.[110] From the argumentative perspective of the *Sophist*, the five forms to which the Stranger restricts his discussion are sufficient for him to make his point, although, contextually speaking, their analogy to the alphabet's five vowels may also explain their number. Teisserenc poignantly qualifies these elementary forms as "vowel forms."[111] For, being "vowel forms," their number cannot, as Theaetetus observes, be fewer than five without jeopardizing the intelligibility of the examination (256d4–5).[112]

Just before beginning the discussion of which forms commune with one another and which do not, the Stranger remarks that in the present discussion he will not be examining all the species so as not to be confused among many, but rather will "choose some of the biggest spoken of" (254c3–4). The list, therefore, is not complete. There are definitely more forms than the five held to be the most important. Their number, five, is determined merely in view of the goal of the whole examination—the demonstration, aimed at Parmenides, that in a way Non-being is, that it too is utterable in an intelligible fashion. But if this list is not complete, it is not only because the five make up a select group among the most important species, but also because of its principial openness to other categories, if not categories of the other, made inevitable by the introduction of one kind in particular, as will become clear in a moment. Undoubtedly, by comparing these forms to the letters of the alphabet, which are limited, the Stranger could be understood as suggesting a finite number of such universal forms of intelligibility. Yet, as already intimated in the context of the debate about those who account for Being in numerical fashion, the thrust of the Stranger's teaching reaches beyond the calculable.

The reason for comparing the "greatest kinds" to the letters of the alphabet, that is, the elements of a kind of writing, alphabetical writing, that already presupposes a highly powerful process of abstraction—a comparison that has led commentators to refer to them as "the eidetic alphabet" or "an ontological alphabet"—is that among these letters, the vowels are letters that make possible any interconnection of the other letters.[113] According to the Stranger, the vowels go "through everything as a sort of bond, so as for it to be impossible without some one of them to fit even another of the rest with an other" (253a6–8). The greatest kinds hold a similar function with respect to all other forms, and share with vowels this universal importance. But there is an additional reason for the comparison, namely, that it serves to show that some of these kinds combine with one another and others do not. Indeed, some of the letters of the alphabet do not fit with one another, while others do. But the comparison in question serves to make still a further point regarding the kind of community that characterizes the "greatest forms," namely, that community is possible in the first place only because not everything is equally capable of linking with everything else. Just as vowels are distinguished from consonants in that they operate as a sort of bond that pervades all the others letters, so that without one of them the others cannot be fitted together, so too do certain kinds in the eidetic alphabet serve as bonds for the others. As a form, Being, for example, is one, but in the sense of just one kind that combines with all the others, with Motion and Rest, for instance, even though Motion and Rest themselves do not conjoin with one another. At this juncture, let me point out that the Stranger asserts that, in the same way that the combination of letters or sounds requires an art, namely, grammar, the combination of the intelligible forms requires a knowledge regarding their mixing. In other words, the combination of the kinds with one another takes place according to certain rules. Inquiring into an appropriate name for this knowledge, which Theaetetus qualifies as "perhaps pretty nearly the greatest," the Stranger suggests that it is "the science of the free" (253c6–9), that is, the science of the dialectician or philosopher. However, this knowledge of the philosopher is a post-Parmenidean, if not post-Socratic, philosophy, a philosophy in a novel sense.[114] But this will become truly manifest only when the Stranger introduces the two other kinds that, in addition to Being (*to on*), Motion (*kinesis*), and Rest (*stasis*), play a highly crucial role in the community made up by the ultimate constituents of intelligibility and, thus, of a community of discourse or *logos*. It therefore remains to be seen what forms of intelligibility lie at the heart of the ontology developed so far.

Before proceeding to the Stranger's explicit discussion of the "greatest kinds," let us remind ourselves again of his comparison of them to the letters of the alphabet. The letters of the alphabet do not mean anything in themselves, and the analogy of the kinds with letters suggests that the same is true of the eidetic forms. Being, undoubtedly, is one of these forms, and it follows that, as such, it too has meaning not in itself but only in relation to other forms. With this, it appears that the debate with Parmenides, for whom only Being is, and Non-being cannot be spoken of without contradicting oneself, has been raised to another level of reflection. Ultimately, the parricidal point is that, without a relation to Non-being, Being is an empty, meaningless word. It remains then to be seen in what sense "Non-being" is to be understood. So far, we have seen that Being, Motion, and Rest are some of the "greatest kinds." As the expression suggests, they are the greatest because they can, as Hans-Georg Gadamer remarks, "be present with everything—in the same way numbers can be present with everything, whatever it is that is so and so many."[115] Yet, as Gadamer continues, such

> Being-with of the greatest kinds does not mean that there is an ultimate general or universal kind, say the One, that would become differentiated and progressively specified. What the greatest kinds are here is of a different sort of generality. [. . .] As that which connects everything, they are, like the vowels, that which binds. Even Being (*ousia* 250b9) is not introduced here as the highest kind or form. It is present with other "things" [*mit da*], even with everything. . . .[116]

As one form among others, the co-presence of Being with other "things," such as Motion and Rest, deprives Being of the exclusive status that it enjoys in pre-xenological philosophical thought.[117] As a kind, Being "is, undoubtedly, the fundamental linkage in all *koinonia* because it makes the forms designed to combine join and participate in one another."[118] But if, as a kind, Being is one of the eidetic letters that holds all the others together, the kind that is the Other of Being is one that, in a complementary and symmetrically inverse way, causes them to divide. "The universal penetration" that characterizes Being as a kind, "accomplishes in every form that which in it remains simply potential. Being makes the terms that must communicate communicate; it makes the forms that are mutually in affinity with one another hold together (*sunechein*, 253c1), exactly as the Other makes terms that are heterogeneous separate from one another."[119] Consequently, Being is no longer the ultimate instance, that is, a general, all-comprehensive concept, nor are any of the other forms that constitute the greatest kinds. No hierarchical relation obtains between them. They do not form a pyramidal system in which one of them is superimposed on the others. The Stranger's doctrine of the eidetic alphabet presupposes the uncompromised plurality, horizontal equality, and co-originarity of the forms in question.

In his pursuit of the examination of the greatest kinds and the modalities of their combinations, the Stranger proposes, first, to look into "what sort [of things (*poia*)] they severally are, next how they are in terms of their capacity [*pos echei dunameos*] of sharing in one another" (254c4–5).[120] But before doing so, he also reminds Theaetetus, as well as the audience or readers of the *Sophist*, of the stakes of this whole discussion, namely, that the investigation in question has been initiated as a response to a formidable aporia regarding Being and Non-being. The Stranger avers that even in the case that he and Theaetetus might be "incapable of seizing [both Being and Non-being] with complete clarity," if they proceed this way they will "not at least fall short of a speech about them, to the extent that the way of the present examination allows it" (254c6–9). He continues, expressing his intention of seeing "whether, after all, 'that which is not' gives way at some point and allows us, in saying that it is in its being 'that which is not,' to get off scott-free" (254c9–d1). First and foremost, the goal of the whole discussion of the greatest kinds and their community is thus to be able to assert against Parmenides that, in a way, Non-being *is* although it *is not*, and thereby to solve the problem of the sophist. Furthermore, the goal is also to make sure that this assertion does not backfire.

So far, the Stranger has referred to Being, Motion, and Rest as three instances of the "greatest kinds," establishing that Motion and Rest do not mix, whereas Being can conjoin with both. Now he holds that "each of them is other than the two, and itself the same as itself" (254d14–15).

As a result, the Other or the Different (*heteron*) and the Same (*auton*) are two additional kinds that raise the number of the greatest kinds to five. As regards the Other or the Different, it should be obvious that in the context of the greatest kinds, these terms refer to what is "other" in a strong sense, rather than to *allos*, that is, other in the restricted sense of elseness. Yet, since "whatever is other [in the eidetic sense] is of necessity that which it is as of another" (255d8–9), in short in difference from it, I wish to keep this intrinsic interrelation intact by referring to *heteron*, the fifth kind, as Otherness or Difference. Now, these two forms of intelligibility—the Other or Different, and the Same—are introduced as forms that always necessarily intermix with the three other kinds, for otherwise they could not remain distinct kinds. The participation of Being, Motion, and Rest in the forms of Sameness and Otherness makes it possible to speak of each of them as the same as itself and as other than, that is, different from, the remaining others. But this is also to say that the newly added kinds secure the community between them all insofar as they are distinct forms of intelligibility. What the forms of Sameness and Otherness accomplish with respect to Being, Motion, and Rest is that each of them is the same as itself insofar as it is different from, or other with respect to, the other. In other words, the community of the greatest kinds (*koinonia ton genon*) is a community based on what we today call differentiality. Indeed, in concluding that Otherness or Difference is a fifth form, the Stranger asserts that its nature "has gone through all of [the other kinds], for it's not on account of its own nature that each one is different from all the rest, but on account of its participation in the look (*idea*) of the other" (255e3–6). The form "Other" thus communes, in a way similar to that of Being, with all the other forms. It is this specific form, rather than the internal nature of any of the other four forms, that makes each one what it is in particular, and it does so only by way of its difference from the others. What the Stranger establishes is that, from the point of view of intelligibility, nothing is what it is all by itself, on the basis of its own nature, but only insofar as it participates in the form of the Other, or Different. Only as such is it the Same as that which it is. For my present purposes, then, I stress that the form of Otherness or Difference, in which all the other kinds participate and which thus pervades all of them, Being included, just as in its own way Being runs through all the other forms, is the form that, together with Being, is responsible for the community of which it itself is a part.[121] Now, as the Stranger says, Difference or Otherness "has been chopped into bits [*katakekermatismenen*] to extend over all 'the things which are' in their mutual relations" (258e2–3). As opposed to the continuity of Being through all other forms, Otherness pervades all of them by making them non-identical with respect to one another. Its universality resides in its lack of the function of continuity by which all other forms become related. Now, even though all the forms are co-originary and equal, the form of Otherness, because distributed among all other forms, bears the burden in the refutation of the Parmenidean doctrine of the identity of Being, and, therefore, would seem to enjoy a particular status. Yet, as will become clear, this impression may only be the result of its "inner" complexity, which we will address expressly hereafter.

Let me pause here for a moment to draw attention to the fact that the notion of Otherness that the Stranger includes among the five genera recasts, from the ground up, the whole problematic of "elseness." What is shown to obtain with respect to the cluster of the five species—namely, that Non-being, and thus Difference, affects and interconnects all of them—limits the concept of elseness to a merely general or undetermined concept of otherness. If Theaetetus suggests that in speaking of the non-beautiful we distinguish it, without turning it into an opposite or contrariety, from nothing *else* (*ouk allou tinos heteron*) than merely the beautiful (257d11–13), then elseness (*allos*) is restricted to unspecified otherness. The myriad of isolated and impenetrable elses which, as the sophists claim, differ from one another on the basis of their nature (*physin*), has, as is demonstrated with respect to the cluster of the five genera, been replaced by a universe of *hetera* that are other because they participate in the idea of Otherness, which not only renders them intelligible but, in the same breath, mutually interrelated. By conceiving of Otherness as difference, and by conceiving of the other as "always relative to another (*heteron aei pros heteron*)" (255d1), others become capable of sharing in one another. This shift from a concern with elseness is also manifest terminologically: the notions of *heteros* or *thateros* ostensibly dominate the Stranger's speech in the *Sophist*, compared to the overwhelming frequency of the term *allos* in the previous dialogue.

However, although Otherness as *heteros* differs from elseness or *allos* in that the former refers to a specific, determined otherness, this distinction, as we will see, does not exhaust the concept or its specificity. The Other as one of the greatest kinds is not an Other over there, exterior to that from which it differs. On the contrary, it is an Other precisely because of the community that is shared with it. In other words, the community in question is one in which the Other is suffered (*koinoniai pathematos heterou*), a community by which something cannot but be affected, and that therefore must, willingly or not, be addressed, named, and engaged (see 252b9–12).

Heteros or *thateros* designates an Other that differs on the basis of the community shared with it, and is thus to be determined in all its Difference.

Before seeking to understand how the doctrine of the greatest kinds represents a radical critique of Parmenides and the beginning of a new way of thinking philosophically, let me caution against the hasty confusion of the crucial thought of "Otherness" or "Difference" that the Stranger introduces into Greek thought with the thought of what is strange or foreign, the foreigner included. Otherness and foreignness are not the same. As Henri Joly notes, if "the Other never catches up with the human Other," it is because "the Platonic Other remains a *category of things* and is not yet a *category of the person*."[122] Indeed, in Plato's time it was not yet possible to link foreignness and otherness as alterity.[123] The Other that the Stranger evokes is a logical category—it pertains at first to genres and, since genres are things, also to things—and thus it is not entirely appropriate to speak of the Stranger as an Other.[124] Let us thus, after what has been said so far about the nature of the Other, look a bit more closely at how the Greeks conceived of difference, or otherness. According to Paul Natorp, for the Greeks,

> What is different is different in relation to something different. The Greek mind conceives of difference as mutual [*Gegenseitigkeit*]; it does not, as we do, speak of contrasting one thing with a different thing, but of contrasting a different thing with a different thing. If A is different from B, then B is no less different from A, A being precisely what is different from B, *its* other, in short. This already implies that difference serves not so much to separate things, but to unite them. The boundary that separates is equally a shared boundary, hence it is a boundary that provides for a transition in thought.[125]

It might seem that Otherness, according to the way its kind or look is introduced (254d14–15), emerges terminologically and conceptually in a process of differentiation in relation to the Same. But if the concept of the other implies mutuality such that what it differs from differs in turn from it, then the Same is not simply the twin correlate of the Other, as is the case with Motion and Rest. As a singular kind, Otherness establishes an Other in relation to another Other. The Other in relation to which an Other is other is, in turn, *its* Other, not an Other mastered by a self, but an Other in relation to which only an Other is other. Thus, a fundamental communality is established between both. By way of this interrelatedness of an Other with an Other that is *its* Other, the category in question differs from that of the Same. Consequently, the participation in the idea of Otherness is what "provides for nothing less than the possibility of relation in general."[126] But this constitutive mutuality or reciprocity of what is Other to an Other, and vice versa, is, in addition to the fragmented nature of the Other, what further complicates the inner complexity of the category in question.

Since, in the *Sophist*, a stranger becomes the author of a doctrine of the Other by showing that the Same cannot be thought without it, the questions of the Stranger and the Other are not only raised to the status of philosophical questions as such; they are also linked together, as it were.[127] Following Seth Benardete's remark on Socrates' suggestion at the beginning of the dialogue that the nameless Stranger might possibly be a god—that is, someone who, like God, is other as such and therefore remains always outside whatever group of humans that he may join—I wonder whether Theodorus' subsequent characterization of the Stranger as only a divine human being does not also imply that he is an other.[128] I also wonder whether, as precisely such an other, as well as foreign, human being, he is moreover an Other in a sense distinct from that which characterizes the individual interrelation of his local guests. Does this particular status of the Stranger's persona, in relation to all the other participants of the dialogue, not also explain why he can be the author of a philosophy in which the form of Otherness plays a significant role? Undoubtedly, one may argue that the concept of Otherness thus introduced is only a logical concept, or the concept of Otherness in general, and therefore that a further parricide might be necessary to make it possible for thought to open itself to the singular human other.[129] But the thought of the Other as it is introduced by the Stranger is, at least on a first level, broad enough to accommodate such an opening within thought. Indeed, as Derrida asks in conversation with Levinas's notion of *autrui*, "how can the 'Other' [*Autrui*] be thought or said without reference—we do not say reduction—to the alterity of the *eteron* in general? . . . The *eteron*, here, belongs to a more profound and original zone than that in which this philosophy of subjectivity (that is, of objectivity), still implicated in the notion of the Other [*autrui*], is expanded."[130] From the beginning, the Stranger's thought also inscribes the possibility of a relation to alterity, in the form of a *foreign* alter Ego, into the core of Greek thought. More precisely, this is the case from the beginning of the new path that the Stranger opens up in the *Sophist*.

In addition to this undoubtedly risky intimation, I venture one more observation. If, ontologically speaking, Otherness in the Greek sense implies a mutuality between others, and consequently their togetherness, then if it is (however improperly) applied to the relation of the Stranger to his Greek hosts, a strange, but also fundamental, community between him (as a stranger) and his hosts comes into view. Certainly, the Stranger can be a stranger exclusively in relation to his Greek hosts, but they differ from him, and can be the Greeks they are, only thanks to him. They are not simply linked with him in a strange unity but, as his presence in the dialogues suggests, it is from the Stranger that the hosts receive the gift of being Greeks—no longer autochthonous but Greeks in an entirely non-native sense.[131]

Now, let us not lose sight of the fact that the whole discussion of the greatest kinds was prompted by the necessity of finding a way out of the aporia regarding Being and Non-being. Therefore, it is time to look once more at Being. The Stranger reopens the question by asking, "Are we to say then fearlessly and contentiously that motion is after all other than 'that which is'?," which elicits Theaetetus' retort, "Most fearlessly rather" (256d6–8). Indeed, the contention that there is something besides Being that *is*, and that is other than Being, is clearly a provocation with respect to Parmenides because it amounts to affirming clearly that something that is not identical to Being—in this case Motion—and thus non-Being, "plainly is in its being 'not that which is' and 'that which is,' since it participates in 'that which is'" (256d9–10). Yet, by extension, this also means that, according to the Stranger,

> it is after all of necessity, in the case of motion and throughout all the genera, that "that which is not" be, for in each and every case the nature of the other, in producing each to be other than "that which is," makes it "not that which is," and on the same terms we'll in this way speak correctly of all things as "not the things which are." And, once more, because they participate in "that which is," we'll say they are and "the things which are." (256d12–e6)

I pause for a moment to gauge the full impact of what is established in these lines, since we are touching here at the core of the Stranger's doctrine. It has been demonstrated that Non-being, understood not as what in no way *is*, but as what is different or other, has Being. Motion has served as an example, but Rest, the Same, or the Different could also have done so. Although all of these kinds participate in Being, they are different from it, not the same as it, and they are, therefore, Non-being.[132] For this very reason, however, Being itself is also only what it is to the extent that it *is not* everything else. In line with the differential logic that constitutes the community between the kinds, the inscription of Non-being within Being itself makes Being what it is in itself—namely, Being. For this very reason, Being stands no longer in a relation of opposition to Non-being, but instead in a relation of Difference or Otherness.

As the Stranger remarks, "Whenever we say 'that which is not,' we're not saying, it seems, something contrary to 'that which is' but only other" (257b3–4).[133] Non-being is the Other of every other. In the community of the greatest kinds, Being is no longer the binary opposite (*antithesis*) of Non-being represented by all the other kinds that, because of their participation in the form of Being, are but merely "its" others. In other words, if Non-being is construed as the opposite of Being, the relation of opposition is no longer one of contrariety, nor is it any longer binary. The negation of Being in Non-being in no way designates a specific essence that could serve to determine the subject to which it refers as an alternative to Being.[134] With the category of the Other, the logic of opposition is thus broken down, and opposition appears only as a relation that is a modification of Otherness or Difference (as in the opposition of Motion and Rest). Rather than a mode of thinking of Otherness, opposition is, on the contrary, to be understood as merely one particular form of Otherness. In advance of all contrariety and binary opposition, the negation expressed by the term "Non-being" requires a (violent) narrowing down or formal-logical restricting of the negation and its subject, before the indeterminateness (and generality) of alterity expressed by Non-being can make room for contrariety and opposition. Furthermore, as Plato remarks, when something stands in a relation to "its" other—as, for example, the Non-great to the Great, or the Non-just to the Just—"the other is not at all more than the other is" (258a5–6). Ontologically speaking, what is other is on the same footing (*homoion*) as that from which it differs, and to which it thus relates; in other words, it is not inferior. The category or kind of the Other is more originary than the structures of oppositional thinking which, in the case of Parmenides, culminate in the conclusion that Non-being is unutterable, unspeakable, and irrational, a conclusion that, in a way, undermines Non-being. The kind of the Other precedes opposition in an a priori fashion, and thus also undermines all hierarchies between opposites, opening a space of intelligibility to the saying of Difference or

Otherness. By breaking down the opposition of Being and Non-being, by recasting Non-being as what is (only) other than or different from Being, it becomes possible to overcome the Parmenidean prohibition, to assert the intelligibility of Non-being, and to speak about it without contradicting oneself. This is what the "look" of Otherness or the Different accomplishes with respect to Non-being, which, in the Stranger's doctrine, refers no longer to what Parmenides called "'the things which are not' [*ta me onta*]" but instead to "the species of 'that which is not' [*to eidos ho tugkhanei on tou me ontos*]" (258d5–7)—in other words, to the Other or the Different.

In resonance with numerous commentators on the *Sophist*, I suggested earlier that the Stranger's parricide is not simply a parricide in the literal sense, but rather a complete and, for a Parmenidean, unmistakably outrageous recasting of the Parmenidean doctrine. But nevertheless, does this recasting of the doctrine in question into an altogether other doctrine not still deserve to be called parricidal? By understanding Non-being in terms of the *form* of Otherness or Difference, Parmenides' contention that *absolute* Non-being is unthinkable and unsayable is, of course, not put into question. The Parmenidean doctrine that the totally non-existent is a non-entity is not challenged, but, on the contrary, is confirmed as it had already been in Book V of the *Republic*. Indeed, the Stranger argues that Non-being, "naked as it were and isolated from all the things which are, is impossible" (237d3–4). It can in no way be applied to anything at all, nor can anything be established about it. As Francis MacDonald Cornford notes, Non-being as the totally non-existent is "a name of nothing at all."[135] Absolute Non-being remains just as unthinkable and irrational as before; it can never become a form.[136] Nor, however, is the Stranger's indictment of Parmenides' claim as a form of storytelling about Being rescinded in any way after he has established the doctrine of the greatest kinds. Rather than somewhat validating Parmenides' doctrine, is the concession regarding absolute Non-being not therefore an admission that, as merely the binary opposite of Being, it is an irrelevant issue? Indeed, at the hands of the Stranger, Parmenides' understanding of Being undergoes a wholesale transformation as well, with the consequence that the whole of his doctrine becomes questionable. As Other, Non-being now inhabits and affects Being, but this expansion of Being implies that the Stranger's rendering of Being is no longer Being as Parmenides conceived it—that is, immutable and unchangeable. Just as Non-being has become a concept of an entirely different logical and ontological order, Being has been transformed into one intelligible form among others for speaking rationally about what is. No doubt, as a kind, Being participates in the other greatest kinds. However, this does not mean that Being spreads out into the four other genres in such a way that would make these forms only modifications or modalities of Being understood in the Parmenidean sense or that, as a result, the kinds would be kinds of Being in an objective sense. To hold that the kinds are five different forms of Being is to construe Being in a pre-xenological sense and, thus, to engage in a mixing and confusion of levels of thought. As forms, the greatest kinds are irreducible to one another and, as we have seen, they are co-originary and therefore of equal importance. Even though some of them mix with one another, no one of them dominates the others. As we have seen, the kinds *are* insofar as one of them, Being, communes with them, but the form of Otherness also makes them totally different from the kind of Being. In fact, from a Parmenidean perspective, they are all forms of Non-being.

Finally, let us also remind ourselves that, in the Stranger's account, the kind of Otherness or Difference prevents all prioritization. What is other or different is on the same level as that from which it differs. Between both, mutuality reigns. As the examples of the non-beautiful, the non-great, or the non-just clearly demonstrate (257b–258a), hierarchy is no longer involved here.[137] But does this permit the assumption, found in Hegel, for example, that Being and Non-being are identical? Certainly, this is not the place to tackle this huge question. I limit myself therefore to evoking only the unique emphasis enjoyed by Otherness and Difference in the Stranger's doctrine. The emphasis placed on Otherness is in no way an indication that it replaces the priority formerly attributed to Being. Instead, this emphasis indicates that Otherness demands to be taken seriously as such. It cannot be "hastily" reduced by identifying it in a speculative fashion with Being by way of a synthesis of the identical and the non-identical, which would save Parmenides' tale about Being and Non-being from the Stranger's radical criticism.[138] Put differently, by understating the Stranger's stress on Otherness, the thrust of his teaching is not only softened; it is folded back into the doctrine of Parmenides, with the result that the specificity of his doctrine is neutralized. The emphasis on Otherness in the Stranger's conception of the greatest kinds lends emphasis as well to the unique strangeness of his doctrine. As the Stranger will explain to Theaetetus, what they have achieved together is not limited merely to a demolition of the Parmenidean thesis. Their accomplishment is more than that, and it is this surplus achievement that makes it all the stranger.

Before concluding this chapter, therefore, a further deepening of the notion of Otherness as a category of discursive and ontological intelligibility is warranted. Following the contention that what is negated by a negative statement is not the opposite of the subject of negation but "only" an other of it, the Stranger observes that "[t]he nature of the other appears to me to have been chopped into bits just as science (knowledge) [*episteme*] has" (257c10–11). The Greek term for "chopped into bits" or, according to another translation, "parceled out"—*katakermatisthai*—comes from the verb *katakermatizo*, which contains the word *kerma*, "coin" or "fragment," and thus means "to change into smaller coins."[139] Literally, the word means *to make change*, that is, to break into smaller parts or morsels. This monetary, if not economic, connotation of the verb, which by extension signifies a cutting or chopping up, will prove significant hereafter. That knowledge is all chopped up is not difficult to understand: even though knowledge is one, it is parceled out into many arts and forms of knowledge. The comparison, undoubtedly, is intended for Theaetetus who, as a mathematician, still finds it difficult to understand that an elementary form such as Otherness is not merely distributed over all "the things which are," but could have "a fragmented interior" whose parts, therefore, are not countable.[140] To the extent that all the "greatest kinds" stand in a differential relation, they are not what they are in themselves and, thus, are not treatable as numerical entities. However, if the fragmented interior of Otherness causes it to be "unlike the other 'greatest kinds'" that "exhibit their look within a single 'thing,'" is it only, as Rosen puts it, because "*otherness* requires a minimum of two 'things' in order to exhibit its look"?[141] As demonstrated by the additional analogies to which the Stranger resorts in order to make his point, the comparisons serve to argue not only that all parts of Otherness have being but also that "the opposition of a proper part of the nature of the other and of the nature of 'that which is' in their opposition to one another, is, if it's sanctioned to say so, no less being than 'that which is in itself,' and it indicates not a contrary to that but only so much, an other than it" (258a13–b4). Here, in my interpretation, the Stranger brings into relief the beinghood of the relation of otherness (*pros heteron*), which is itself multiple, if not made up of infinite parts, and which constitutes the form of Otherness itself. The kind of the Other is made up of an infinite, noncalculable number of relations to Otherness, and these relations that have being make up this form as a form with a "fragmented interior." The name for the nature of these relations is, as Theaetetus says in response to the Stranger's question of what to call it, "[c]learly [. . .] that very thing, 'that which is not,' which we were seeking on account of the sophist" (258b7–8). In the Stranger's explication of the relation to Otherness that itself has Being, Non-being as the incalculable cluster of the relations constitutive of the form of Otherness is just as existent, just as real, as Being itself, and as such this very relation to Otherness makes for the possibility of *logos*.

Having set out to demonstrate that Non-being, in the same way as Being, also has being, the Stranger has in fact accomplished more than just refuting Parmenides' restriction of philosophical thought to the thinking of Being. By pressing onward in their inquiry, they have, he says, "disobeyed Parmenides to a further extent than his prohibition" and have done "[m]ore than just examining what he forbade us to do" (258c7–10). By taking on father Parmenides, and especially by pressing on in the inquiry into Non-being, the Stranger (together with Theaetetus) discovered or rediscovered philosophy, as it were, in a surplus discovery. What this novel philosophy is becomes clear in the Stranger's following remark:

> We not only proved that "the things which are not" are, but we also declared what is in fact the species of "that which is not." Once we had proved that the nature of the other both is and has been chopped into bits to extend over all "the things which are" in their mutual relations, we had the nerve to say that this very thing is in its being "that which is not"—a proper part of the nature of the other in its opposition to that which severally is. (258 d5–e5)

The philosophy that the Stranger introduces is a philosophy *of* the Other, first, in an objective sense. By considering Non-being, which for Parmenides *is* absolutely *not*, as a form—the form of the Other—the nature of Non-Being changes, not only insofar as it is said to be on an equal footing with Being, but also insofar as it is a form that is all chopped up so as to be distributed through all the things that *are* in their mutual relation to one another. When Paul Friedländer, in his commentary on the *Sophist*, speaks of the form of Non-Being as "not-*this*-being," he means, of course, to highlight that the negativity of Otherness is always a negativity in relation to a determined reality.[142] Yet, by using the formula of "not-*this*-being" to characterize Otherness, he also touches, I think, on something essentially new in the Stranger's doctrine. Non-being is not only raised to the status of "a *single* Form, an *Eidos*, among the things that are"; in being all chopped up, this form of intelligibility is broken down, like a coin, into the smaller units that serve to make single otherness—"not-*this*-being," but an *other* being—intelligible and meaningful for its part. The form of Otherness or

Difference pervades all things not like an abstract generality, but instead always only in a way that reflects things' specific relation to other things. It is always only in relation to another being that a being can be recognized in its single, if not singular, otherness. The form of Otherness or Difference is other than all of the other "greatest kinds" in that, by nature, it is a differential form, as a result of which Otherness is each time other. In a way, it is unlike all the other forms not only in that it is differential in a passive way; it is also actively differentializing—in short, it is a force of Othering. In sum, then, the Stranger's philosophy is in essence the opening of an economy of otherness within thought—an economy, no longer calculable, of relations of otherness.

As we have seen, if the Stranger develops his philosophy by limiting his discussion to five of the greatest kinds, it is not only in order to avoid confusion but also because the five kinds in question presumably suffice for the point he wishes to make with respect to Parmenides. But it is also clear that there are not only more kinds, but also more kinds that could be considered the greatest. The thrust of the dialectician's philosophy is to argue, I submit, for a non-countable number of forms, even of those that belong to the greatest kinds. However, I would like to consider here the possibility that their list is not complete because one of them, namely, Non-being, is recast in terms of Otherness and Difference. The kind of Otherness is not only infinitely chopped up; furthermore, although an Other is always only in relation to another Other, for structural reasons the kind of the Other inscribes within itself the possibility of illimited and unpredictable instances of Otherness, with respect not only to already constituted Others but also to the kinds themselves. I venture the claim that the Stranger's philosophy of the Other potentially inscribes within itself the space for as yet unheard-of kinds, forms of intelligibility that are not yet manifest or have not yet found their way into *logos*—that is, kinds *of* the Other, in a subjective sense.

One observation that the Stranger makes while establishing Otherness as a fifth look should, therefore, draw our attention. In the process of advancing his point, he reminds Theaetetus that, among the things that *are* and which thus have the form of Being, "some of 'the things which are' are spoken of by themselves, and some are always spoken of in relation to different things" (255c14–16). Those that are said to be themselves by themselves participate in the form of Sameness, whereas those that are always only in relation to others participate in the form of Otherness. Now, "the other (is) always relative to another" (255d1). It follows that Otherness cannot be another name for Being. Otherness, in the same way as Sameness, causes that to which the form of Being applies, and which thus has being, to be either the same or other. Otherness must, therefore, be entirely different from Being. At this point, the Stranger makes the following observation: "if the other participated in both of the pair of species, just as 'that which is' does, then at some time or other there would also be some other of the others not in relation to another, but, as it is, it has simply (artlessly) turned out for us that whatever is other is of necessity that which it is as of another" (255d4–9). Consequently, the Stranger can conclude that the Other must be a fifth form. However, we should pause here for a moment at the suggestion of a non-relational, non-differential other. Even though the Stranger's whole argument thoroughly and on solid grounds excludes such a possibility, because this other would be other on the basis of its sameness rather than in relation to something other, it raises a question, however controversial. Is this evocation of a non-relational other not also the acknowledgment of the opening up of the form of Otherness to what is other than the other, other than the differential other, that is, the other within a system of otherness? The Stranger's elaboration on the form of Otherness, I dare suggest, opens this thought not only to an infinity of others but also, in a virtual fashion, to an other that, although not other on the basis of its own nature, is other in another way. In short, the Stranger's doctrine of Otherness may thus harbor the possibility of extending to the thought of an other that is no longer simply categorizable in terms of an other that is what it is only in relation to an other.

In any event, the Stranger's xenological reworking of philosophy has an additional aspect that needs to be brought into relief. Before returning to the question of the nature of the sophist in the last part of the dialogue, the Stranger sums up what he and Theaetetus have accomplished in the ontological investigation by saying, "let no one say of us that we have the nerve to say, in declaring that 'that which is not' is, that it is the contrary of 'that which is.' We have long ago dismissed all talk of any contrary to it, whether it is or is not, admitting of speech or altogether failing of speech (*alogon*)" (258e8–259a2). Recall that the ontological investigation in the *Sophist* grew out of the encounter with the aporetic nature of both Being and Non-being. After the refutation of the Parmenidean notion of Non-being, the Stranger reminds us here again of Parmenides' conception of Being, arguing that in the process of refuting Non-being he has, at the same time, also refuted Being as Parmenides understood it. Indeed, by stating that Being has no contrary, another concept of Being comes into view, one that knows only Otherness and Difference. But this insight also has implications for the status of opposition within philosophical thought itself. The Stranger holds that Being and Otherness

> mix together with one another and the pair of "that which is" and the other has gone through everything and each other—the other, because it participates in "that which is," is (on account of its participation), yet it is not, however, that in which it gets to participate but other, and in being other than "that which is" it is most plainly and of necessity "that which is not." . . . (259a5–b1)

However, if Being and Otherness are coextensive, then there is no relation of opposition or contrariness between them. As a result, "opposition" is relegated to a subsidiary role in the community of the greatest kinds, namely, to the set of Motion and Rest, which in particular cannot intermix because, if they did, each would revert into its opposite. The philosophy of the Stranger is thus a philosophy that, by endowing Otherness with being, takes the oppositional character out of the Other in its relation to Being, and thus draws Otherness from the start into the community of the kinds. In other words, it is the form of the Other or the Different that, thanks to the absence of contrariness, ensures the communing of things to begin with. The Stranger's new take on philosophy, therefore, consists in establishing the relation of Difference or Otherness as the fundamental relation, and inscribing opposition as a derivative possibility within its web.[143] His is a philosophy predicated on relation—that is, a philosophy of the Other.

A moment ago, I suggested that the philosophy of the Stranger is a philosophy *of* the Other in an objective sense, but this philosophy, as I have emphasized again and again, also originates with him. Plato's stroke of genius is to have a stranger—*the* Stranger—discover philosophy as a mode of thinking and speaking dominated by the relation to what is different or other—a stranger who, as his qualification as "divine" suggests, is also *other* than the people of the cities in which the philosophers roam.[144] By having a stranger articulate such a new way of philosophizing, one that overcomes the sterility of the Parmenidean principle of identity and of the absolute difference between Being and Non-being, Plato not only compels his contemporaries to reconsider what is to be understood as philosophical thought but also, in principle, suggests that such thought, as the thought of a stranger or an Other, transcends in a fundamental way all native thought, and therefore has a universal thrust, in principle at least. In offering the leading role in the dialogue to a stranger, Plato inscribes into philosophy the place of the foreigner, if not of the Other, from which philosophy can uproot itself and thus become able to account for what is Other. More radically put, by inscribing the place of the Other into philosophical thought in this way, Plato makes philosophy the *logos of* the Stranger, the non-native, the Other. Rather than a demand of universality that, because it originates with the sons of the earth, is oppressive with regard to all others, this philosophical demand comes from the Stranger and thus implies openness. Philosophy, then, would belong to the Stranger—a stranger who, rather than spinning tales about Being that, like those of "his" Greek predecessors or, for that matter, of any other civilization, are intelligible only to those that spin them, philosophizes according to the rules of correct speaking (*orthologia*) about the Same and the Other, that is, the rules of intelligibility (239b4). Consequently, in this Greek "thing" that is philosophy, Greek thought expropriates and expatriates itself. It is not only the opening *to* the thought of the foreigner but also the very thought *of* the foreigner *within* Greek thought. Here the full implications of the Stranger's parricide become manifest. If the radical critique of Parmenides amounts to a parricide, it is for the reason that he is an indigenous father. With the parricide, philosophy emancipates itself of its native roots, and ultimately also from Greek language as a particular idiom, opening itself to a saying that is discursive and structured by intelligibles that are no longer idiom bound.

Undoubtedly, most cultures welcome strangers. Yet, in most cases, the relation to the stranger is merely a modality of a given culture's relation to itself, one that does not in the slightest way disturb the latter relation but, on the contrary, reinforces it. By contrast, what we encounter in Plato's welcoming of the Stranger is of the order of a relation that radically unsettles Greek self-identity. It is an openness that does not leave the host's identity intact.

Returning very briefly to my opening remarks regarding the beginnings of Europe, I would like to suggest that, besides the notions of "rationality," "the political," "democracy," "freedom," and so forth that Europe, or the West, has long claimed as its Greek roots the thought of the Stranger as we have encountered it in the *Sophist* has also been bequeathed to Europe. Needless to say, however, this heritage which, as we have seen, is also the heritage of philosophy understood as the thought *of* the foreigner, is not just one more legacy among others. It is the legacy that Europe has least assumed or lived up to. Nevertheless, as a significant aspect of the Athenian heritage that has been handed over to Europe, and that Europe claims (in addition to the equally important legacy of Jerusalem) as part of its foundation, Europe has a responsibility toward it. However, unlike the question of Being whose forgetting, according to Heidegger, has been instrumental in the formation of Western metaphysical thought, and unlike the forgetting of the political experience of Greece that, following Arendt, is at the core of Western political thought, I do not wish to suggest that the Stranger's doctrine has been simply forgotten throughout the West. The category of forgetting or oblivion might not be sufficient to describe the case regarding the thought of the Stranger. Indeed, the figures of the stranger and the foreigner have been topical issues in European thought since the Renaissance, where they did not serve (as they did in almost all other cultures) merely as a foil against which the culture could define itself and to celebrate its own humanity. Instead, these figures provided a critical perspective on the West's complacency and cultural arrogance. But the Stranger's thought cannot be classified in terms of a handed-down model, that is, a pattern or measure that, as an integral part of a patrimony, could be forgotten. The philosophy that the Stranger teaches presupposes, as we have seen, the parricide of the founding father, and hence at the very least a suspension or *epoché* of inheritance and the property one owes to ancestors. This philosophy, even though bequeathed to Europe, therefore does not fit the category of the patrimonial. It implies a way of thought that changes the relation to what is handed down. If Europe, or the West, has not lived up to this thought, which requires the radical abandonment and transgression of all autochthony, of all rootedness in oneself, and of all self-identifying retrenchment, it is because, rather than a model that implies the representation of an end, this thought is a formidable injunction and responsibility to disown oneself and to become other than oneself. As a responsibility to this injunction, the thought of the stranger is not a model or anything like an ideal to be progressively approximated, which still implies a reservation or withholding; instead, it is an unconditional demand at every present moment. It is in itself the realization of the demand in question. Needless to say, such an extreme or hyperbolic exigency is impossible to realize. But it is precisely for this reason that it also remains a responsibility and a challenge that must be met. Before it can make the claim that certain of its origins lie in Greece, Europe has to "measure itself up" against the "legacy" of the Stranger's *logos* and the performance of a self-disownment that alone, strictly speaking, generates philosophy.

Chapter Three

The Statesman

According to the history of its reception, the *Statesman* has not enjoyed considerable attention; in other words, its historical influence has not been particularly extensive.[1] As A. E. Taylor remarks, "since the days of the Neoplatonists the dialogue seems to have been little read [. . .] Perhaps no Platonic work of the same largeness of conception has been so completely neglected by most students of Platonism."[2] For instance, Gilbert Ryle contends that, unlike the *Sophist*, this "weary dialogue" "does not also tackle interesting philosophical issues, with one diminutive exception."[3] Is this because it is a dialogue that deals with a "practical" subject matter? Those interested in Plato's conception of statehood generally limit themselves to the views expressed in the *Republic* and/or the *Laws*. Written in the interval between those two works, the *Statesman* undoubtedly makes for difficult reading. Presumably composed after Plato's return from his second visit to Syracuse, the dialogue has been characterized as bizarre, rambling, and methodologically flawed; some scholars have even believed that Plato did not write it. When it is read at all, commentators have largely tended to focus on this late Platonic work's refinement of the method of dialectic, rather than on the problematic of the statesman and his peculiar art. This is all the more bizarre as there is an unmistakable parallelism between the philosopher's knowledge and that of the statesman, both of whose arts consist in interconnecting either ideas or contrary virtues.[4] In recent years, however, this situation has changed. The number of excellent studies devoted to this previously neglected dialogue has increased, as has the interest in the complexity of the figure of the statesman and his art.

After having inquired, in the *Theaetetus*, into the nature of knowledge without achieving a definite answer, the *Sophist*, the *Statesman*, and the announced (but never written) dialogue on the philosopher represent attempts to determine three forms of human activity through the specific forms of knowledge that characterize them, thus acknowledging a certain plurality of knowledge. These are *sophistike*, *politike*, and philosophical *episteme*. In the *Sophist*, as well as in the *Statesman*, this inquiry into three types of human activity and the three corresponding and distinct forms of knowledge is conducted by a stranger, the *xenos eleates*. As Cornelius Castoriadis reminds us, *xenos* in Greek means not only a stranger or foreigner "but also and especially he who receives the treatment reserved to foreigners, that is to say hospitality. There is a Zeus Xenios, protector of foreigners; and *xenia* is hospitality. *Xenos eleates* is therefore both the stranger as well as the guest, the invited visitor from Elea."[5] But why, in order to elaborate on the specific nature of the knowledge that characterizes the sophist, the statesman, and the philosopher, does Plato need a stranger to perform this inquiry? I have tried to respond to this question in the context of the *Sophist*, and I expect to address this unique feature of the dialogues—which has drawn very little attention in Plato scholarship—in the case of the *Statesman* as well. Is a stranger required only because the shift from an inquiry into the essence of knowledge as such to one into different forms of knowledge requires a different set of questions than the Socratic ones?[6] The question regarding the strangeness of the figure of the Stranger, and what links him to the rather un-Socratic account of politics in the *Statesman*, will remain on the agenda throughout this chapter. It is, indeed, in light of the Stranger that I intend to elaborate on what the dialogue has to say about the statesman's knowledge, thus also restoring and highlighting the "strangeness" characteristic of the Stranger's conclusions.

I recall that, to a large extent, the *Theaetetus* is not merely a debate about how the Protagorean theory of homo mensura has devastating consequences for a theory of knowledge. It is also a debate about how, with the statement that what one perceives is also immediately true for oneself, the homo mensura theory also subverts all meaningful interaction of human beings. Indeed, in the second half of the dialogue, the practical consequences of the doctrine are regularly examined by the Stranger by way of explicit references to the *polis*. As Protagoras offers, "what we're saying, in declaring that all things are in motion, and that which is the opinion of each, this also is for a private person and a city" (168b4–6). Indeed, the sort of things "that are just and beautiful in the opinion of each city, these also are for it as long as it holds them to be so" (167c4–6). The roles of the wise man (*sophos*) and the good public speaker (*agathos rhetor*) consist in "mak[ing] cities be of the opinion that the good things in place of the poor things are just" (167c2–4). In accordance with his speech, Protagoras includes the sophist in the list of those who are wiser than others and who, without opining false things, cause good things to be for the common good, which lasts as long as do the state's beliefs about what is good and just.

If, in the *Theaetetus*, the thrust of Protagoras' doctrine—namely, that what appears to me is also what *is* for me—is shown to serve as the foundation for the sophist's claims to knowledge, it is first of all in view of the subsequent investigation in the *Sophist* of his art, an investigation that at one point shows him to be a character almost indistinguishable from the philosopher.[7] Precisely because he resembles the philosopher to a confusingly dangerous degree, it became necessary to clearly separate him from the latter. But if Socrates already brings to light the political implications of Protagoras' doctrine in the dialogue preceding this inquiry, it is also in advance of the *Statesman* and in order to set the stage for a discussion of the sophist's business in the city, which shows him to be also almost indistinguishable from the true statesman, and thus to be rivaling the king. As is argued in the *Statesman*, among all those who pretend to have a part in running the state—the very large crowd of all those who partake in "the chorus that deal[s] with the affairs (*pragmata*) of the cities" (291c2–3), and who "quickly exchange their looks (*ideai*) and capacity with one another" (291b3–4)—is made up of the sophists, the greatest imposters regarding political art. Thus, they stand out as the actual rivals of the genuine statesman, from whom they must therefore be thoroughly distinguished. In other words, with the examination of what kind of knowledge characterizes the true statesman, the Stranger returns in his second dialogue as leader to a question already broached in the *Theaetetus* and which, although following necessarily from what had been established there with respect to Protagoras' doctrine, had been left in abeyance.

Prior to directing our attention to the *Statesman*, a distinction made in the preceding dialogue needs to be addressed. As we have seen, Protagoras already distinguished between the wise man, the rhetorician or public speaker, and the sophist. The *Sophist*, by contrast, concludes with a discrimination of the statesman (*politikos*), the public speaker (*demologikos*), and the sophist. This distinction is arrived at in the context of a discussion of the art of imitation, in which all three figures participate. Imitation, it is shown, consists of two kinds: "imitation with opinion as opinion-mimetics [*ten men meta doxes mimesin doxomimetike*] and the one with science as a mimicry by acquaintance [*ten de met' epistemes historike tina mimesin*]" (267e1–3, translation modified). More simply put, the distinction is one between those who know what they imitate, and those who, for professional and commercial reasons, only pretend to have the knowledge in question. Compared to the statesman, who is sincere and whose imitation is based on insight, both the public speaker and the sophist are described as insincere imitators of the wise man, in different ways: the public speaker, who deceptively pretends to be wise, mimics wisdom publicly in long speeches, whereas the sophist does so in private and in short speeches.[8] Having thus separated him off from both the public speaker and the sophist, the dialogue sets the stage for an inquiry into the figure of the statesman himself, and the kind of knowledge that characterizes him.

It is important to realize that, in this process of discriminating between the different figures, the sophist is proclaimed a master of imitation. This is of particular significance since, in the dialogue devoted to the statesman, the entirety of all those who actually rule—no matter the constitutions over which they preside—are referred to as "being the greatest imitators and greatest enchanters, they prove to be the sophists of sophists" (303c4–5). With this, the goal of the *Statesman* becomes clearer. Its aim is to distinguish the true or ideal statesman not from the philosopher but from the sophist imposters who merely imitate him with no genuine knowledge of his art. The difficulty of distinguishing the sophist from the philosopher, whom he imitates, already showed that the whole investigation demanded by Socrates of the Stranger at the beginning of the *Sophist* is predicated on the problematic of mimesis and its modalities. This holds true of what is at stake in the *Statesman* as well, since the problematic of mimesis is exacerbated here not only insofar as the statesman too is an imitator—he imitates the art of the true statesman—but also because his art is pitted against that of the sophists, the masters of unlimited imitation who furthermore mushroom in the cities. Apart from the many who, with more or less legitimacy, claim to play a role in the constitution of the state, the sophist is by his very nature plural, and forms a "very large crowd" (291a2–3), or a "chorus" dealing with the affairs of the cities (291c2–3). In the *Sophist*, the sophist was one "many-headed" animal (*polukephalos*, 240c5) from which the philosopher was to be distinguished. In the *Statesman*, he morphs into a throng of all kinds of beasts.

So, let us bear in mind that the inquiry in the *Statesman* is intended to define the specific knowledge that is the statesman's own, and the kind of knowledge of which it is a scientific imitation. Only on this condition will it be possible to demark him from the sophist—and especially "the sophists of sophists"—but perhaps while looking for the statesman to also find, unawares, the science of the philosopher. Recall that at the beginning of the *Sophist*, Socrates invited the Stranger to elaborate on the forms in which a philosopher appears in the cities, whether as sophist, statesman, or madman. In the homonymous dialogue, the sophist was shown to be a deceptive imitation of the philosopher. Yet, if he now needs to be distinguished from the statesman, it is first of all because the sophist also lays claim to statesmanship and the knowledge that it involves. But in distinction from the sophist, who has been shown to possess a false resemblance to a philosopher, the statesman, though not being a philosopher himself, resembles him in a much more positive way. If one way in which the philosopher appears in the cities is as the sophist, this is a wholly deceptive way; however, when he takes on the appearance of a statesman, the philosopher certainly has much more in common with him.

In Plato scholarship, the positions articulated in this late dialogue through the voice of a stranger have led scholars primarily to one of two conclusions. Either, as some scholars aver, the Stranger does not represent genuine Platonic positions,[9] or, according to others more concerned with the unity of the Platonic corpus, those positions duplicate or resonate with things established in previous dialogues and, consequently, are not completely new positions. Throughout this book I have insisted, and continue to insist, on the novelty of the Stranger's teaching and, in particular, on the novelty that derives from the rupture with all the major currents of Greek thought. Consequently, a few remarks on how to understand "novelty" here are certainly warranted. Plato is the author of these two late dialogues, both of which call upon a stranger to break with the entirety of the pre-Socratics. And that is not all: even the Socratic method itself appears to undergo a critical reevaluation in these dialogues. Having a stranger or foreigner perform these tasks inevitably endows the foreigner's philosophical doctrine, and his outline of the nature of the royal art, already with a sense of novelty. What a stranger teaches must as such be new, unfamiliar, unexpected, and surprising. In my reading, the didactic nature of the two dialogues in which the Stranger sidelines Socrates further suggests that the dramatic effect of such novelty is purposively intended. Plato wishes us to approach the elaborations of the Stranger, as well as how he arrives at them, as something new. But the novelty of the positions defended by the Stranger in no way puts the unity of Platonic thought in question, nor does the fact that certain of the

Stranger's theses are reminiscent of developments in the earlier dialogues diminish the innovative nature of the accomplishments of the late dialogues. There is no question as to the continuity of Plato's work, even though some of the Stranger's statements imply some Platonic self-criticism. In Campbell's words, "the spirit of Socrates is still working under the Eleatic mask."[10] But Taylor's observation, according to which the real difference between the early and the late dialogues is "that Plato's centre of interest, as we may call it, has shifted," is not forceful enough.[11] This does not speak to the sense of novelty effectuated by the Stranger's break with both Protagoras and Parmenides, a break from which emerges a fresh understanding of philosophy and politics that, all differences considered and albeit belatedly, will have been the unifying spirit of all of Plato's thought—and for that matter, the thought of a non-Platonist Plato.

Without denying that Plato, in earlier dialogues, has anticipated some of the insights of the Stranger—at times in the context of positions that Plato severely criticized (Protagoras on the learning of political virtue, for example)—I thus proceed on the assumption that through the Stranger's teaching in both the *Sophist* and the *Statesman*, Plato elaborates a rather novel conception not only of philosophy but, as demonstrated in the *Statesman*, also of political knowledge that in many aspects (and notwithstanding crucial differences) anticipates the ethical and political writings of Aristotle, Plato's most significant disciple. I am thus cautiously sympathetic to Cornelius Castoriadis's contention that in the *Statesman* Plato is, in a way, similar to what I already have argued with respect to the *Sophist*, involved "in something like a second creation of philosophy."[12] In this late dialogue, the rudiments of a new philosophy are sketched out, new in the sense that philosophy recognizes here a place for a kind of knowledge distinct from its own—but not therefore inferior to it, like opinion—and that concerns the affairs of the commonwealth. Unlike *dialektike*, *politike* is a knowledge that does not concern the whole as such, the *cosmos*, but only a part of it—the *polis*—even though that partial whole might have a cosmological foundation; furthermore, this partial whole is not therefore simply subordinate to the *cosmos*.[13] If I cautiously endorse Castoriadis's claim, it is also because this second creation does not come easily for Plato. Indeed, to cite Auguste Diès, in this dialogue Plato "must discuss and battle—with himself, first of all—to establish the features of the doctrine" in question.[14] If he puts this second creation into the mouth of the Stranger, this might be not simply because only a foreigner could overcome the resistance to such a conception, and to highlight its novelty, but perhaps also because, in this way, Plato can still keep a certain distance from it.[15]

It is well known that, in the *Theaetetus*, Plato makes the point that philosophy originates in the pathos of wonder (*thaumazein*). However, few scholars seem to have remarked that in the *Statesman*, whose aim it is to define the royal art and the knowledge that it presupposes, the Stranger—after having admitted (rather late in the dialogue, it is true) that bad things happen to cities and their political regimes, and that this is not particularly astonishing—asks his interlocutor Young Socrates whether we should not "be more astonished [*thaumasteon*] as to how a city is something strong by nature [*phusei*]." And he adds that even "though the cities have been undergoing things of this sort now for endless time [that is, all sorts of bad things], still and all some of them are stable and do not get overturned, though at times many do sink below like ships and perish and have perished and will still go on perishing on account of the sorry state of their captains and crews" (302a2–8). The wonder in question, about how the ever-changing and restless entities that are polities can survive even in the absence of the genuine art of statesmanship, is one that not only deserves philosophical reflection but also induces a form of reflection distinct from philosophical reflection. In the *Statesman*, I hold, the wonder in question is *the* eye-opener, not of theoretical thought, as in the *Theaetetus*, but of a different form of knowledge—the knowledge of political philosophy as an attempt to find an answer to the enigma in question.[16]

As a result, we should not be surprised to encounter in the dialogue a number of insights that we normally associate with the realm of the political, and also hints that the exploration of the domain in question must take on a different methodological form than in the case of theoretical thought. At this point, however, it is appropriate to first say a word about the protagonists. Apart from the Stranger, there is, of course, the elder Socrates, Theodorus the Cyrenaic mathematician, and two of his students, Theaetetus and Young Socrates. Having assigned Young Socrates to the Stranger as his interlocutor—the former's name, as the elder Socrates acknowledges, entails kinship with him in some sense—the elder Socrates falls silent until the very end, when he thanks the Stranger for the beautiful and complete exposition of the royal art and who, or what, the statesman is.[17] Even though mathematics, and geometry in particular, is the prime paradigm of philosophy—as is evident in the *Republic*, for example—this does not make the theoretician Theodorus or, for that matter, his student Young Socrates, philosophers per se. On the contrary, one might say—for indeed, throughout the dialogue the pertinence of mathematics in the approach of practical matters such as statesmanship will be a constant issue. Of course, as a student in the Academy, Young Socrates should also be knowledgeable in politics.[18] But as is demonstrated by the dialogue, precisely because he is a mathematician Young Socrates proves not only to have difficulties understanding philosophical arguments, but his geometrical approach to politics, which goes hand in hand with his uncritical subscription to popular opinions about the political, also impedes his understanding of the Stranger's account of political art.[19]

The *Statesman* is unquestionably a highly pedagogical dialogue. It has been argued that, unlike what is the case in the *Sophist*, the Stranger "speaks to the younger Socrates like a schoolmaster."[20] Be that as it may, the inquiry is not conducted only to determine the statesman's essence but also to make Young Socrates skilled at dialectics—that is, to make him a philosopher. Why is it that this task is incumbent on a stranger, and why must his interlocutor be a young man who shares the same name with the elder Socrates, who conjectures that he must therefore "have a kind of kinship with me" (257d2)? Is the purpose of this not to make Young Socrates think philosophically like a stranger, rather than like the native elder Socrates, and thus also to become estranged from what he, as a mathematician, already believes to be true?[21] In distinction from Mitchel Miller's conclusion that even though Young Socrates repeatedly misses the points that the Stranger makes, he finally passes the test at the end, I hold that his mathematical training and uncritical adherence to opinions regarding the political make him ultimately unable to fully understand the Stranger's teachings. This is perhaps not by accident, because what the dialogue establishes about a true statesman must have been hard for contemporary Athenians to grasp. It is difficult to make out what, at the end of the inquiry into the sophist, Theaetetus will finally have grasped about the philosopher; and the same holds true in the case of Young Socrates as regards the nature of the statesman. If *legein* is a showing, Young Socrates does not see what is shown to him. His repeated failure at "seeing" what the Stranger advances about politics is important not only because it reveals that he has not yet become a dialectician but also because it tells us something significant about Plato's reasons for having a stranger argue about the nature of genuine statesmanship.[22] It suggests that only a stranger can be up to the task of telling the Athenians something other (*allotriae*) than what they already believe with regard to statesmanship, and also that this is an almost impossible task, given that, as we will see, the Stranger's point is that none of the existing Greek constitutions is in fact a *politeia*. Considering that even the gifted young mathematician—who is incapable of distancing himself from his theoretical approach and his inveterate believe in popular opinions about statesmanship—proves unable to understand what the business of a statesman is from a philosophical point of view, the task that the Stranger faces in his attempt to bring to the discussion what Xavier Marquez qualifies as a "Stranger's Knowledge" is huge, to say the least.[23] Since there is no permanent place for it in a political community, as Marquez remarks, does this not also mean that this knowledge has always again and again to confront such a community from the outside in order to prevent it from indulging in debilitating self-identity? A political community requires the incessant intervention, always new again, of a statesman, after the preceding one has withdrawn. Such intervention, I hold, is the responsibility of each of its individual citizens.

This being established, it may now be appropriate to list some of the most distinct philosophical features of this remarkable Platonic dialogue. First, there is the highly complex nature of its constant methodological shifts, which are as much motivated by the Stranger's attempt to make Young Socrates a good dialectician as they are required by the subject matter of the dialogue.[24] The repeated interruptions of the examination by methodological reflections concerning the way and the tempo of the investigation, until the king "appears[s] to have for us a perfectly complete figure" (277a6), are a function of the discursive requirement of making the nature of statesmanship vividly plain to "those capable of following it" (277c5–6). The merely external outlines of the subject matter do not suffice. Like the portrait of a living creature (*zwon*) that comes alive only when painted with "the vividness as it were that's in pigments and the mixture of colors" (277c3–4), the portrait of the statesman and his art can be made to come fully alive only under the condition of shifts of perspectives and the speed of the exposition.[25] It is precisely these methodological interruptions that discursively secure the coming alive of the statesman's portrait—that is, of what defines him. But as this subject matter also concerns every citizen of a commonwealth, the frequent methodological reflections, the interruptions they represent, and the new directions that are thus taken are also intended to bring the portrait of the true statesman alive for as many as are "capable of following" the definition (277c6). Can one assume that, compared to the *Sophist*, the inquiry into the statesman concerns a subject matter that, in principle at least, also virtually has a broader range of addressees in view? Is this the reason why the Stranger must have recourse to the technique of *skiagraphia* that, as the imitator's art, manipulates colors and shadows in paintings so as to produce the illusion in our souls of their conformity with reality?[26] As I have already emphasized in my reading of the *Theaetetus*, Socrates seeks to arrive at his conclusions regarding the nature of knowledge together with his interlocutor. The ideal of synergetic dialogue in which every proposition, including its foundations and presuppositions, must rest on mutual agreement by the speakers is, perhaps, even more critical in a dialogue devoted to a matter as practical as statesmanship.[27]

The methodological shifts do not solely comprise reflections on which routes to take and the pace of the investigation but also consist of divergences or digressions. The interruption of the diairetic analysis with a myth would seem to amount to a complete change of discursive register, a shift to the register of telling imaginative stories; thus, this shift also acknowledges the role that persuasion plays in the philosophical examination of issues of politics, before establishing rhetoric as the art of "persuad[ing] a multitude and a crowd through mythology" (304c11) as closely related to statesmanship, though subservient to it. But first, we should note that the shift from *logos* to *mythos* imposes itself because of a deficiency in the first *diairesis*. According to the Stranger, due to the form of division practiced so far, the method of philosophical investigation into the statesman borders on the ridiculous, perhaps even becoming disgraceful of *logos*. Hence the recourse to myth as a "supplement to *logos*," contrary to what is commonly the case in the Platonic dialogues, where myth and *logos* are not only opposed to one another, but where, rather than preceding myth, *logos* comes after as a response to the myth's limitations.[28] The passage from argumentation to storytelling is here primarily a shift to "some other way [*kath' heteran hodon*]" (268d6), by which the methodological deficiencies of the first *diairesis* are to be corrected by another form of investigation. But both ways in which the examination of statesmanship is carried out, the first *diairesis* as well as the subsequent mythological approach, are shown to be insufficient. Both the theoretical elaboration—seemingly in conformity with the Socratic method of division—and the recourse to storytelling to explain its genesis fall short of making sense of the political. From the beginning, the Stranger thus tries to make Young Socrates aware that both approaches fall short in grasping the specificity of the realm of human affairs, and in particular the art of statesmanship. Only after this has been made plain does the Stranger develop a methodological approach to the main topic under investigation that, all differences considered, is on par with his accomplishments in the *Sophist*.

One of the remarkable features of the *Statesman* is the Stranger's relinquishing of the Socratic form of division (*diairesis*) which, together with composition (*synagoge*), characterizes dialectical science—in other words, philosophy. This abandonment of the Socratic method of investigation par excellence, namely, the dichotomous procedure of dividing or halving (wholes) through the middle—an abandonment necessitated by the insight that division is a more complex and subtle process—occurs after the first failed attempt to define the species or idea to which the statesman belongs. As will be shown, both the long and the short way of division lead to results that ridicule the *logos* itself. But since the Stranger in the *Statesman* leaves behind the dichotomous method of division—which, as already indicated, is intrinsic to the understanding of Socratic philosophical investigation, as is generally acknowledged—this highly important topic warrants at least a brief reflection.

In the context of elaborating on dialectics in the *Phaedrus*, Socrates had pointed out that dividing according to concepts (*kat' eide*) requires "following the objective articulation: we are not to attempt to hack off parts like a clumsy butcher."[29] From this it follows that a *diairesis* divides a whole not arbitrarily, but into eidetic parts, but also that these eidetic parts stand in a relation of contrariety to one another, and are thus dichotomous; furthermore, since after each division the concept that is bipolarly opposed to the one in which one hopes ultimately to find one's object of the search is abandoned on the (left) side, *diairesis* is also bifurcatory. The division ends only after having arrived at a genre that cannot be further divided, and to which the object to be defined belongs. Thus understood, *diairesis* is a technical method for the analysis of logical concepts and their aspects, a formal exercise at classification, as it were. Now, though the image of the clumsy butcher suggests that rather than cutting off parts from a whole, division by concepts or *eide* should proceed by way of natural cleavages, the principle of division is regularly referred to as one of "halving," or cutting down the middle. Indeed, when Young Socrates takes a part for an *eidos* within the first division intent on defining the statesman, the Stranger reminds him of the need to cut through the middle because in this way it is more likely they will encounter generic concepts. He adds that it is not safe to cut off a fragment from a whole: "it's safer to go cutting through the middle [*dia meson*]; it's there rather that one might encounter looks (*ideai*)" (262b8–9). Let me draw attention to the fact that, though it is safer to cut through the middle, it is only more likely (but in no way certain) that one will come across looks this way. As Rosen observes, "it is important to note that cutting through the middles is not the same as cutting at the natural joints."[30] As opposed to cutting through the middle, the safest way, and the one that the

Stranger chooses—when, after abandoning bifurcatory division, he resumes dividing from now on in an entirely new form that is appropriate to the subject matter of the dialogue—is to cut a whole (that is, a living whole) according to its natural articulations. In the case of a living whole, such as a city and the integrated whole of its arts, the second-best way of dividing it proceeds along such natural joints. Consequently, the Stranger proposes to "divide them, as if it were a sacrificial victim, limb by limb, since we're incapable of doing it in two, for one must always cut into that number that's as near as possible to two" (287c4–6).

In the case of the different arts from which statesmanship is to be set apart, it is thus impossible to divide this whole into two, through the middle. As we will see, the reason for this is that the royal art that is to be defined does not stand in a bipolar, dichotomous relation to all the other (subservient) arts. As Mitchell Miller avers, the Stranger "*aims to do more than isolate the statesman.*"[31] Indeed, even though his aim is to account for a particular art, this art, "while on the one hand one amongst many, on the other hand is charged with the supreme task of harmonizing the others; this art—the statesman's—would be devoted to securing and preserving the cooperative order of the arts and the citizens who perform them."[32] Therefore, the statesman's is an art that does not stand in a dichotomous relation to all the other arts, but is an art within the arts, one that interlinks all of them into an organic whole.

As the principle of *diairesis*, halving or cutting through the middle aims at the contrariety of genres that are separated from one another. Though this may work for the theoretical analysis of ideas, it does not work for the analysis of human affairs. Reminding ourselves of the propaedeutic role that, according to Socrates, mathematics and geometry hold for philosophy, the question therefore arises as to the affinity of the method of *diairesis*—as a halving—with mathematics and geometry. Does division through the middle divide a thing into equal parts, like the division of a number or the bisection of a line?[33] The subsequent developments perhaps provide a minimal hint as to the important question of whether mathematics and geometry stand as a model for the form of *diairesis* which, after a first attempt, the Stranger abandons.

In the course of the first attempt to define the statesman through division, the Stranger emphasizes that the division in question cannot consist in slicing off a part from a whole, but can succeed only on the basis of kinds or species, and that furthermore the latter, rather than just words (*onoma*), require concepts (*ideais*).[34] Parts and species are not the same, but are other (*all' heteron alleloin*) (263a4–6). However, as applied so far, the method has not taken this philosophical difference into account and, as the Stranger intimates, it has been modeled after the mode of walking or gait (*poreia*) of bipeds as opposed to quadrupeds—in other words, after a mathematical (pseudo-)procedure of measurement (266a1–b7). It is at this juncture as well that the Stranger reminds Young Socrates that, in the dialogue on the sophist, it was shown that the method of division must, when properly applied, "always on its own terms [get] on with the truest," and not let itself be distracted by value judgments regarding "the more august" or "[deny] honor to the smaller in preference for the bigger" (266d8–11). But what is more, the mathematical jest about dividing "[b]y the diameter, of course, and again by the diameter of the diameter" (266a10–11) shows forcefully, though perhaps not very elegantly, that so far the Socratic method of division has not been oriented by ideas but has instead proceeded to halve wholes according to some comical geometrical principles. The result of doing so is "that we have left, as the closest competitor of that dignified being a monarch, the breeder of pigs," a pleasantry indicative of the abstractness and limits of Socratean *diairesis* when applied beyond theoretical and formal analysis.[35]

In a radical shift in discursive genres, the Stranger interrupts the investigation, first resorting to storytelling (and thus appealing to Young Socrates' barely overcome childhood), before taking up the method of division again in an entirely refurbished fashion, reflecting a new conception of dialectics or philosophical science that is in accord with the subject matter. The recourse to myth was required not to supply the idea of the true statesman, but to provide the theological foil against which his idea—as one pertaining to a mortal rather than a godlike being—can come into view. Once this has been achieved, the division can be taken up again. From here on, however, it no longer proceeds by sectioning through the middle in a geometrical sense, but through what is closest to it, the natural joints of the whole that is to be analyzed. This abandonment of the dichotomic method of inquiry into the *eide* or looks of things in its Socratic version, and of the paradigmatic role that mathematics plays in pinning down the object of the search, does not happen by accident. It is the object of the search itself—the kind of knowledge characteristic of the *basileus politikos*—that demands these changes. Indeed, if the dichotomic division through the middle is abandoned in favor of a division according to the natural joints of a whole, as in the case of the sacrificial animal, is it not because what is to be determined is a living whole—namely, the *polis*, as well as the political being (*ton politikon andra*) as a living human being?

After severing the statesman's art from all the arts that have to do with herds, and just before exploring how the paradigm of weaving is suitable for defining the specificity of his art, the Stranger asserts that, in addition, his art must be divided from all "the cocauses and causes throughout the city itself [*kata polin auten*]" (287b7). The statesman's art, having already been differentiated from all the arts that pertain to a whole, such as those of herding, and which are entirely exterior to his own, must now be set apart from certain arts *within* the whole that is the city, and for which all these other arts pretend to be responsible. Although the Stranger, in the *Statesman*, began the process of narrowing down his subject in a way similar to what he had done in the case of the sophist, the difficulties that the arts in question pose to being divided in two cause him to quickly abandon this method, which had been successful in the case of the strange animal that is the sophist, whose form continually changed, refusing to let itself be pinned down by a "look."[36] As opposed to the sophist's many disguises, which made it so difficult to catch him by finding the idea that defines him, the problem with the statesman is that so many others, *if not all*, lay claim to that title. The idea of what a true statesman is must thus orient the process by which he can finally be distinguished from the entirety of those who pretend to care and tend to the conservation of human beings in a *polis*. This is one more reason why a change in method is required.

When Plato allows the Stranger to declare "the dissimilarities of human beings and of their actions and the fact that almost none of the human things is ever at rest," and, as a result, that no art of legislation whatsoever is capable of issuing "in any case anything simple about all and over the entire time" (294b2–5), it is no longer in order to dismiss the political realm altogether as one in which only sophists are at home. As the Stranger acknowledges, human things make up a realm of dissimilarities in which nothing is "ever at rest," and therefore laws (*nomoi*), if they presuppose the immutability of things, cannot apply to them "for all time." And yet, even though this realm is certainly that of popular opinion, it also harbors the possibility of what the Stranger refers to as "true opinion [*alethe doxan*]" (309c6), a kind of knowledge distinct from philosophical *episteme*, a knowledge that secures this domain's independence and its own kind of lawfulness.[37] If in the late dialogues Plato has a stranger inquire into the knowledge that characterizes the sophist, the statesman, and the philosopher, this is at first the result of a recognition that there are different kinds of knowledge.[38] It is true that the sophist proves only to possess fake knowledge, and thus that he is not an *epistemon*, as opposed to "the science of the free" (253c9), which characterizes the philosopher. In the case of the *Statesman*, it is clear as well that there is a kind of knowledge that has its own legitimacy, and that a specific experience of wonder compels us to investigate. This kind of knowledge—political knowledge—must remain distinct from philosophical knowledge, even if it is only second best (*deuteros plous*) compared to the latter, if one is not to abandon the realm of human things and prevent it from realizing in its own way the just, the good, and the beautiful. This knowledge is above all that of "the kingly and intelligent" [*ton meta phroneseos basilikon*] (294a7), but is perhaps not only his alone.

Immediately at the beginning of the dialogue, the program of the *Statesman* is announced: to determine, by way of sectioning knowledge differently from how it was sectioned in attempting to define the sophist, "the political straight-of-way," and once one has "separated and removed it from everything else, stamp a single look (*idea*) on it" (258c3–6). It is not only an issue of finding the specific nature of the statesman's knowledge, but of finding it in a way that is demanded by the very specificity of the knowledge in question, and that conforms to an art intrinsic to actions, thus concerning the genesis of certain things. The novel section of the arts from which the definition takes its start is between mere insight (*gnostikos*) and an art that "inheres in [. . .] actions [*praxesin*]" (258e1) insofar as they are to bring something into being. Needless to say, the royal art belongs to the latter form of art. But before beginning to determine the statesman's knowledge and art in a more precise fashion by following the process by which this knowledge inherent (*sumphon*, that is, naturally inhering, congenital with, innate, inborn) in actions is distinguished from the actions themselves, two of the Stranger's observations should interest us, though I will return to them at length only later in this chapter. First, the Stranger argues that there is only "one science" that deals with "a large household [*oikesis*] or in turn the bulk of a small city," and he adds, "this science, whether one names it royal, political, or economic, let it not make for any difference between us" (259b11–c4). In short, "the statesman and king and slavemaster and, further, household-manager [*oikonomon*]" (258e8–9) all possess the same science. But needless to say, this does not mean that a statesman and a household-manager are the same, or that anyone heading a household would per se be capable of presiding over a state.[39] What they share is only the knowledge of self-injunction—an art, however, that is inevitably different in each specific case.[40] The second observation made here by the Stranger is that anyone who, "though himself in a private station, is competent to advise" someone in his art deserves "to be addressed with the same name of the art as the one he advises has" (259a1–4). The Stranger asks, "Whoever is skilled enough, though himself private, to advise a man who is king of a land, shall we not say of him that he has the science which the ruler himself should have been in possession of?" (259a6–9), and without hesitation Young Socrates agrees.

As we have seen, Plato distinguishes the knowledge peculiar to statesmanship from insight, the paradigm of which is mathematics—theoretical knowledge, in short. But the knowledge characteristic of the statesman is not therefore simply practical. The paradigm to which the Stranger resorts to explain the knowledge in question is that of the master-builder or architect who is not himself manually or practically engaged in the work, but only gives appropriate directions to the workmen in view of the completion of the assigned work. His knowledge, rather than being practical, is one that naturally inheres (*symphonos*) in the assigned work, and concerns the telos that is to be accomplished. It is a theoretical knowledge, no doubt, but one that—contrary to the knowledge of the mathematician, who has completed his task after a discriminating (*krinein*) assessment of what he has cognized—is injunctive (*epitactic*) in that, following the insight regarding the work that must be accomplished, he knows how to direct his workmen in realizing it.[41] What characterizes the science or knowledge of the master-builder is that he knows how to direct the workmen, those who have the power to act, in making his insight into the principle or cause of its practical realization in a work. The injunction that comes with the knowledge of the master-builder consists in "enjoin[ing others] for the sake of some kind of coming-to-be [*geneseos tinos heneka*]" (261a13–b1). In other words, his injunction is aimed at making something happen. The paradigmatic role that the master-builder occupies in the definition of the statesman not only highlights from the start the communality with which he and the citizens bring a work into being but also that this cannot happen without their mutual agreement or consent.[42] In any event, with the division of all insightful knowledge into discriminative (or critical) and injunctive knowledge, only the general species of knowledge has been found in which the art of statesmanship fits. A long process of further divisions—such as the division of the art of injunction into the self-injunctive art and borrowed authority to give orders—as well as several methodological twists, will be required to arrive at a satisfying separation of the statesman's art from all the arts, and pretenders to his art, that vie with it.

Plato's take on politics in the *Republic* has been frequently characterized as merely theoretical. For example, think of Hannah Arendt and

Jacques Taminiaux, among many others. However, the determination of the statesman in the homonymous dialogue by way of a knowledge inherent in action approaches politics from an entirely different angle which, as I hold, is not by accident developed by a stranger. One of the fundamental differences between the *Republic* and the *Statesman* is that, in the later dialogue, cities are not the result of a natural disposition of human beings but, as we will learn from the myth about Cronus and Zeus, are something that humans themselves create by themselves through art; thus, rather than being natural, cities are of the order of artifacts. Whereas in the *Republic*, which has no place for political art, "human life, including its political and civil dimension, is fully inscribed in nature," and whereas Socrates is oblivious to any difference between nature and artifice, the Stranger considers civil and political life to be primarily and exclusively human.[43] As Michel Narcy remarks, "[t]he Stranger can offer his own definition of the political only by refuting Socrates, and by refuting him as Socrates did himself in the case of Protagoras, by first elaborating on his own position."[44] If the *Statesman* thus occupies a distinct position in relation to the *Republic*, it is because Plato, in the later dialogue, allows the Stranger to do what only a stranger might be permitted to do—that is, to rebuke Socrates, and to do so in the same way the latter did with respect to Protagoras in the *Theaetetus*.

Plato scholarship more or less agrees that the statesman, as he is defined in the late dialogue, is no longer either the philosopher-king of the *Republic* or the legislator of the colony to be created from scratch in the *Laws*. Whereas it is Socrates—who in the *Gorgias*, in the context of a stinging critique of Athenian democracy and its democratic politicians, claims to be the only true politician—who develops the notion of the philosopher-king in the *Republic*, the statesman is exclusively the Stranger's creation. Mitchell Miller argues that by having a stranger develop the notion of the statesman, Plato revises and even disavows his understanding of the philosopher-king, not least in order to ward off the attraction of the young Academicians—represented in the dialogue by Young Socrates—to the idea of an autocratic ruler who would solve Athens' political problems. Distinct from the philosopher-king, the Stranger's statesman is not a *dunastes* or sovereign.[45] But if the genuine ruler, whose concept is developed by the Stranger, is also different from the philosopher-king in that he is not one who builds an ideal city from scratch, it is because his task as a citizen of an actual city consists in setting an already existing city on its right course, as demonstrated by the repeated references throughout the dialogue to the Athenian *polis* with all the turmoil it underwent in the fifth and fourth centuries.⁴⁶ The statesman is *not* a philosopher with knowledge of the idea of a just, good, and beautiful city but, as we will see, possesses a different kind of knowledge that, even though it is qualified as a second sailing, is the best knowledge possible of the most perfect order of which an actual human city is capable. But before more precisely defining this knowledge, which is second best specifically because it is that of a statesman who is a full member of a city, I tentatively submit that the statesman as understood by the Stranger is not a maker of human polities. Hannah Arendt has forcefully argued that the *Republic* not only demonstrates that Plato models the philosopher-king after the household head, thus ignoring the difference between the constitution of a household and that of a *polis*, but also that the application of the doctrine of the ideas, which originates from experiences in the realm of fabrication, to the realm of the political makes of the philosopher-king of the *Republic* a craftsman; more precisely, the philosopher-king is a maker, a fabricator. However, in her brief reference to the *Statesman*, which she reads entirely from the perspective of the earlier dialogue and as further evidence of Plato's misunderstanding of the political, she ignores the fact that, right from the beginning, the statesman is distinguished from both the household-head and the slavemaster. As we have already seen, both have in common an injunctive or directive art, but that is as far as the comparison goes. In addition, Arendt does not allow for the possibility that the statesman does not *make* the city in the way the philosopher-king does.⁴⁷ The statesman's task is defined by the inadequacy of all the regimes of actually existing poleis to what a *polis* is supposed to be. Furthermore, as a member of an actual community, the statesman is a finite human being, just as all those whom he is to unite into one whole, and therefore he is not some kind of supreme authority like the philosopher-king.⁴⁸ His authority must be of a different sort. But in order to demonstrate that unlike the philosopher-king, the statesman is not a maker of cities from scratch, and that this is a distinctive feature of the later dialogue, it is, of course, necessary to follow the dialogue through its progressive refinement of the specific kind of knowledge that characterizes the statesman.

Although I will defer a response until the end of the chapter, a question might be warranted at this point. In order to establish the true nature of the sophist, the Stranger had in the preceding dialogue to refute the latter's claim, based on the sophist's appropriation of Parmenides' thought according to which only Being is and non-Being is not, that all of his statements are true. To demonstrate that false statements exist, and thus that the sophist is a fake, the Stranger had to refute father Parmenides; in short, he had to commit a parricide of sorts. Given that in the *Statesman* the Stranger recalls on three occasions what he and his interlocutor were up to in the preceding dialogue, the question that needs to be raised is whether, in order to establish the true nature of the statesman, a similar outrageous act—one also that only a stranger to Athens could dare perform—is required. The question, then, is whether there is something about the dominating opinions of theoreticians and others about the statesman that needs as radical a criticism as the one performed in the *Sophist*, a criticism without which it is not possible to establish the true nature of the statesman, and which raises the second inquiry to a specific level of knowledge philosophically equivalent to what is accomplished in the *Sophist* but, of course, different. In fact, since the Stranger holds that finding the true statesman is a much more arduous task than locating the sophist (284c7), more than just one parricide might be necessary.[49]

I return to the notion of the true statesman. Compared to the large crowd of all the politicians who deal with the affairs of the *polis* and whose chorus, in the Stranger's words, is "[t]he greatest enchanter of all the sophists and most experienced in this art" (291c5–6)—an art grounded on the mere imitation of knowledge—the true statesman, by contrast, is a rare commodity. Because of the kind of science that statesmanship presupposes, the possession of this art and the pretention to the title in question are limited to "some one, two, or altogether few" (293a4). Plato is rather straightforward on this point: the knowledge of statesmanship is of such a nature that only one individual in a state, or at best two, are capable of it, implying also that some states might lack statesmen of this kind altogether. This scarcity of true statesmanship needs our attention not merely because it inevitably suggests a congenital superiority of some over all others, but also because things might prove to be a bit more complex. Indeed, let us immediately point out that it is not the office that one holds that makes one a true statesman. Already from early on in the dialogue it is recognized that "[w]hoever is skilled enough, though himself private, to advise a man who is king of a land" (259a6–7) merits the title of a true statesman, perhaps more so than the royal one whom he advises. The possession of this royal art, in which one can excel without exercising it, blurs the distinction between the private and public.

A further implication of the decoupling of the knowledge in question from institutions of kingship is that, however scarce it is due to its difficulty, it is not therefore the result of a natural distinction that would set the true statesman apart from all other human beings and make him a god among men, as it were. This point is forcefully made in the *Statesman* when it is asserted that, unlike what is the case with bees, "there is no king that comes to be in the cities [. . .] who's of the sort that naturally arises in hives—one who's right from the start exceptional in his body and his soul" (301d9–e3). It is true that in Book IX of the *Laws* the Athenian stranger briefly considers the possibility that, "by God's mercy," a man could be born with the natural capacity of putting the interest of commonwealth above his own, but such a possibility is soon dismissed.[50] True statesmanship is not a natural or native talent.[51] Like the art of one who is competent in advising a physician without ever being one, the statesman's art is a talent of counseling, of giving advice, one that presupposes broad and deep experience rather than being distinguished by a natural talent. It is a talent for *sumboulia*, for giving advice in the royal art to other human beings who are not political by nature per se, who in other words are not political animals, and whose political disposition therefore cannot be taken for granted.[52] The passage quoted above, asserting that no king comes to be in cities like the one that arises in the beehive, concludes as follows: "they [the cities] must, it seems, once they've come together [*sunelthontas*], write up writings while they run after the traces of the truest regime" (301e3–5). Because of the lack of a natural king, the members of a city must come together and, presumably in concert with a kingly advisor, and since no rules arise among them by nature, decide in common about laws, thus becoming political beings in the first place. As I see it, it becomes clear here that the advice conveyed by a kingly individual takes place in a process of deliberation with all the prospective citizens of a city and that his advice, rather than being despotic, is prescriptive or injunctive because of the citizens' free and mutual agreement to follow his counsel. But, although the Stranger leaves no doubt regarding the paucity of actual individuals in a city capable of true statesmanship, there is one more thing I wish to hazard: since statesmanship is not a natural distinction, but is based on profound and extensive experience and, furthermore, since the one who is capable of it is a mortal just like those he cares for, anyone in a multitude could, in principle, possess this art concerning humans while themselves remaining human. Therefore, as may already have become clear, this art is intrinsically democratic. "Democratic" not in the sense of the particular regime Plato was familiar with but, perhaps, in a more fundamental sense.

The statesman, the political man, is a knower (*epistemon*) (258b5) in that he has an art or science specifically his own. It is on this presupposition that the dialogue begins, and proceeds, narrowing down the definition of the one who possesses this art by progressively setting him apart not from all others, but from all the other arts involved in the care of the state and all competitors and pretenders to his art. This occurs in a process during which, as we have seen, a variety of methodologies are tried out and abandoned until, finally, at the end of the purification process, the statesman—or, perhaps more appropriately, his art—reveals his (or its) look like shining gold. The Stranger starts with the arts or sciences and the knowledge they represent, and after having divided them into manual (or practical) and theoretical (cognitive or gnostic) sciences, he divides the latter again into "discriminative (critical)" arts (like mathematics) and "injunctive (epitactic)" arts (260b6–7). Statesmanship, as the Stranger and Young Socrates agree, is not practical knowledge but a sort of theoretical art—one, however, that in distinction from mathematics, which here serves as the paradigm of discriminative or critical gnostic art, is prescriptive, injunctive, or epitactic in nature. That is, on the basis of a certain theoretical knowledge intrinsic to action, the statesman's art provides instructions, injunctions, orders, to convert insight into being.

For my purposes here, I will skip the further distinctions made that at the end of the first *diairesis* culminate in the dubious definition of the statesman as a herdsman in charge of the totality of his herd's needs. The Stranger begins to correct this definition with the help of a striking myth about the periodic reversal of the entire universe, a myth unique in Plato's work—namely, the myth about the respective epochs of Cronus and Zeus. This myth serves to situate such a figure of fatherly authority in a mythic age preceding the contemporary world; in the contemporary world, furthermore, everything happens in reverse of what obtained in the preceding cosmic age. This mythic age is an age in which a god—Cronus—nurtured human beings and all other creatures without distinction, in all respects, directly, and without laws. At that time, the Stranger emphasizes, "there were no regimes [*politeiai*]" (271e10–272a1)—that is, no political regimens and no statesmen, because there was no need for humans to form societies to begin with. In the same way as they required no arts whatsoever to survive, they also had no need for an art of statesmanship. They formed a herd of individual bodies, like a herd of other animals, lacking any structure among them as individuals. The conception of the statesman as a herdsman of human beings is characteristic of this mythical age alone; only a god, and not any mortal, can occupy such a position. In the dialogue, the myth thus provides a foil in contrast to which the present epoch under Zeus can come fully into view, an epoch from which the nurturing Cronus and all the daimons have withdrawn, and in which humans have been abandoned to themselves and are themselves in charge of shaping their fate.[53]

Since political art is missing from the several gifts, such as the different crafts, that the gods provide them to survive in the new world where they are exposed to nature, it is clear that the political art is an art that humans have to invent themselves. In Taylor's words, the myth in the *Statesman* "has nothing to do with speculation about either the 'first' or the 'last' things. It is simply that the all-sufficient ruler by the Grace of God, who needs no help from the laws, belongs to that 'other time' when beasts could talk, when men knew nothing of work, of clothes, or of sex, and everything happened backwards [. . .] Such an autocrat belongs to fairy-tale, not to authentic history."[54] In short, with this myth, the Stranger forces Young Socrates both to acknowledge that instead of being natural, states or cities are manmade, and to resolutely look for the statesman exclusively amongst human beings and within the existing conditions of mankind, rather than as a despotic paternal figure. To conceive of the statesman as a herdsman is to think of him in a backward way. The statesman's task is not to lead humanity back to the paradisiac Cronus age. The Stranger urges Young Socrates to look for the statesman not as someone distinct in nature from his subjects, and therefore as a divine household-head, but as someone who leads a polity over whose subjects he does not—unlike a household-head, a slavemaster, or a herder—hold property rights. Indeed, as is clear from the retold myth of Cronus in Book IV of the *Laws*, Cronus and his daimons rule the human world like an *oikos*.[55] One purpose of the myth is to make Young Socrates aware that all the concepts by which they have so far approached the statesman describe a state of affairs that is not that of the present, and the statesman as the head of a large household is one such anachronistic concept. The interpretations of the statesman as a shepherd and as a father-figure both unmistakably belong to a pre-political era. In distinction from the myth, "a second course" regarding statesmanship thus comes into view, where statesmanship is an exclusively human affair and where, rather than nurturing beings of a different species as would any shepherd, the statesman is no longer a divine and paternal figure who as such would also be the breeder of his flock. Instead, he himself belongs to those he rules. But something else becomes clear here as well. With the rejection of statesmanship as a herding of the human flock, the "second course" proposes also a new conception of communality, one significantly different from a herd of tamed animals. Having given "the common nurture of many together, which belongs to animal-nurture, the name of herd-nurture or a kind of common nurture [*tes zootrophias ten ton sympollon koinen trophen ageleiotrophian he koinotrophiken tina onomazomen]*" (261e1–3)—a designation that perfectly describes the kind of communality (or, rather, the lack thereof) that existed between the individuals of which Cronus and his daimons were in charge during the golden age—it follows that another name, different from *koinotrophiken* as *ageleiotrophian*, is required to speak of the community over which a statesman rules. It can no longer be a name denoting collective animal husbandry, in which the community of a herd as a plurality of individuals is a merely quantitative concept. A statesman does not preside over a community in the sense of a herd. He must be not only one among the citizens of a *polis* but must also belong to the community that they form together with one another. As a community, rather than a herd, a polity excludes nurturing by a benevolent or despotic patriarchal figure. By contrast, it demands care, or tending, as the Greek term *epimeleia* is commonly translated. Statesmanship consists of the "care of an entire human community" (276b9)—in other words, the care not of a multitude of human bodies, but of the community they freely (*hekousios*) form. This also implies that the exclusively human art of statesmanship requires its free recognition by the citizen body that is subject to it. If a community voluntarily accepts being tended, rather than raised or nurtured, by one who belongs to the community of free men— whether as a citizen or as a foreigner—then the community is no longer a herd. In Taylor's words, such a state would imply the "Greek equation of law with *suntheke politon*, arrangements agreed upon by the citizen body."[56] Care, or tending, differs from raising and nurturing in that it presupposes human autonomy: its object is the preservation of human beings' ability to direct themselves, and shaping their life politically is a condition *sine qua non* of statesmanship. Statesmanship is a royal art only when the free consent of everyone, and everyone's (active) participation in it, is assured. As the Stranger points out at one point in the yet incomplete process of defining statesmanship as a political art, it is "the voluntary herd-grooming of voluntary two-footed animals" (276e13–14). In spite of the conceptual ambiguity of this statement, it is safe to say that all the features characteristic of statesmanship are tangible by way of the difference codified by the Greek notion of *epimelaia* as opposed to *trophike*.[57]

The function of the myth in the dialogue, then, is to introduce the distinction between the theocratic "care of human nurture [(*oi politkoi*) *tes trophes epimelountai tes anthropines*]" (268a1–2)—that is, care for the material well-being and conservation of human beings as natural or animal beings— and the care (*epimeleia*) of the specifically political needs that arise among them once they have been forced to rely on themselves for everything. In other words, the myth about the ages of Cronus and Zeus sets the stage for the introduction of the dimension of the political, cosmically situating it in distinction from a mythical theocratic epoch that was all about human nurture and that preceded our own epoch, the epoch of Zeus, in which humans are left to fend for themselves and in which alone there is a need and a place for a statesman and his art.[58] The myth makes it plain that, for Plato in the *Statesman*, "[w]hat is natural is the sick or disordered city," and, by contrast, "healthy political life is not natural."[59] To conclude, the role of the myth in the dialogue is to bring into full view the originality of the realm of the *polis* and of the "political" in distinction from animal husbandry, including that of human beings. Thus, in a "second course," the myth's role is to elaborate on the categories specific to all things that depend on human agency alone, so as to be able to secure the singularity of this domain by keeping it free of all theocratic concepts that obliterate its uniqueness, such as paternalism, herds (*agelaioi*), herding or nurturing (*trophe*), and so forth.

With the opening lines of the dialogue, in which Socrates accuses the mathematician Theodorus of a mistake in calculating the relative worth of the sophist, the statesman, and the philosopher, a limit of mathematics is from the start established, and frames the whole discussion to come about the political and the statesman.[60] In John Sallis's words, the dialogue marks this limit "in various fashions, it will do it again and again, for example, by way of comedy, of myth, and of parody."[61] I would like to draw attention to what may be another (perhaps only indirect) reservation regarding mathematics that also occurs toward the very beginning of the dialogue, one that seems to have been overlooked by commentators. At the moment when the Stranger is about to begin defining the look of the statesman by way of the Socratic method of *diairesis*, he asks Young Socrates whether there is not "a kind of natural joint [*diaphue*]" (259d11) in theoretical art that permits divisions to be made "in a harmonious way" (260b8). This natural break, joint, or suture is one between the art of counting (*logistikos*)—that is, mathematics—and the art, for example, of a master-builder, an art that serves as the first paradigm for defining the statesman, as we have seen. It is to this term, a "natural joint," that I propose paying a bit more attention, because with it the Stranger shows himself from the beginning to approach his subject in terms of a method of division that has its "organic" wholeness in view, but whose necessity becomes inevitable once its dichotomous divisions, without attention to the subject's natural joints, have led to the conclusion that the statesman is a herder of unhorned and featherless bipeds. From the failed definition of the statesman by way of the first *diairesis*, it has already become clear that if *diairesis* is a method that proceeds by halving wholes, such as the totality of the arts, without heeding the specific nature of the wholes but instead cutting them through the middle into contraries, its bifurcatory or dichotomous nature, which appealed to Young Socrates, inevitably ushers in absurdity. Yet it is only after the passage through the myth that the Stranger abandons this mathematical understanding of the philosophical or Socratic method of investigation, since in attempting to establish the nature of the statesman, it has become manifest that they have been "incapable of doing it in two." From here on, the Stranger proceeds explicitly to divide wholes "limb by limb [*kata mele*]" (287c5). Undoubtedly, *diaphue* (which, in its figurative sense, also simply refers to distinctions) and *mele* are not identical terms, but they both denote natural joints. If, at the very beginning of the first *diairesis*, the Stranger thus already speaks of joints rather than halves, is it not in order to confront Young Socrates from the start with the need to break with the mathematical model of the method to which, as a mathematician, he cannot but be attracted, especially when it comes to defining an art that concerns living wholes like statesmanship?[62] A theoretical or mathematical approach to the art in question will necessarily fail to define it, and thus the need arises of first telling the young man a story to correct the error. Let me also note that upon Young Socrates' agreement that they should look for a natural joint along which to divide the gnostic arts, the Stranger observes that, indeed, "it's desirable for those who are doing anything in common to be unanimous" (260b10–11), especially if such doing implies "dismiss[ing] the opinions of everyone else" (260b13–14) about what constitutes statesmanship. Does the very subject matter of the dialogue—statesmanship—not also require that, while exhibiting the look of the statesman, an injunction unknown to mathematics emerges and has to be observed—namely, an injunction to do this exhibiting in common, meaning also discursively?

What the myth recounted by the Stranger has brought to light is that, during the reign of Cronus, human beings were nurtured by the god in all possible respects; they were thus not in need of any arts, such as agriculture or, in particular, the art of politics. Furthermore, not only were they not in need of sexual generation since they sprung forth fully formed from the earth, but they were also not in need of one another other to begin with since, nurtured in all respects by the god, they were fully independent of one another. They also had nothing to expect or fear from each other. During the epoch of Cronus, human beings had no motivation whatsoever to congregate, and it was a thoroughly apolitical age. However, all of that changes once the god withdraws: the cosmos is on its own, and begins revolving in the opposite direction. At that moment, in order to protect themselves from nature and from themselves, human beings had to invent the arts (some of which they received from the gods), and it is through the arts that they entered into relation with one another.[63] The cities became complex entities of interconnected arts and, through those arts, of human beings. It is in this context that the Stranger proposes to approach statesmanship, as the art of all arts, by way of the paradigm of weaving.

The purpose of weaving is to create protective wear against a hostile nature, but by making it the paradigm of statesmanship, it is also understood as a protection against the dangers that man poses to man—the dangers of *polemos* and *stasis*. I have to pass over in silence the complex process of purification that statesmanship, as a form of weaving, will have to undergo before "royal plaiting [*basiliken symploken*]" (306a1) will have been fully exhibited in all its purity at the very end of the dialogue. But before I can focus on this art, what its goal is, and how, precisely, it accomplishes its task, I must first return to a question I left in abeyance—that is, whether or not, in order to properly define the statesman, the Stranger must perform something akin to the parricide that was required in the *Sophist*.

In the *Statesman*, the Stranger suggests at certain moments that without risking or daring (*tolmeteon*) to make certain arguments, no progress in the definition of the statesman can be achieved. This language clearly resonates with that of the *Sophist*. Furthermore, at a particular juncture in the discussion, the Stranger makes explicit reference to the former dialogue, from which one can infer that the statesman will never be found without a refutation of a paralyzing assumption regarding the arts, a refutation as radical as that of Parmenides' doctrine on Non-being (284b8–c4). This one particular reference to the *Sophist* follows the Stranger's introduction of the question of true measure, or "the mean" (*to metrion*). The question is introduced after a strict definition of weaving has been reached, one that can serve as the paradigm for statesmanship. Of course, it is not by accident that the question arises at this precise point for, indeed, it concerns a standard for the genesis of a successful product of art one that can be judged to be good or beautiful and, more generally, for coming into being, whether of beings or of discourse. Having, in a long and seemingly cumbersome process, separated off all the subsidiary arts involved in woolworking as the co-causes of weaving properly speaking—including the art of twisting combed wool into a hard thread (the warp) and a softer thread (the woof)—that is, from the very art that brings the product of weaving (the woolen garment) into being, weaving itself is finally shown to consist of the interlacing of soft and hard threads that are distinct because they are different in nature.[64] In the Stranger's words: "Whenever the proper part of the syncritical art engaged in woolworking produces a plaited web by a straight plaiting of woof and warp, we address the entire plaited thing as a woolen garment, and the art that supervises it as weaving" (283a4–8).

At this precise point, the Stranger, reflecting back on the long and tangled speech through which they arrived at this result, begins a digression about the nature of excess (*hyperbole*) and deficiency (*elleipsis*) in the speech they have woven, asking whether it was too long or too short. Obviously, the inquiry concerns a standard for how to proceed discursively, whether through disproportionally lengthy divisions or in telling too long a story—in other words, it is an appeal to "the art of measurement [*metrike*] [that] deals with all these things" (283d2). With the reference to measurement, one cannot but recall Protagoras' doctrine according to which man is the measure of all things, and the Athenian stranger's statement in the *Laws* that, rather than man, God is this measure. In the *Statesman*, however, the question of measurement and its standard arises in the context of the formation of speeches and, subsequently, the genesis of a polity. It concerns the coming into being of the arts, in particular the art of statesmanship, and what such political art is to engender. In other words, the just measure concerns the accordance of what is brought into being with the form or idea of the intended product—a polity, in the case of statesmanship.[65] But to return to the specific context in which the question of true measure arises, it is thus not just any art of measurement that is capable of making a fitting judgment about excess and deficiency, whether in the art of debating or in any other art. The art in question is to be divided into two, one in which the greater and the smaller are simply evaluated in relation to one another, and "one in terms of the necessary (indispensable) being of becoming," that is, one that proceeds in relation to a mean or standard (283d8–9). If Young Socrates does not understand what is meant by the second kind of measurement it is because, as a mathematician, he is obviously familiar only with the first form of measurement. However, the form of measurement required when it comes time to philosophically debate the nature of the arts, and especially the knowledge of the statesman, requires a non-mathematical approach to non-quantifiable things such as excess and deficiency, the bigger and the smaller, and so forth, so as to be able to make judgments about them—that is, to praise or blame them. Here, in other words, with respect to political knowledge or, more generally, to the whole domain of the practical, mathematics is an obstacle to any philosophical comprehension of the domain in question. The core studies that the elder Socrates established in Book VII of the *Republic* as a propaedeutic to philosophy—mathematics, geometry, and kinematics—no longer have pertinence here. "Essential measure," as Miller translates *to metrion*, or "the mean," requires a knowledge different from that of the "erudites," including Theodorus and his students.[66] As Rosen notes: "For the first time in the dialogue, we are about to be introduced to the exercise of phronesis, good sense or judgment. This exercise is the art of measurement."[67] Whenever it is a question of becoming, in other words, of the coming into being of something—in short, of what the arts do, including the art of the statesman—mathematical measure is inappropriate and incapable of assessing it; for, in this case, to judge about the greater or the lesser requires a third term, not a leveling middle term between extremes, but a mean or true measure with respect to which excess and deficiency can be evaluated.[68] The knowledge of this standard is a non-arithmetical knowledge, one required wherever there is a question of genesis, of bringing something into being, as is the case with all the arts, including, needless to say, that of the statesman. It is called *phronesis*, good sense or judgment, the ability to judge what is good and bad, appropriate and inappropriate, and it concerns both moral virtue and technical efficacy. The full significance of this notion of the mean or "essential measure" is highlighted by the Stranger when he asks Young Socrates, the mathematician, whether by "allow[ing] the nature of the bigger to be relative to nothing other than to the less," and thus never to be relative to the mean, they "won't [. . .] destroy by this speech the arts themselves as well as all their works, and in particular [. . .] make vanish both the political art that's now being sought and the art of weaving that's been described? For all arts of this sort surely keep a close watch in their actions on the more and less of the mean [. . .] And it's in exactly this way, by preserving the mean, that they produce everything good and beautiful" (284a1–b3).

Now it is exactly at this point—when it has been established that, *qua* arts, weaving and statesmanship require a non-arithmetical standard for evaluating excess and deficiency, and thus for producing fitting objects—that the Stranger evokes the *Sophist*, saying, "Then, just as in the case of the sophist we compelled 'that which is not' to be, when the speech slipped by us along this line, so also now, in turn, mustn't the more and the less be compelled to become measurable relative not only to one another but also to the becoming of the mean? For it's really not possible for either a statesman or anyone else to have been proved to be indisputably a scientific knower of matters of action if this is not agreed upon" (284b8–c4). Establishing that extremes must be able to be measured in relation to a non-mathematical standard for action to be possible is thus a feat of a similar order to proving in the *Sophist* that Not-being, in a way, is.[69] If the latter was accomplished by the parricide of father Parmenides, who is targeted by the present polemical argument? The Stranger refers to them as "many of the clever"—or, in J. B. Skemp's translation, "our 'erudite' friends"—who, "in the sheer belief that they're pointing out something wise, say on occasion, 'After all, there is an art of measurement about everything that becomes'" (284e11–285a3), including the whole of human life, without, however, making a distinction between the two arts of measurement. These "erudite" friends are, unmistakably, the Pythagoreans, the mathematicians, and, mutatis mutandis, also Plato, with his earlier understanding of the paradigmatic role of mathematics for philosophy.[70] If the more or less is not compelled to become measurable in respect of attainment of a norm of due measure, of the "fitting" (*prepon*), the art of statesmanship disappears and, as the Stranger warns, the "search after this for the royal science" becomes *aporos*, without a solution (284b5–6). What is at stake, then, with the distinction between true measure and relative measure, is nothing less than the very existence of the human domain itself—that is, of the arts—and the possibility of action: without a true measure the arts cannot exist, but if they exist, then this is also proof of the existence of such an absolute measure.[71] Thus, Young Socrates, the young mathematician, not knowing what he is saying, avers: "Then we must as best as we can do the same thing now as well" (284c5–6). In other words, he says, they must do what was done in the case of the sophist—namely, kill father Pythagoras, the father of mathematics.

By introducing the notion of another genus of measurement, one without which the realm of the arts and human affairs (including statesmanship) would collapse, the Stranger manifests himself as a stranger, as someone who, from the outside, challenges Greek popular beliefs—one of which concerns the very distinction between the barbarians and the Greeks themselves—and Greek philosophical thinking. It is precisely in this section on measurement that one can gauge Plato's reasons for charging a stranger with the task of delineating the limits of mathematics as the paradigm of political philosophy. When the Stranger refers to the mathematical art of measurement as that which is concerned with "number, lengths, depths, widths, and speeds relative to their contraries," as opposed to arts of measurement "relative to the mean, the fitting, the opportune, and the needful, and everything settled toward the middle and away from the extremes" (284e4–8), he refers to the core study of philosophy as a theoretical inquiry into the essence or ideas of things that Socrates establishes in the *Republic*. By arguing that it is impossible to apply this approach to the imprecise and fleeting entities and actions characteristic of the public domain, and that it is not appropriate as a standard for production via *technai*, the Stranger asserts the resistance of that domain against the theoretical approach, and puts this latter approach into its place. But though everything that depends on human agency is imprecise from a theoretical point of view, it has a precision (*akribes*) and a perfection or completeness (*teleios*) of its own (284d2).[72] However, for the exactitude or precision of the public domain to fully show forth, the subsequent division of the art of measurement into mathematical measurement and measurement concerning "the necessary (indispensable) being of becoming" (283d8–9) is required. As Young Socrates acknowledges, each part "is a big section and far different from each other" (284e9–10). The magnitude of this section is an intimation as to the scope of the parricide it involves.

The sort of knowledge entailed by the genesis of anything belonging to the order of a product of the arts, and above all a product of statesmanship, is not the knowledge of the theoretician and mathematician, nor is it that of the philosopher who models his search for the ideas after mathematics. It remains that only a philosopher—one who, like the Stranger, is not infatuated with mathematics—can possibly become aware of the distinct nature of such knowledge. Based on true measure, this knowledge involves, as we have seen, *phronesis*, a kind of judging not only intent on finding the middle between extremes but, ultimately, on accomplishing a mediation between the universal and the particular, the law and the singular case, of which theoretical knowledge is incapable.[73] The knowledge of a statesman concerns the precision (*akribeia*) with which the law applies to a particular case.

Finally, I can now begin to address what can be accomplished by the statesman—in other words, I emphasize, what can be accomplished by him or *her*, of whom only very few are found in a multitude. If I also refer to the statesman as a she, it is because we know from the *Republic* that women too can be rulers.[74] Furthermore, according to the *Laws*, by choosing spinning and woolworking as the arts that characterize him or her, the statesman's skill is one over which, in ancient Greece, women had superintendence.[75] But it is not simply the case that the Stranger "illustrates the political art by an emphatically domestic" and "characteristically feminine art," rather than "by such 'outgoing' arts as herding and piloting," as Leo Strauss remarks; the Stranger does so, indeed, by an art that is also the distinguishing craft of a masculine god such as Zeus.[76] Weaving is thus an art in advance of the male/female distinction, one, as we will see later, that concerns the interlacing of both sexes. I do not make these observations only in passing, since the risk I wish to take is indeed the thesis that, when speaking about the statesman, the Stranger is—in spite of the scarcity of statesmen in any actual polity, and thus in defiance of what was actually the case in Athens at that time—implicitly speaking about *every* member of the polity as potentially a statesman, women included. However, this supposition can be made only once statesmanship has been completely purged of all the arts that are subservient to it, including the three that resemble it most—generalship, rhetoric, and the activity of judges—until it shines forth in all its purity. Even then, however, it is not certain that this hypothesis can be sustained without friction. Nevertheless, I believe that, since a number of textual hints allow for this speculation, it is worth trying.

Because of the precariousness of this suggestion, it may be appropriate to reflect once again on the nature of the Stranger in order to bring out certain implications of his intervention. These implications may not, strictly speaking, have been intended by Plato, but they are not therefore arbitrary and in fact, I contend, necessarily follow for textual reasons. Although I have taken care to explain that the Stranger is no barbarian—which, at the time of the dialogue, the Athenians would have associated with the Persians—I have also consistently stressed the Stranger's strangeness. Plato's contemporaries, who had recently defeated Persia's attempt to conquer Greece and subject it to its despotic power, would not possibly have liked to learn how to live politically from a barbarian. To be able to confront the Athenians with another take on philosophical and political thinking, the Stranger cannot be altogether different from them. In spite of all its novelty, the new philosophy he teaches builds upon the tradition, and owes its intelligibility to what it rejects. For the same reasons, what he offers regarding statesmanship cannot be something outlandish. If the Stranger's lessons on politics were altogether other than what the Greeks were familiar with, they would not have been able to recognize what parts of it could concern them. The Stranger's political doctrine must take its departure from facts and conceptions recognizable by the Athenians, and his break with these facts and conceptions must build on them. It is in this context that I wish to return once more to the contention that, within a city, only one, two, or at most three are capable of the art required of a genuine statesman. This claim is justified by the complex nature of the art in question, but does it not also imply a distinct conception of the nature of the individuals who could possibly possess the required knowledge? Apart from the demanding nature of the art in question, there is perhaps another reason why the Stranger and his respondent can imagine only one, two, or three potential statesmen in an existing polity.

Let us therefore remind ourselves that throughout its history the Greek *polis* was made up by a number of tribes, the *phylai*, which were corporate bodies based on real or notional ties of kin. These tribes were themselves often subdivided into smaller kinship groups called *phratriai*, brotherhoods, to which their members were largely loyal. Yet, under these conditions, no member of these social groups and fraternities could ever become an individual capable of statesmanship. Since only individuals free from the constraints and loyalties of the groups in question could meet the criteria of being a statesman, a possibility that is hard to imagine, it is impossible to look for the one or few who possess the art of statesmanship among the members of these factions in the *polis*. As a dramatis persona, the Stranger—without a patronym, and moreover, if we follow the reading of the dialogue that holds that he has also no kinship with the Eleatic tribe, without a faction—is thus the model for the implicit demand in the *Statesman* that a genuine polity can only be one that is free from all local and regional tribal identifications. With the persona of the Stranger, Plato makes an attempt of thinking "free men"—that is, individuals free of the authority of thinking fathers, and free of the constraints of ethnical allegiancies in the realm of the political. Only a stranger could possibly confront the Athenians with such an exorbitant demand which, although difficult to imagine, is nonetheless based on the Greek idea of freedom and self-determination. Furthermore, although he is not totally other, the Stranger is foreign enough to have to quit after he has, *qua* foreigner, lectured the Athenians. He is foreign enough to advise them, but too foreign to become one of them. However, an Athenian individual, or rather all members of the *polis*, as political beings free from all the baggage associated with tribalism and fraternalism, will have to be in charge of realizing the idea that necessitates finding the true measure for what is excessive and deficient according to his doctrine. Whether or not this is what Plato explicitly intended to suggest is evidently debatable, but as a figure in the dialogue the Stranger has a dynamism whose effects cannot all be calculated in terms of Plato's intention.

In seeking to define what characterizes statesmanship in distinction from the lengthy list of all the other arts that claim this role, and after having separated off statesmanship from the entirety of all of them, including the false arts, the *Statesman* concludes by defining statesmanship as royal weaving. Weaving is not simply a paradigm in general for what the royal art consists of; it is also, as we will see in a moment, a metaphor for such an art under its specific form of woolworking. And as such, the royal weaver alone possesses the kind of art in question. Yet, paradoxically and however unjustifiably, the many (if not all members of a polity) lay claim in one way or another to the title in question! They certainly mistake the art that they perform within the state for that of the royal man or woman, and may erroneously confuse their respective competences with the singular art of the statesman. But does this misjudgment, by seemingly the entirety of all the other members of the polity, not also suggest that all of them are in one way already factually involved with the commonwealth, and that, at least in principle and under certain conditions, each one could become a true statesman?

In preparation of the development that awaits, I must return once more, though briefly, to the Stranger's choice of the paradigm of weaving. Weaving, he proposes, is "the smallest paradigm [. . .] with the same business as the political" (279a7–8) and, by being set alongside this greater thing, can serve to elucidate it. But it is also chosen, admittedly, for lack of a better paradigm.[77] Now, the Stranger is quick to say that it is not weaving as a whole but, within the class of things that are crafted as "repellents for the sake of not being affected" (279c9), only that kind of "weaving that deals with robes woven from wool" (279b4–5) that will serve as the paradigm. In other words, only the latter narrower or stricter form of weaving can serve as a paradigm for the royal art. Crucial here is that in the *diairesis* of all the arts involved in making repellents and coverings, the Stranger locates woolen clothmaking in the genus of *problemata* (shields) made of hairy elements that are said to "bind themselves together by themselves [*auta hautois sundeta*]" (279e7–280a1). Only woolworking meets this criterion. But before elaborating on the various reasons why weaving thus understood can serve as a paradigm to illuminate what the statesman does, I recall that, in the age of Zeus, "just as the cosmos had been ordered to be an independent authority [*autokrator*] over its own movement, so too in exactly the same way the parts themselves were ordered to grow, generate, and nurse, to the extent that they could, through themselves [*autois di' hauton*] by a similar conduct" (274a5–b2).

That is, once human beings "through themselves had to manage their way of life and their own care for themselves just as the cosmos as a whole, in joint imitation of" it (274d4–6), the foundation was laid on the basis of which weaving can meaningfully be made into a paradigm of statesmanship. Indeed, specifically in the case of woolen cloaks, weaving, by producing fabrics that "bind themselves together by themselves," is paradigmatic of an activity that, like that of the way of life that comes into being under the regime of Zeus, has authority over itself. Weaving, the Stranger holds, receives its name from the protections it produces—clothmaking—and so too the royal art and statesmanship are named from what they accomplish—the political (*politikes*)—that is, from what makes cities into cities.[78] If it is so important to characterize weaving as the making of fabrics in which the threads bind themselves together by themselves, the reason is that this characterization brings to light an illuminating parallelism between clothmaking and caring for the city. The paradigm establishes that cities too are made of elements that willingly, and ultimately free from any preexisting traditional bonds, "bind themselves together by themselves." Undoubtedly, it will be objected that in actuality the Greek polity was a unity based on all sorts of already unified segments of the population. But here, the Stranger is speaking of the formation by a statesman of a community in advance of such divisions. Yet, one may wish to know where, if the members of such a community are to bind themselves by themselves into such a commonwealth, the statesman comes in. Is his role that of securing the possibility for the members of the cities to weave themselves freely together? Does it consist in joining together that which, by itself, binds itself together by itself? And in what capacity, and by what means, does he or she accomplish this task? The art in question, as it is manifest in the dialogue, is one of caring for citizens, rather than nurturing or nursing a herd of human animals. Is care, then, not also a function of what the statesman's art must accomplish first and foremost, and which, in modern terms, would have to be characterized as the citizens' self-determination—that is, their willingness to let themselves be interwoven into a *polis*?

In our dialogue, the Stranger fulfills his promise of examining the figure of the statesman, as whom, in addition to appearing as the sophist and the madman, the philosopher was said to appear to the ignorant in the cities. In both cases, it is a question of distinguishing the philosopher from those figures whom he sometimes dangerously resembles, as in the case of the sophist. But compared to the sophist, the statesman is the good other of the philosopher. Though Socrates thanks him at the end of the dialogue for having successfully completed the inquiry, the Stranger never exclaims, as he did in the *Sophist*, that in the *Statesman* he has also inadvertently discovered the philosopher. The art characteristic of the philosopher, which concerns epistemic knowledge, had shown itself to be dialectical science, the art of division and composition. But apart from the fact that, in the context of the discussion of the art of measurement, the Stranger explicitly evokes both procedures of the scientific method—on the one hand, dividing a manifold by species, and on the other, comprehending them within one genus—as calling upon one another (285a–c), his systematic distinction of the royal art from all rival arts revealed the statesman to be involved in a counterpart of the art of the philosopher by selecting the potential citizens of a city according to their contrary virtues in order to weave them into the fabric of a polity.[79] His art is not one of division and composition, nor is it theoretical; rather, it is an art that concerns the *polis*. He finds the divisions factually given, and his task is to combine them in view of a community. Although he does not possess knowledge in a philosophical sense, the statesman, unlike the sophist who simply pretends to be omniscient, has "true opinion." In the *Theaetetus*, true opinion was established as part of philosophical knowledge, and thus the statesman, in possessing it, proves to resemble the philosopher, all differences considered. His art is not dialectics; he does not string together, as does the philosopher, the elementary building blocks of intelligible speech in view of knowledge in an emphatic sense. On the contrary, his art consists of interweaving opposite virtues existing among those who make up the city by balancing their excessive and respectively deficient features, thanks to his knowledge of the mean, into a political fabric that, on the level of human things, does what the philosopher does on the level of discursive speech.[80] Therefore, his art compares favorably to that of the philosopher. Toward the end of the dialogue, his art is called "royal plaiting" (306a1). It is the counterpart to the philosopher's art of the weaving of *logoi*.

Since, with this, both the differences and resemblances between the philosopher and the statesman have become clear, I wish, before looking into what exactly the latter's art consists of, to engage in a brief and schematic reflection on the respective differences of both figures from the sophist. From the beginning of the *Sophist*, the philosopher is a figure related to—but distinct from—both the sophist and the statesman, one of whom is the philosopher's bad other, with the other being his good counterpart. The philosopher's dialectical art—the art of division *and* combination—is what permits this comparison. In the case of the statesman, the divided is ready at hand in the city, but he has the skill of weaving it into a solid fabric. The sophist's art must necessarily be distinguished in relation to such an accomplishment as the philosopher's art of meaningfully interweaving concepts in discourse. From the definition of the sophist at the end of the dialogue by which finally he has been nailed down, it is, at first, difficult to see in which way he has to be construed as a perversion of the art of division and combination. Instead of a lengthy analysis, let me just point out that the conclusion that the sophist, in his being, is a master of the art of making contradictory speeches originating in an insincere kind of conceited imitation of semblance-making intended as a shadow-play of words, presupposes precisely that his art rests on opposition and contradiction, and that this is what he claims to be able to teach. His whole art descends from his skill at contradicting any claim whatsoever, and at making everyone else as capable of it as he himself is (232c9–11). It is a divisive art, inhibitive also of all mixing. Does it not follow from this that his art is one of division alone, for the sake of division, in complete abstraction from the other side of the philosopher's art, that of comblination? Furthermore, since making others capable of contradiction is an art that aims at the young members of the elite within a city, it is also an art in direct conflict with that of the statesman.

Thus, I begin the discussion of "royal plaiting"—that is, the discussion of "what sort [of plaiting] it is, in what manner it plaits together, and what sort of woven thing it hands us" (306a1–3)—with the Stranger's observation that, in order to do so, "we must have the nerve to declare a somewhat amazing speech [*touton de peri thaumaston tina logon apophainesthai tolmeteon*]" (306b7–8) about virtues such as courage (*andreia*) and moderation (*sophrosyne*). This remark recalls the point in the *Sophist* where, before engaging Father Parmenides, the Stranger tells Theaetetus that "we now must have the nerve to set upon the paternal speech" (242a1–2). Indeed, the argument that he is about to make regarding virtues is one that goes against the grain of "usual speech"—in particular, it goes against the grain of the elder Socrates' contention elsewhere that all forms of virtue are in a friendly relation to one another.[81] A bit later in the dialogue, the Stranger returns to this contention, and remarks that "proper parts of virtue, not small, are as a pair at variance with one another by nature [*allelois diapheresthon phusei*], and, in particular, act on those who have them in [the] same way" (308b7–9). In what seems, then, to be another parricide—necessary this time to be able to define the specificity of the statesman's kind of weaving—the Stranger declares that the pair of virtues that are courage and moderation "is in a certain sense with a well-founded enmity toward each other and admits of a sedition of contraries in many of the things which are" (306b10–12). Left to themselves, these virtues would destroy, each in its own way, all human community: both too much courage and too much restraint would result in the destruction of the community by outside forces. But since these virtues are also at war with one another, they threaten the whole arrangement of life from within the *polis* as well. And yet, a "compounding science" such as the royal art brings these virtues, "which are both similar and dissimilar," "all together into one, craft[ing] some single power and look (*idea*)" (308c6–7). However, similar insofar as they are virtues, and yet bipolarly opposed as are woof and warp, can these radically contrary virtues serve as the material for the statesman to weave together a city?[82] The royal art faces the challenge of interconnecting, in a unifying fashion, virtues that left alone would lead to *polemos* and *stasis*; paradoxically, however, it is those virtues themselves—which by nature are at variance with one another—that allow for the creation of a web by means of which they commingle. Indeed, it is their very perfection that harbors the potential of allowing themselves to be intertwined with one another. Therefore, let us underline the fact that for the Stranger, that which at first glance seems to make a city utterly impossible is also its very condition of possibility. By combining material that is similar and dissimilar into one, the royal art is to "craft some single power and look (*idea*) [*mia tina dunamin kai idean demiourgei*]" (308c7), that is, a work that is perfectly unified thanks to its proprieties and structure—in this case, a city. And yet, as is obvious from what has been said about the opposite nature of the virtues, the material out of which the city is to be created is marked by excess and deficiency. To aim for the "self-consistency (*homolegoumenon auto hautoi*)" of the product, a standard is thus required; in other words, true measure is required, a standard in view of which what is opposed in the contrasting virtues lends itself to being interlinked into a *polis*.[83] It is only thanks to the knowledge of such true measure for balancing the extremes of opposite virtues that the statesman can possibly accomplish what is a seemingly impossible task.

Regarding the human material from which a city is to be woven, the Stranger submits that "all those whose natures are able in obtaining an education to become settled in the noble and grand and to receive with art a mutual commingling, when some of them tend more toward manliness—the royal (art) holds the view that their solid character is like a warp growth—and some tend to the orderly and enjoy in accordance with the semblance a wooflike thread, rich and soft, and their natures are straining in contrary directions to one another, it (the royal art) tries to bind and plait them together in some sort of way" (309a7–b8). Needless to say, the royal art, as a weaving, is possible only if its material lends itself to being woven into a fabric. But the paradigm for this art also presupposes that some material is useless, and needs to be discarded, for the benefit of only those threads that through themselves lend themselves to interweaving. Thus, in distinction from those who "are perforce pushed off towards godlessness and insolence and injustice by a bad nature" (308e13–209a1), and who therefore have to be expelled from the city, the remaining others have a good nature that allows them to be educated to become woofs or warps in a political fabric.[84] Let us note that these others, who are to form the stock of a city, are not good by nature; rather than being political animals—that is, political by nature—they only lend themselves by a natural disposition to becoming so through education. I wish to stress here this natural disposition of the human elements to becoming part of a political whole—that is, paradoxically, part of a non-natural, although living, whole. They lend themselves by themselves to becoming part of a polity, a manmade entity. But they also lend themselves to being woven into a commonwealth only on the condition of a good education.

Yet the role of the statesman is not that of an educator. He is, at best, the one who tests (*basanizo*) children through child play to determine whether they will let themselves be educated, before handing them over to "the lawful educators and nurses" under his supervision (308d1–e8). In the arts of woolworking, education is the analogon of the art of twisting combed and carded wool into hard and soft threads.[85] As a syncritical art, it is the business of a class of practitioners who are important, and yet subservient, to the art of statesmanship. But in the same way as the threadmaking of woof and warp is not yet the art of weaving, so too the education through which human beings are prepared to become fit to be woven into the social web is not yet itself a political art. The statesman's science, as a science of weaving, builds on the human material as it is prepared under the supervision of the educators, or perhaps better, in view of what the ultimate goal of statesmanship is. But it is such an art only if, thanks to the education, human beings by themselves make themselves available to become threads in a social and political fabric. In this way education, as the formation of natural dispositions in view of interlacing, is what makes consent possible.

It is not by accident that royal plaiting consists in forging two kinds of bonds between virtues at variance with one another: one concerning the soul, and the other concerning the body of human beings—in other words, a divine and a human bond. In reference to human beings, the Stranger holds that the royal plaiting "makes fit together by a divine bond, in accordance with the kinship, that part of their soul that is eternal-in-genus, and after the divine it fits together in turn their animal-genus with human bonds" (309c1–4). For reasons of economy, I limit myself to a discussion of the divine bond, not only because what Plato advances about the human or marital bond is easy to understand, but also because these bonds are really human (rather than animal) only on the condition that they are already grounded in the divine bond.[86] So what is that part of the human being's soul that is divine? It is, as the following statement by the Stranger suggests, a kind of knowledge: "Whenever that which is in its being true opinion [*alethe doxan*] with steadfastness about the beautiful, just, and good things (and about their contraries) comes to be in souls, then I say that a divine (opinion) is coming to be in a more-than-human genus [*doxan . . . theian . . . en daimonioi gignesthai genei*]" (309c6–9), literally, in a daimonic genus or lineage. Strictly speaking, only the gods can have true knowledge of what is beautiful, just, and good, but if humans have a true opinion about it, then the part of their soul that has this opinion makes them more than just members of an animal species. I also think that the Stranger's reference to it as a daimonic genus is not accidental. When human beings have a true opinion of what is beautiful, just, and good in their soul, a daimon speaks to them, and they are thus more than a physical, natural lineage.

Now, this true opinion is that which the statesman, by way of the muse of his royal art, is to instill (*empoiein*) in those who have been correctly educated and whose natural inclination to virtue has been developed accordingly.[87] Such production of true opinion regarding the beautiful, the just, and the good in human beings prepared through education is *the* defining feature of a genuine statesman (309c6–9). As has already been seen, education is not part of his art; this is incumbent on "lawful educators and nurses." But the true opinions that are to engender the divine bonds between citizens "have been nurtured through laws" that only the statesman, *qua* legislator, could have instituted (310a2). The true opinions that form the divine bond of the educated are implanted by the laws. It is at this precise point, the point at which statesmanship is to be exerted in concrete conditions, that one touches also at the indispensable function of laws.

Only with this feature of the statesman's action of engendering laws concerning "true opinions" does his full exhibition get underway. As the Stranger asks, "[i]f a manly soul takes hold of the truth of its own sort, doesn't it get tamed, and would it not be most willing in this way to share in the just things" (309d10–e2)? And vice versa, if a soul characterized by orderliness "partakes of these opinions," does it not "become in its being moderate and intelligent, within the limits of a regime" (309e6–7)? By contrast, souls that refuse the gift of the opinions in question, whether possessing courage or restraint, become wild or foolish, respectively. Differently put, if true opinion takes hold in the souls of contrary virtues thanks to the genuine statesman's art and good laws, these souls let themselves be tamed or moderated, and thus find their true measure. However, tamed in this way by what the Stranger refers to as "a drug by art [*techne pharmakon*]," the souls that had been at variance with one another have also already potentially been woven together and made to bond, or have already woven "themselves together by themselves," in what is termed "the more divine binding together of the dissimilar and contrarily diverging parts of the nature of virtue" (310a3–5). In full awareness that laws can be both a remedy and a poison, statesmanship thus consists of instilling in humans a true opinion of the beautiful, the just, and the good by which they (humans) become woven together or, as I hold, which allows them to freely weave themselves together.[88] This, I contend, is the true nature of the statesman: to allow for human beings, thanks to good laws, to weave themselves into a living whole.

At this point an additional reflection on weaving may be warranted, for its function as a paradigm set next to the greater thing that is statesmanship, in order to dis-cover it, has run its course, and its limits have become tangible. Indeed, weaving as an art is a form of making, but what so far has become visible about the royal art is that it is no longer an art in this sense. I recall also that, in the final stage of the process in which statesmanship is separated off from all the arts that lay claim to it but are subservient to it, the Stranger brings the look of the statesman into full view by distinguishing him or her from the general, the rhetorician, and the judge. These are already arts no longer involved in making artifacts in a strict sense and, as a result, the statesman's art is to an even lesser degree an art involved in making. Furthermore, does the fact that only contrary and opposite virtues lend themselves properly to the art of the statesman, unlike woolen threads—however much they have been twisted, and in spite of what has been said about them in relation to clothmaking—not reveal the limit of the paradigm for understanding statesmanship?[89] With Ernst Moritz Manasse, I point out that although "the warp and the woof threads might have been produced specifically in view of a woven fabric, they are in their separateness (that is without being woven together) nothing bad. By contrast, the human *ethe* (that correspond to the singular parts of *arete*) require unification, since in isolation they lead to onesidedness, that is, are pernicious."[90] Although the Stranger continues to refer to the royal art as an art of weaving, it is a weaving beyond the artisanal activity. It is the art, inherent in all active arts involved in a polity, of directing its participants to interrelate by way of the bonds that make them citizens. An expertise that compels citizens, by way of injunction, to "bind themselves together by themselves" is not a weaving in any of its common senses.[91]

According to the Stranger, "the single and whole work of royal weaving [*basilikes sunuphanseos ergon*] [is] never to allow moderate characters to stand apart from the manly, but by tamping them down together by means of joint-opinions, honors, dishonors, reputations (opinions), and mutual betrothals of hostages, and bringing together out of them a smooth web with—as the saying goes—a good hand, always to entrust to these in common [*koine*] the offices of rule in cities" (310e8–14). Negatively speaking, the sole task of the statesman's art is "never to allow moderate characters to stand apart from the manly." What, precisely, does this mean? In my reading, it means that the art of the statesman consists first of all of never allowing human beings to be isolated and independent from one another, as they were in the apolitical age of Cronus. The statesman's art serves to prevent natural relations, based on the animal needs and inclinations of isolated individuals, to shape the relations among human beings, and instead to foster bonds between them that are social and political in an elementary way. The true opinion he instills in them is a way of bringing those whose virtuous nature has already been developed through education into relation with one another. In other words, it is a way of bringing one into relation with others as beings that are dissimilar to oneself. In sum, his or her art consists in making citizens out human beings, and if he or she succeeds in this, he or she has in the same breath created "the smooth web" of a body politic. As a being belonging to the same species he or she is to care for, the statesman's task thus amounts to bringing about and securing what is—according to the myth told by Protagoras in the homonymous dialogue—besides all the arts inequitably distributed among human beings, an additional gift of Zeus bestowed on all human beings without difference, namely, "respect for others and a sense of justice" as the foundation of political skill, enabling them to survive in a hostile world.[92] Further, the statesman's task is accomplished when he or she has succeeded in making the human beings he or she is in *care* of into citizens, and thus the statesman can entrust the administration of the state to them collectively, to be shared among them in all cases. This moment corresponds to the statesman's withdrawal—not *from* the city, but *into* it—disappearing, as it were, in the multitude of its citizens.

To conclude, then, the statesman's art is one of making human beings, as natural or animal beings, into citizens. Such a thing, however, is possible only if this is an art by which the citizens are allowed to relate to themselves by themselves, so that they can "bind themselves together by themselves." In doing so they thus form, by way of the dissimilarities between them, a collective out of themselves that is not of the order of a natural gathering like that of a herd but, by contrast, already a minimally political entity. In spite of the critique leveled against democracy throughout the dialogue, what the statesman's art accomplishes—namely, to bring human beings to interrelate by themselves—is to make a certain fundamental democracy into the foundation of the city. Given Plato's judgment about democracy in our dialogue (and elsewhere), a claim like this would seem to be entirely incongruous. So, before I return to the status of the statesman in our dialogue—that is, his status in distinction from the philosopher-king, as well as the pair of the philosopher and the enlightened autocrat—let us consider the following. As the Stranger explains, none of the political regimes that he distinguishes—I limit myself here to the forms of monarchy, oligarchy, and democracy—are right (*orthes*) regimes since, rather than being ruled by the knowledge of a statesman, they are ruled by factions, whether of one, some, or the many, and which pursue their particular interest over that of all others. As is explicitly stated in the *Laws*, rather than constitutions, oligarchy, democracy, and autocracy are "'party ascendancies,'" in which "a willing sovereign is controlling reluctant subjects [in the case of a democracy, the multitude of the poor controls and oppresses the rich] by violence of some sort."[93] When the Stranger muses that criteria such as the "few or many, [. . .] the voluntary or the involuntary, [. . .] poverty or wealth" are not the distinctive features of a right regime, but instead only "a kind of science" (292c6–8), it is made clear that none of the actually existing forms of political regimes can be the right one. In none of them can one find the art of the statesman. On the contrary, all three regimes so far distinguished are regimes not only of inequality but regimes in which one party violently rules over all the others. But the deeper problem of why none of the existing regimes can be correct is that true statesmen who could secure the rightness of such regimes are, as we have seen already, a rare commodity. Therefore, perhaps only a monarch could incarnate the knowledge required, but neither the multitude (*plethos*) in a city nor a smaller number of citizens would ever be able to acquire it.[94] From this the Stranger, returning to a claim made earlier in the dialogue, infers that "the right rule, whenever it proves to be right, must be sought as the rule of some one, two, or altogether few" (293a3–4). Regimes in which the many or the multitude exert power cannot possibly hope to become right regimes; this distinction is reserved only for the regime in which one knowing individual has power, and if this were the case, it would not matter what its particular form would be. Let us then note that only where a knowledge geared toward the whole of a polity exists, a knowledge that concerns the care and conservation of this whole, can a political regime be correct.

In light of this devastating judgment regarding democracy—and in light of the possibility that "if there is some royal art," and if "no multitude is [ever] capable of getting any art whatsoever," especially not "the multitude of the rich and the entire people together" (300e5–8)—it would seem to be utterly hopeless to link the statesman and his knowledge to the possibility of democracy. In addition, this would seem to unambiguously confirm the way Plato has been read as hostile to democracy, and a monarchist at heart. But let us remind ourselves that the exposition of the art of statesmanship in our dialogue takes place by a stranger. The daring hypothesis I advance is that with the Stranger something else becomes manifest, in that "democracy" is no longer one regime among several, but indeed concerns the nature of the political itself. The core of the Stranger's teaching on statesmanship is not only that the possibility of the political is not based on a choice between regimes but, further, that it is based on an elementary democracy.

So let us take note of the following: according to the Stranger, all existing regimes are imitations and, moreover, they are all bad—if not even perverse—imitations of true statesmanship. According to the myth told by the Stranger, the cosmos when abandoned by the God proceeded "in its reordered state, into its own usual course, with its own care of and authority over those things in itself as well as itself, remembering to the best of its ability the instruction of its craftsman and father," and "at the beginning, it performed in a more precise and finished way, but finally with less keenness" (273a8–b4). Does it not follow from this that the royal statesman was initially conceived as a divine shepherd, but as the memory of the golden age began to fade, the statesmen from then on to the present—although resembling their mortal subjects—arrogated to themselves a power that corresponded to the previous and "contrary circuit, and, what's more, of a god instead of a mortal" (275a1)? Correct in this conception of statesmanship, and in conformity with the exigencies of the new age, is only that it supposes the statesman to be "the ruler of the entire city [*poleos archonta*]" (275a3). Yet all the forms of statesmanship, and all forms of political regimes in the current age—monarchy, oligarchy, and democracy—are regimes in which a part of the whole (either one, some, or many) holds power over the rest of the members of the cities: parts, the monarch included, that without exception are perverse usurpations of a kind of reign over human beings that has its fictive place in a mythical age. These parts rule over the cities as their households, which in the new era of Zeus can be interpreted only as a perverse imitation of the age of Cronus. Is the fact that only one or very few among the many who are present in an actual polity can have the knowledge required to be a statesman not because, rather than incarnating the idea of a king, they are only parts of the whole they are to let rule itself? Would it not therefore be relevant to bring the crucial distinction made by the Stranger, between parts of a whole and kinds, to bear on what it takes to be a statesman if, to be one, he or she must be one of the polity but cannot simply be a part of it? Does the statesman, in order to be one, not have to participate in the look of what has been established about his art—namely, to encourage the citizens of a commonwealth to themselves foster the bonds that bind them together?

In the meantime, a distinction may be warranted that, although Plato does not explicitly make it in the *Statesman*, can be found in the *Laws*, just preceding the Athenean stranger's retelling of the myth of Cronus. It is the distinction between a polity and the arrangement of a dwelling place or house—in short, it is the distinction between a *politeiai* and a *polewn de oikeseis*, which, as opposed to a constitution, refers to "settlements enslaved to the domination [*kratos*] of some component section, each taking its designation from the dominant factor."[95] Plato continues: "But if a society must take its name [that is, the name of monarchy, oligarchy, or democracy] from such a quarter, the proper course is to call it by the name of the god who is the master of rational men."[96] In sum, the power exercised by a section or sections of a polity over the whole is an imitation of Cronus' reign, a reign over its subjects as members of some large household. It follows from this that a polity or constitution is something essentially different from what is the case with the regimes of the current states (monarchy, oligarchy, and democracy), and that a statesman is in principle not comparable to the one, the few, or the many who dominate them, a being endowed with power (*kratos*); in short, the statesman is, unlike them, not a sovereign. Because of his knowledge, a statesman has an authority *within* a polity rather than *over* it. Because he is an organic "part" of the whole, he is not merely a *part* of it.

Yet, if a polity differs from the arrangement of a household, however large, it necessarily follows that its founder has to be thought without any of the concepts that define divine herdsmanship and its surrogates in contemporary societies. Only on this condition will he or she have the ability to be the founder called forth when the cosmos begins to move in the direction opposite that of the reign of Cronus—that is, as it moves today—and when all of mankind, meaning also (even though Plato does not say it in this manner) when every individual, as an individual, becomes responsible for how to live together. In conformity with the new age a statesman must, in principle, rely exclusively on his knowledge or insight. It is in this context that the Stranger makes an observation that leaves Young Socrates perplexed—as it would have any contemporary Athenian—an observation that has continued to irritate some Plato scholars until today, namely, that a true statesman should be able to rule without laws.

Before I address the question of the law, I recall that in the *Sophist* the Stranger's new understanding of dialectics is based on a radical refutation of all previous authority and all customary and native ways of thinking. In this the Stranger continues what Socrates, whom Plato characterizes in the early dialogues as one who like no other fought against the merely traditional and customary, began in the *Theaetetus* but did not dare to take to its full conclusion. In the *Statesman*, in which the Stranger extends his radical uprooting of Greek thought by turning from the concern with the ideas to the phenomenal and concrete world of the *polis*, the law of a city has to become necessarily the object of his critical resistance to the merely customary. As Manasse poignantly remarks, in order to understand the Stranger's statement that "the one who knows must break the power of the *nomos* by way of his knowledge," it is necessary to be aware of the fact that "in the concept of *nomos* the entire power of the traditional is condensed." The statesman's knowledge is an "autonomous knowledge, incommensurable as such with respect to everything customary."[97] The Stranger's statement, often qualified as outrageous, according to which the true statesman must be able to ignore the law and act according to his insight alone, is thus the direct and necessary condition of a way of conceiving of the knowledge required by the phenomenal realm of the *polis* in an innovative way no longer framed by customary beliefs.

But, generally speaking, the Stranger's statement should, after all, not be so surprising because the new epoch—in which the statesman is supposed to care for how human beings are to live together—is not only one in which the God has withdrawn but is also an epoch where humans are to rule over themselves. But if this is so, then only a human being like all others can possibly reign over human beings. This, however, comes with the implication of not only no divinity, but also no timeless law, which in its abstraction and rigidity is as aloof from human things as is a god, can confine the statesman's actions. Nor, furthermore, can the statesman oversee the whole of human beings by representing a part of humankind, which, as we have seen, is possible only through violence. He must walk the thin line between an abstract universal and an excluding particular.

Instead of expounding in detail this important question in the dialogue, I limit myself to three observations. The first concerns the precise moment in the dialogue when the Stranger makes the statement that the best polity is one without laws. After the discussion of the several political regimes, the Stranger argues that what makes a true ruler is not criteria such as whether the one or the few who rule "rule the willing or the unwilling, whether in conformity with writings or without writings, and whether they are rich or poor" (293a6–8), but exclusively whether they rule with a certain critical and supervisory knowledge, and are intent on "sav[ing] the things treated" (293c2) "by supplying his [or their] art as law" (297a1–2). The royal ruler is still defined here in complete abstraction from actual forms of government simply as what he is in himself—that is, according to what he is *qua* the idea of a statesman—but already in view of actual polities. Defined in abstraction from actuality, with the sole focus on his knowledge, a statesman ought to be able to rule without laws wherever he rules and whether the government he supervises has written laws or not. However, once he is at the head of a government, things change. First, because in an actual state no statesman could ever hope to be able to attend in minute detail to what is required by each individual case under his supervision, it is "necessary to legislate, inasmuch as the law's not most correct [*orthothaton*]" (294c12–d1), and to "set down the law for individuals in a somewhat coarser way" (295a8) rather than tailoring it to specific cases to ensure its correctness. Even though this kind of lawgiving does not meet such a desideratum, the prohibition of "doing anything whatsoever contrary to [the laws] is a second sailing" (300c3–4). Second, the argument in the *Statesman* is based on the recognition of the aporetic nature of the law: it is to be the law for all particular cases, but because of its universality it also fails to do justice to the particular. According to the Stranger, "[a] law would never be capable of comprehending with precision [*akribos*] for all simultaneously the best and the most just and enjoining the best, for the dissimilarities of human beings and of their actions and the fact that almost none of the human things is ever at rest do not allow any art whatsoever to declare in any case anything simple about all and over the entire time" (294a10–b5). To do justice to a concrete case, and to precisely apply the law to an individual case, the true statesman must ignore the law in all its abstraction, especially when in its written form it has become unflexible, and must instead rely (as any good physician or captain would do) on his insight. Precision in this case does not refer to mathematical exactitude, but to the ideal statesman's ability to do justice to a concrete situation by precisely relying on his own judgment.[98] Even though in the end he is forced to become a legislator, he alone possesses the necessary *akribia* that the written and codified law lacks because of its rigidity in relation to human things, which are perpetually changing.[99] In one commentator's words, "After all the law is not what is most correct, '*orthothaton*.'"[100] Yet—and this is a third observation about the change that comes about with the statesman as head of a government—when the statesman is considered in the context of factually existing regimes that he is supposed to reorganize, rather than in the ideal space in which he could create a polity from scratch, laws show themselves to be absolutely indispensable. From what we have seen so far, laws are not a good thing per se. If the Stranger condemns their abstraction, but then also acknowledges that a good statesman must be a legislator, it is because laws are *pharmaka*, both a medicine and a poison.

With this portrait of the statesman as one who, in conformity with his concept, idea, or look, must make his art into the law, but who cannot accomplish this without doing the next best thing—namely, giving laws, however coarse they are—it might be necessary to remind ourselves again that unlike what happens in beehives, statesmen do not naturally arise in cities as "one who's right from the start exceptional in his body and his soul" (301e2–3). But if someone were to arise in this way in a city and deserve to be named a king, "he would be welcomed warmly and in piloting with precision would be the only one to manage with happiness the right regime" (301d5–7). This would be a regime under which human beings would be happy to live. Yet, since the possibility that a statesman could arise naturally in cities is essentially excluded, the inhabitants of the city have, instead, to "come together [*sunelthontos*]," and once they have done so, "write up writings while they run after the traces of the truest regime" (301e3–5). From the context, this reflection serves manifestly as an explication of why, according to the Stranger, "all the bad things" occur in those regimes (301e8). Indeed, if in the cities all the inhabitants come together to decide about themselves, they "perform their actions without science in conformity with writings and usages" (301e9–302a1). Entrusted to writing laws formulated, moreover, on the basis of local and regional customs, this cannot but amount to the enshrinement of an oppressive particular. And yet, perhaps this passage merits a closer look. Indeed, what about the fact that, in the absence of a genuine statesman in the city, its members must come together to deliberate and decide? In human cities, no statesman arises in a natural way as would the queen in a beehive; therefore, its citizens must draw together and, banded together in association, give themselves laws that, notwithstanding their articulation in writing, are furthermore said to be an imitation of the truest regime—namely, a regime that would have been organized by an ideal statesman had he been around. Despite that what the citizens do in his absence leads to "all the bad things" that happen in the regimes they create, it remains that they come together, deliberate, and give themselves laws that seek to emulate as best as possible what they remember regarding the truest regime. Do these essentially democratic features not deserve highlighting? The comparison with a beehive unmistakably suggests that in the post-Cronus era humans are no longer simply animals but rather are living creatures who, with no divine help, must care for themselves alone, and that no statesman—not even one, not to speak of two or three—will ever be able to arise in this new era. Yet, by bonding together and being bound together, the subjects of the cities themselves do what a statesman would do—namely, they unite themselves by themselves into a city. In the absence of a statesman who would naturally arise within the cities, the city, or more precisely its numerous citizens (rather than just one), have no option other than to shape themselves by way of laws, just as a statesman would do, were he to eventually arise among the citizens, into a polity—by themselves, that is, in some democratic way. Yet this possibility, barely sketched out, is also immediately abandoned in order to continue inquiring into the distinct nature of a genuine statesman until he has shone forth in all of his purity, like shining gold. But in the remaining pages of the dialogue, completing the task he had promised to his Athenian hosts, the Stranger does not return to the intrinsically democratic features of citizenship.[101]

At the end of this section of the dialogue, I wish to ponder one more time the question that has driven my reading. In particular, why, in the *Statesman*, does Plato have a stranger teach the Athenians who or what a statesman is, and what his art is about? As I have pointed out, the Stranger—rather than being a barbarian associated, according to the Greeks, with despotic regimes—is a foreigner who is other enough to teach his guests something about philosophical and political thinking that is not, however, altogether foreign to them. Indeed, the doctrine he lays out for them is rooted in the implications of Greek thought itself—implications that, given the nature of the *polis* with all its ethnic divisions, required that a "stranger" reveal them to his Athenian hosts. As demonstrated by the obsession in Greek political thought with the distinction and classification of the different political regimes, there is a concern within Greek thought with "democracy," not merely as a regime, but in a fundamental sense, a concern that the actual *polis* with its inherently ethnic and fraternal divisions does not allow to gain traction. Distinct from the Athenian Stranger of the *Laws*, the Stranger is a stranger *in* Athens, not only a guest of his Athenian hosts, but a foreigner in his own house as well.

If a statesman arises within a city and its political regime—in comparison with the philosopher-king and the pair of the philosopher and the enlightened despot who, as "outsiders," precede the city they seek to create—he does so within an already existing regime, and as a figure internal to the city. Undoubtedly, he or she is one of the many—that is, one of the citizens of a regime, but also one of the very few capable of such a science. Is he or she, therefore, not at the same time necessarily a stranger of sorts among all his or her fellow citizens, comparable in a way to what Socrates says of himself during his defense? Is he or she not something like a "stranger" within the *polis*, a stranger who comes not from the outside, but from within the city itself? But if statesmanship is not a natural talent, and if no statesman will ever arise in a city like the queen in a beehive, then however rare the knowledge that his art presupposes, it is a knowledge that, precisely because it is not a natural talent, each citizen could potentially have. Notwithstanding its difficulty, there is nothing inherent in such knowledge that by its nature would prevent it from being possessed by any particular citizen. Supposing that this is correct, would it then not also follow that every citizen, precisely because he or she is potentially a statesman, is also potentially a stranger with respect to all others? Furthermore, would it not also follow that the fabric in which they partake, rather than being marked by what they share in common, is marked by their intrinsic difference? If Plato has a stranger elaborate on the royal art, is it not because only a stranger would dare tell the Athenians that, in order to unite themselves by themselves into a polity rather than into a macro-household, they must set their local and native differences apart and become, in a way, strangers to themselves? Does it not therefore take a stranger to propose a theory of statesmanship that makes the foreigner, and the relation to him, an intrinsic structure not of political regimes specific to a nation or *ethne*, but of a polity in which citizens themselves come together by themselves—democratically—to take charge of their destiny?

We know from the dialogue that once the statesman has accomplished his or her work, he or she can withdraw—like only a stranger can do—allowing the citizens to choose together, on an essentially democratic foundation, the specific political regime in which to live. Indeed, *qua* art, the art of the statesman must remain within the limits of what is fitting. Weaving together the contrary virtues of human beings in the way we have seen—and only this, no more and no less—is what the statesman's art is to accomplish. Everything else he must leave to the citizens. It is the citizens who are to decide whether one, a few, or many are to be in the position of archonts, and they are to choose their city's rulers according to the knowledge or true opinion that makes them citizens, that is, rulers who themselves combine contrary virtues (311a3–8). Indeed, once a democratic foundation has been put into place, it is of secondary importance which regime the citizens opt for—monarchy, oligarchy, or democracy—since, *qua* citizens and collectively in charge of the affairs of the state, they should in principle be able to protect themselves against the perversions to which the different forms of regimes can lend themselves. Does this not also indicate another important distinction regarding the philosopher-king in both the *Republic* and the *Laws*? In other words, are both of these dialogues not inquiries into regimes, as opposed to the *Statesman*, which inquires into a polity? Could one not venture to say that the different political regimes that citizens might choose for themselves—citizens, that is, of a *polis* that has been shaped by a statesman in a fundamentally democratic fashion—have then only a name in common with the several regimes that the Stranger distinguishes in the dialogue?[102]

I recall that Young Socrates and the Stranger were in accord regarding the factual scarcity of statesmen in a multitude, but also regarding the fact that anyone who had the insights required to be a statesman merited this title, whether or not he or she holds public office. The statesman, as exhibited in the dialogue, is one of these very few who causes others to combine and form a polity. He or she is a special figure, a god among human beings in a way, but not a god of a different species, and for this very reason also one who, once he has accomplished his task, can disappear again within the web of citizens that he has compelled to come together by themselves.[103] Unlike what is the case for the philosopher-king, nothing is left for the statesman to do once the city has been plaited except to plait himself back into the web he or she has woven, becoming one thread among others. Once his or her job is finished, he or she is only a citizen among citizens in the whole that has been fashioned. But does this not also imply as a correlate that any one of the citizens will, as a citizen, have been a potential statesman? Or again, more simply, that anyone who truly is a citizen *is* also potentially in the position of a statesman? Certainly, Plato does not explicitly say this. On the contrary, his repeated claims "[t]hat a multitude of no matter whom would never be able to get the science of this sort [that a statesman requires] and manage a city with mind," (297b10–c1), or even that "the multitude of the rich and the entire people together would never get this political science" (300e7–9), seem to limit the possibility of acquiring the art in question to only one or a few. But the Stranger distinguishes this one or few from large groups of men, or multitudes. Multitudes *qua* multitudes are incapable, of course, of developing this science *as such*, but if this multitude is made up of citizens, is it not also implied that everyone in it is already potentially a statesman?

In this final chapter, I have tried to be attentive to the lesson of the Stranger, and have sought to restore the strangeness to the *Statesman*. This strangeness, I contend, culminates in the goal pursued throughout the dialogue of exhibiting the art of the statesman as, ultimately, an art of citizenship, and the statesman him- or herself as one who deserves to be called "just" an exemplary or, rather, a model citizen. Is this not also the reason, after having completed his task, he can withdraw and merge with everyone else in the city? Certainly, only very few within an existing *polis* qualify for the title "statesman," but does not the definition of the statesman reveal that he or she is what a citizen is to be per se? Certainly, this is not what Plato says in an explicit fashion, but is it not what the Stranger's words allow us to infer? In my reading, what the Stranger offers to his Athenian hosts—but to us today as well—is the conception of an unheard-of democratic foundation of a body politic that merits its name. It is the conception of a polity in which the participants are no longer parts of a herd manipulated by the one, several, or many in power, but instead are citizens in the full sense of the word, with all the responsibilities that this title bestows on any person belonging to a state—to any statesman, in short.

Notes

Introduction

1. According to the identification of perception and knowledge, hearing someone speaking in a foreign language means that one knows those foreign words yet does not understand them.

2. Although at one point Socrates holds out the prospect of a dialogue on the philosopher, in which he presumably would have explored this topic together with Young Socrates, Plato did not make good on this implicit promise. What was perhaps planned as a tetralogy thus became a trilogy.

3. Notwithstanding that the *Theaetetus* is a dialogue in which the dramatic context (in a Straussian sense) is kept to an absolute minimum, *qua* dialogue between highly concrete individuals, the marginal conditions that it offers for its understanding are dramatic. See Wolfgang Wieland, *Platon und die Formen des Wissens* (Göttingen: Vandenhoek & Ruprecht, 1982), 54. As one commentator avers regarding the *Theaetetus*, "the personality of the young man is the point of departure for the inquiry, leading to the question: What is knowledge?" (Paul Friedländer, *Plato, Vol. 3: The Dialogues, Second and Third Periods*, trans. Hans Meyerhoff (Princeton, NJ: Princeton University Press, 1969), 150. By contrast, both dialogues in which the Stranger is in the position of the questioner are also largely bare of any dramatic context, but the simple fact that it is a stranger who leads the discussion is in itself a singularly dramatic feature. Both dialogues are, as has also frequently been observed, barely distinguishable from presentations of a theory that only formally respects the requirement of the dialogical. Indeed, the Stranger acknowledges right from the beginning that a vast, drawn-out speech is required in order to answer Socrates' questions, but that for reasons of the hospitality granted to him, it would be "unbecoming to a stranger and savage" (218a) not to agree to observe the dialogical form. This, of course, is also an indication that he would have preferred to present an uninterrupted speech.

4. Hannah Arendt, *Between Past and Future: Eight Exercises in Political Thought* (New York: Penguin Books, 2006), 120–127.

5. Ibid., 120–121.

6. Christian Meier, *A Culture of Freedom: Ancient Greece and the Origins of Europe*, trans. Jefferson Chase (Oxford: Oxford University Press, 2012).

7. For a detailed exposition of these and several other beginnings, see Christian Meier, *Athens: A Portrait of the City in Its Golden Age*, trans. Robert and Rita Kimber (New York: Henry Holt and Co., 1998).

8. Meier, *A Culture of Freedom*, 8, 14.

9. As Bernhard Waldenfels writes, "that which is foreign penetrates the core of reason and the core of what is held to be one's own only in the eighteenth and nineteenth century in explicit and irrevocable fashion, and fully so only in the twentieth century." See Waldenfels, *Topographie des Fremden. Studien zur Phänomenologie des Fremden*, Vol. 1 (Frankfurt/Main: Suhrkamp, 1997), 16–17.

10. Plato, *The Collected Dialogues*, ed. Edith Hamilton and Huntington Cairns (Princeton, NJ: Princeton University Press, 1980), 80–81 (99c5–e3).

11. This schematic presentation of the radical nature of the Stranger must suffice here. Later in my discussion of the *Sophist*—in which, on the invitation of Theodorus and Socrates, he is made the sole questioner—I will expand in more detail on the radicality of his "strangeness."

12. Plato, *The Collected Dialogues*, 61 (78a4).

13. Rhetoric is part of the art of enchanting, an art in which spell is set against spell. See Plato, *The Collected Dialogues*, 403 (289e5). See also Heinrich Niehues-Pröbsting, *Überredung zur Einsicht. Der Zusammenhang von Philosophie und Rhetorik bei Platon und in der Phänomenologie* (Frankfurt/Main: Klostermann, 1987), 160.

14. All Stephanus references in this book are to the translations by Seth Benardete of the three dialogues of the trilogy: *Plato's Theaetetus*, *Plato's Sophist*, and *Plato's Statesman*, Parts I, II, and III, respectively, of *The Being of the Beautiful* (Chicago: University of Chicago Press, 1986).

15. In the same way as the three tragedies were presented in successive sessions to a continuing audience, the dialogues too were presumably acted out on the occasion of the Games in a similar way for a three-day audience. See Gilbert Ryle, *Plato's Progress* (Cambridge: Cambridge University Press, 1966), 34.

16. The stylometric difference is discussed by Ryle at the end of the last chapter of *Plato's Progress*, 295–300.

17. "This stranger whom Theodoros introduces was not anticipated" when at the end of the *Theaetetus* the discussants agreed to meet again on the following morning. "He is one more [*en plus*] without one being able to say that he is one too many [*en trop*]" (Jean-Luc Nancy, "Le Ventriloque," in *Mimésis. Des articulations*, eds. Sylviane Agacinski et al. [Paris: Aubier-Flammarion, 1975]), 280. Yet, as will be argued hereafter, the *Theaetetus* prepares the coming of the Stranger. With its open ending it even creates the space in which a stranger could arrive.

18. I quote here from the standard translation of Theodorus' introduction of the Stranger. Later, in my discussion of the *Sophist*, I will question the validity of that translation.

19. Nancy, "Le Ventriloque," 313.

20. Whether the group is simply homogenous is somewhat questionable: apart from the age differences between Theodorus and Socrates on the one hand, and Theodorus' students on the other, Theodorus is originally from Cyrine, and hence is a stranger, but an invitee at Plato's academy; the relation between the two older men, that is, between the mathematician and the philosopher, is somewhat uneasy.

21. For the concept of a proleptic reading, see Charles Kahn, "Plato's *Charmides* and the Proleptic Reading of the Platonic Dialogues," in *Journal of Philosophy* 85, no. 10 (1988): 541, and especially 546.

22. Benardete, "Theaetetus Commentary," in *Plato's Theaetetus*, 141–142.

23. Auguste Diès, "Notice," in Platon, *Le Théétète, Oeuvres Complètes*, trans. Diès, Vol. 8 (Paris: Les Belles Lettres, 2010), 125.

24. Benardete, "Theaetetus Commentary," 89.

25. The distinction between *mythos* and *logos* needs a reconsideration here, since *mythos* is associated, as far as its form (and not only its content) is concerned, with authoctony, nativeness, ethnicity, and tribal nature. Furthermore, since the Stranger speaks of the doctrines of the pre-Socratics as tales or stories, *mythos* is also the form that characterizes the sayings of the so-called wise men, as opposed to the philosophers.

26. Christian Meier, *Entstehung des Begriffs 'Demokratie'. Vier Prolegomena zu einer historischen Theorie* (Frankfurt: Suhrkamp Verlag, 1970), 19–20.

27. Ibid., 17. If Solon is the first to discover the idea of civil responsibility, this does not mean, of course, that he had already a full-fledged abstract conception of the *demos* as a completely different power and rule. For the development of the concept of democracy, see ibid., 39, 48–49.

28. Bonnie Honig, *Democracy and the Foreigner* (Princeton, NJ: Princeton University Press, 2001), 14, 39.

29. Ibid., 72.

30. Ibid., 18.

31. Ibid., 8. See also Michel Agier on how immigration in Europe has led to the invention of novel forms of hospitality not only on the level of the private welcoming of foreigners, but especially on the level of the village, and the city as well. As a prologue to his anthropological approach to the question of hospitality, Agier embraces Jean-Luc Nancy's argument that a stranger is a stranger only on the condition that he or she remains an intruder (*intrus*) from the outside. As a stranger, he or she must not lose his or her exteriority to the place of welcome. By contrast, Agier rejects Jacques Derrida's contention that hospitality deserves to be hospitality only on the strict condition that it is unconditional. Furthermore, in his polemical discussion of Derrida's conception of hospitality, Agier does not once

refer to the notion of the conditional which is inseparable from hospitality according to its concept, that is, in its unconditional sense. See Michel Agier, *L'Étranger qui vient. Repenser l'hospitalité* (Paris: Seuil, 2018).

32. Julius Stenzel, *Studien zur Entwicklung der Platonischen Dialektik von Sokrates zu Aristoteles*, 3rd edition (Stuttgarts: B. G. Teubner, 1961), 131.

33. Agier, *L'Étranger qui vient*, 144. See also 145, where Agier concludes his book with the perspective that "we will have to invent a nomad citizenship for everyone."

Chapter One

1. In my reading of the *Theaetetus*, I will not take into consideration the discussion in the "Prologue" between Euclides and Terpsion, not so much because of its possible inauthenticity, or because the dialogue is supposed to originally have had an entirely different introduction that has been lost, but because the complex reconstruction of the dialogue that it suggests is of no particular concern for the argument I wish to make here. Myles Burnyeat asks, "Is Eucleides telling us what Socrates and Theaetetus said to each other, or are we listening to them directly? Perhaps Plato's meaning is that we can read the dialogue either way. We can be passive recipients of testimony, or we can be actively present with the discussion" (*The Theaetetus of Plato* (Indianapolis: Hackett Publishing Company, 1990), 127. I choose here the last option. It remains, however, that because it confirms Theodorus' prediction that Theaetetus would prove to be capable of great deeds, deeds that concern his life as a citizen, attention to the Prologue would help emphasize the political dimension of the dialogue, as well the implicitly "political" reading of it that I will propose in preparation of the *Statesman*. Furthermore, it has been pointed out that a Megarian thread is part of the fabric of the dialogue. Lewis Campbell holds that the argument, for example, that knowledge is true opinion with a definition is Euclidian in origin. Taking the Prologue into consideration would thus certainly be helpful for figuring out the theories that Plato fused together in his own propositions. See Campbell, *The Theaetetus of Plato* (New York: Arno Press, 1973), xxviii–xxix.

2. A. E. Taylor, *Plato: The Man and His Work* (New York: Meridian Books, 1956), 323.

3. Ibid.

4. Distinct from the rather general agreement of scholars regarding the aporetic nature of the *Theaetetus* are the studies of Ronald M. Polansky, *Philosophy and Knowledge: A Commentary on Plato's Theaetetus* (Lewisburg: Bucknell University Press, 1992), and Rosemary Desjardins, *The Rational Enterprise: Logos in Plato's Theaetetus* (Albany, NY: SUNY Press, 1990). Both argue that the dialogue provides, in Desjardins' words, "a carefully worked-out answer—an answer recognized as explicit, however, only if the dialogue is taken self-referentially" (15).

5. During the discussion of Theaetetus' third response to the question of what knowledge is, Socrates observes that there is one thing in the theory as stated that he finds objectionable, and yet he poses the rhetorical question: "what would knowledge still in fact be, apart from (the) speech and correct opinion?" (202d7–8). As Mitchell Miller remarks, "whatever difficulties Theaetetus' understanding may turn out to have, he [Socrates] regards true judgment and *logos* as at least necessary for knowledge" ("Unity and *Logos*. A Reading of *Theaetetus* 201c–210a," in *Ancient Philosophy* 12, no. 1 (1992), 90. In other words, although no final determination of the nature of knowledge is provided, Socrates' treatment of Theaetetus' third response is not negative, as has been the case for both of his previous definitions, and despite the shortcomings of its justification a positive determination of at least one necessary condition for knowledge has been established. For an account of the "completeness" of the dialogue, according to which it holds the fullest Platonic account of knowledge, see Polansky's *Philosophy and Knowledge*. Polansky writes that "its negative conclusion notwithstanding, the *Theaetetus* contains a positive answer to the question of knowledge" (18–19).

6. Is this not the prime reason why, in the *Theaetetus*, the inquiry into the nature of knowledge must remain incomplete?

7. Benardete, "Theaetetus Commentary," 91.

8. Such playfulness does not inhibit the dialogue's radical interrogation of authoritative doctrines and the dominating force of common opinions; on the contrary, a certain playfulness in the dialogue is indicative of the break with authority and everyday beliefs, accomplished on a rigorous discursive level.

9. In Theaetetus' first reaction to Socrates' question of what knowledge is—that is, before he ventures his three definitions—he makes no distinction between geometry and the art of shoemaking; both are said to be mere skills, practical and theoretical techniques.

10. Although "wisdom" (*sophia*) seems, at first, to refer only to expertise or being knowledgeable in something, as indeed the notion did in pre-Platonic thought (even though it meant from the beginning something more spiritual than mere *techne*), Socrates' suggestion that the wise are wise by wisdom (*sophoi oi sophoi*) implies that another meaning of wisdom prevails here: the dialectical knowledge sought by the philosopher—that is, its highest form. Is it not because Socrates has a higher and philosophical conception of wisdom in mind that he has a "small issue" with the alleged sameness of wisdom and knowledge, and refuses to accept the opinion that one is wise if one is an expert in arts such as geometry, harmony, or astronomy, not to speak of the art of the cobbler? For the pre-Platonic meaning of *sophia*, see Bruno Snell, *Die Ausdrücke für den Begriff des Wissens in der vorplatonischen Philosophie* (Berlin: Weidmannsche Buchhandlung, 1924), 1–20.

11. However, Campbell notes that "the distinction between the race and the individual, between the general term 'man,' and the singular term 'this man,' was probably not distinctly present to [Protagoras'] mind." For a "popular teacher," such

as Protagoras, the term "man" "would naturally call up the idea, not of human nature or of the human mind, nor of the race collectively, but of 'a man,' 'this or that man,' an individual, 'you or me,' not however conceived of as an individual, nor consciously distinguished from any abstract or generic notion of man, but simply present to the imagination" (*The Theaetetus of Plato*, l–li).

12. Taylor, *Plato: The Man and His Work*, 326.

13. In the *Theaetetus*, Protagoras' theory is filtered through Socrates' eyes. I will not, hereafter, be concerned with how the historical Protagoras differs from his portrayal in our dialogue, or whether Plato's representation of him can be trusted. Nor will I explore the known schools with which the propositions Socrates attributes to him could be identified.

14. At one point in the *Sophist*, Theaetetus uses the term *sunakolouthein* (224e4).

15. Although it is in the two dialogues in which the Stranger leads the investigation that the notions of an "account" and "true opinion" find an adequate explanation that in principle allows for a stricter definition of knowledge, I do not see what the Stranger *qua* stranger contributes directly to this development.

16. Jacob Klein, *Plato's Trilogy: Theaetetus, the Sophist and the Statesman* (Chicago: University of Chicago Press, 1977), 145.

17. Benardete, "Theaetetus Commentary," 89.

18. In Book IV of the *Laws* Plato writes, in what is clearly a reference to Protagoras' statement: "it is God who is, for you and me, of a truth the 'measure of all things,' much more truly than, as they say, 'man'" (*The Collected Dialogues*, 1307 [716c5–7]). Although this statement is no doubt the horizon within which Plato's criticism of the formula takes place, I will not, hereafter, elaborate on it.

19. After having explained to Theaetetus that Protagoras' secret confiding, to only his disciples, that his statement that man is the measure of all things implies that "nothing is one alone by itself" (*auto kath'hauto ouden estin*), and that this is nothing trivial (152d2–e7), Socrates begins to unpack (beginning at 156a3) the mysteries of the initiated (*kompsoteroi*). His purpose in doing so is, first of all, to make Protagoras—and, through him, Heraclitus—into an opponent worthy of debate. As Desjardins observes, "it is only in light of this subtler elaboration of *kompsoteros* theory that it becomes possible to understand the deliberate ambiguity of meaning hidden beneath that original, and superficially simple, proposition that 'everything is motion and there is nothing else besides this'" (*The Rational Enterprise*, 54). But when Desjardins construes this remarkably sophisticated theory as Plato's positive answer to the question of knowledge in the dialogue, one cannot but wonder what remains of Socratic irony, and above all what happens to his unrelenting and multifaceted refutation of one of the dominant currents in Greek philosophy. If the Protagorean argument that "nothing is one alone by itself" is not trivial, is it not because—apart from the fact that it represents the ground of the flux theory, and thus the opposite of the Parmenidean thesis of the Oneness of Being—the argument gestures toward a between of the extremes of change and

rest or, more precisely, toward a doctrine about the interrelation of the same and the other to be developed in the *Sophist*?

20. In his commentary on Socrates' refutation of the thesis that knowledge is perception, Francis MacDonald Cornford is certainly right to emphasize that Plato does not reject in totality Protagoras' and Heraclitus' understanding of knowledge: it is also a contribution to the knowledge characteristic of the restricted sphere of the sensible world. Plato criticizes the theory as one-sided, and demolishes it where in its extreme version it is applied to all things, thoughts, opinions, and judgments included. See Cornford, *Plato's Theory of Knowledge* (London: Routledge & Kegan Paul, 1935).

21. But the flux theory is not simply to be discarded, for still another reason. If the theory is not a trivial one, it is also because motion is identified with life, and rest with perishing and non-being. As Socrates posits, "So the good is motion both in terms of soul and in terms of body, and the (bad) the contrary?" (153c4–5). As demonstrated by all the imagery, including the Homerian imagery, regarding this aspect of the flux theory, the theory in question is indebted to popular beliefs, and thus seems to have their authority for support. Criticism of Protagoras' speech thus also demands putting into question these articles of popular belief. But it also shows that what his doctrine has going for itself is, in distinction from Parmenides' more theoretical concerns, its "practical" or, if you wish, "utilitarian" nature. Protagoras, "like other popular teachers, [. . .] had a keener eye for the immediate wants of those who came to him than for the truth, of which, however, he is not to be supposed a careless lover" (Campbell, *The Theaetetus of Plato*, li). This concern with the "practical" is especially tangible in Protagoras' self-defense, in particular in the context of the emphasis on the wise man's ability to induce change (*sophon hos . . . metaballon poiesei*) at 166d–167c. However, to the end, this more practical bent of his thought will allow Socrates to associate Protagoras' theory with sophism and the daily concerns of life in the *polis* in the fifth and fourth century BC, as Plato experienced it.

22. Polansky, *Philosophy and Knowledge*, 92. The reference is to Socrates' introduction of the notion of relative change to explain that quantities too are constantly in movement, and hence change.

23. As I have already emphasized, I will not be concerned here with the faithfulness of Socrates' portrayal with respect to the historical Protagoras. By contrast, it is important that Protagoras is not a fictive, but rather a real person in fifth-century philosophy, with whom Plato takes issue.

24. In the preceding parts of the dialogue, Socrates' message to the mathematicians is that the homo mensura formula is not compatible with mathematical truth. One of the prime reasons Socrates strengthens Protagoras' doctrine is not only to make Theodorus and Theaetetus aware of the fact that it puts their authority into question (see, for example, 169a2–6, where the question is raised whether just anyone, or only experts, can be the measure of geometrical theorems), but

also to provoke in the young man a sense of dizziness and wonder in the face of the seemingly irreconcilable statements to which the man-measure doctrine leads, a pathos required for the young man to be able to question its truth. Here, a remark is warranted about the reason why a digression about philosophy (or rather, about the state of mind of the philosopher in distinction from the "practical" man) is placed at the center of the dialogue. Rather than an unnecessary interruption, or as something totally irrelevant to the topic of the dialogue as some have claimed, this marks the point where Socrates, after having established the practical dimension of Protagoras' doctrine, wishes to pass on from an eristic position to a more philosophical examination. In contrast to what obtains in the practical sphere, such an examination requires leisure, a topic that the dialogue evokes right before Socrates begins his elaboration on philosophy as a kind of inquiry that is free and also playful, in contrast to what is possible when time is regulated by an hourglass. In a philosophical investigation, the eyes are fixed on the whole, and it is an inquiry that focuses on what something is in itself, such as justice or injustice, and in what respect they differ from each other, and everything else (175c2–4). For a negative appraisal of the digression on philosophy in the *Theaetetus*, see, among others, Ryle, *Plato's Progress*, 278.

25. What are the implications for the whole Protagorean thesis that this doctrine needs assistance? Is there a provision in his thought that allows for such help? In any event, Socrates comes to the help of Protagoras' thesis by letting Protagoras himself speak to defend his own position.

26. See Lewis Campbell, *The Sophistes and Politicus of Plato* (New York: Arno Press, 1973), lii.

27. However, such respect does not exclude the total demolishing of the opponent. Throughout the *Theaetetus*, the Socratic cross-examination is primarily negative, and in this, Socrates' method is after all eristic. As Campbell notes, the *Theaetetus* can therefore be fairly regarded as a Megarian dialogue. "[A]lthough it is no mere sophistical sham-fight, it is characterized by the predominance of that dialectical exercise which consists in refuting theories." "[T]he Megarian method of criticism which reigns almost unquestioned in the Theaetetus, in the Sophista becomes criticized in turn" (*The Theaetetus of Plato*, xiii, lxvi). This criticism of the Socratic elenchus, and the replacement of a merely negative dialectic by one that yields positive results, is one of the Stranger's accomplishments.

28. In the apology of Protagoras, it is the latter who (through the voice of Socrates) refers to the examination as one about "whether knowledge and perception (are) the same or maybe different [*tauton eite kai allo*]" (168b7–8). Since for Protagoras there is no such thing as the entirely other, the question can concern only the identity of knowledge and perception, or whether each of them is something else.

29. Henry George Liddell and Robert Scott, *A Greek-English Lexicon* (Oxford: Oxford University Press, 1968), 70.

30. With this the question arises, of course, of how the infinite mass of the things generated, and of the generating things—"the nameless of which (are) without limit, and the named very many" (156b8–9)—differ or are other with respect to one another, given that none of them is what it is in itself.

31. In doing so, Socrates acknowledges that the Protagorean thesis is a response to a genuine problem, a problem which, therefore, demands serious consideration.

32. Theaetetus having said that he has no opinion about what the Protagoreans would say in this case, Socrates responds: "Well, in that case, listen to me as to what sort of things they would say about them, those who determine that the opinions at any moment are true for him who is of that opinion. I suspect that they speak, by questioning, in this way" (158e5–8).

33. In no way, they continue, is it even conceivable that, although something differs in all respects from it, in another respect it could still be the same as it. Insofar as it is completely other, it is, paradoxically, no longer other (*allos*) compared to something else.

34. Polansky notes that the claim that for something to be wholly other also entails its being unlike an other is an illicit inference by Socrates (see *Philosophy and Knowledge*, 105). But let us keep in mind that Socrates here is only the mouthpiece for Protagoras.

35. Jacob Klein comments, "We notice that the words 'same' and 'other' are emphasized by Socrates." He is also to my knowledge one of the very few to observe that in the discussion that follows, "the emphasis on the word 'other' persists." But Klein does not pay attention to the different voices—of who speaks for or against whom—involved in the argument, nor in what sense, or senses, the word "other" persists (*Plato's Trilogy*, 92–93).

36. I thank Kalliopi Nikolopoulou for this observation.

37. The attentive contemporary reader will likely notice the similarity between the Protagorean theory as formulated in the *Theaetetus* through the voice of Socrates and Gilles Deleuze's philosophy of difference.

38. Had the difference between a healthy and a sick Socrates been made in the introductory presentation of the flux theory, both, I surmise, would have been presented as numerically other, as two different cases among others. But once the possibility of false perceptions is acknowledged—the observation that a healthy and a sick Socrates are not the same men, because they are dissimilar to one another—the difference between both becomes one of complete otherness, health and sickness being exclusive of one another.

39. It might be appropriate to quote here the passage also in its Greek original: "*Oúkoun egṓ te oudèn állo potè genḗsomai oútōs aisthanómenos toû gàr állou állē aísthēsis, kaì alloîon kaì állon poieî tòn aisthanómenon. Oút' ekeîno tò poioûn emè mḗp' ot' állōi sunelthón tautòn gennêsan toioûton génetai. Apò gàr állou állo gennêsan alloîon genḗsetai.*"

40. Although Plato, hereafter in the dialogue, continues to make use of the two expressions for the other, he does so perhaps interchangeably; but when Protagoras makes a distinction between an appearance that is infinitely *better* or sounder than that which another has, he resorts consistently to the expression *heteros*: "*heteron heterou autoi toutoi*" (166d4; see also 167b5). Let me also point out that when Socrates broaches the two definitions of movement according to Protagoras, locomotion and alteration, alteration is referred to as "another species [*heteron eidos*] of motion," whereas the changing of place in locomotion is referred to by the term *alloiosin* (Schleiermacher translates it as *Ortsverwechselung*) (181d4). In all these instances, it is clear that the two terms refer to different conceptions of what is other.

41. Cornford strongly objects to casting the "common terms" as "categories." I agree, but not because he conceives of them as objects of the knowledge that originates in the soul, since interpreting them as *noeta* does not take sufficiently into account the transformation of Plato's conception of ideas that begins with the *Theaetetus* and is further developed in the *Sophist*. See Cornford, *Plato's Theory of Knowledge*, 105–106. I will return to this issue in the following chapter devoted to the *Sophist*.

42. When, with respect to what all things have in common, Theaetetus remarks that the soul examines especially the relations between the beautiful and the ugly, the good and the bad, "calculating in itself the past and the present things relative to the future" (186a11–b1), the Stranger's inquiry into the interrelation of the greatest kinds is dimly anticipated. I also note that the distinction made in this context between the senses as *organa* of perception, and the things like being and non-being, sameness and otherness, oneness or multiplicity, etc., which the soul examines "itself through itself" and which, therefore, are not of the order of *organa* by means of which the soul would elaborate on what all things have in common, is already indicative of the special status of the *eide* (185d7–e2). They are forms of thought and language. The present study proceeds on the assumption that, in the *Theaetetus*, Plato's "theory" of the ideas undergoes a transformation that will become explicit in the Stranger's doctrine of the "greatest kinds." It is a change from understanding knowledge as a direct witnessing of the forms *auto kath'hauto* to an understanding of knowledge as regarding the forms required to give valid reasons or accounts. See also Amélie Oksenberg Rorty, "A Speculative Note on Some Dramatic Elements in the Theaetetus," *Phronesis* 17, no. 3 (1972), 236.

43. Burnyeat, *The Theaetetus of Plato*, 90.

44. The determination of knowledge as true opinion is not simply dismissed. It is found to be unsatisfactory because of the impossibility of accounting for the possibility of false opinion. Even though it is agreed upon that false opinion is a fact, all its explication shows is that it is impossible. Yet with his second response, Theaetetus has for the first time touched on something that, since it makes room for the soul, is essential to knowledge. However, this cannot simply be opinion (true

or false) because, ultimately, opinion will be shown to be something that one has been made to believe, and by which one has been persuaded (by common opinion or public speakers, for example) to opine certain things (201b8–c8). Knowledge, by contrast, requires a mode of representation that, like the soul's inquiry by itself into what things have in common, takes place without *organa*, and is free.

45. See also A. T. Cole, "The Apology of Protagoras," *Yale Classical Studies* 19 (1966), 108.

46. See also Polansky, *Philosophy and Knowledge*, 181.

47. Gareth B. Matthews, "A Puzzle in Plato: *Theaetetus* 189b–190e," in *Philosophical Analysis: A Defense by Example*, ed. D. S. Austin (Dordrecht: Kluwer Academic Publishers, 1988), 8.

48. The same occurs at 199d–e when false opining is attributed no longer to taking one thing for another, but instead to the interchange of knowledges.

49. Martin Heidegger, *The Essence of Truth: On Plato's Cave Allegory and Theaetetus*, trans. Ted Sadler (New York: Continuum, 2002), 193. Let me also point out that in his reading of the *Sophist*, Jacob Klein pays systematic attention to this word "both" in the dialogue (*Plato's Trilogy*, 40ff).

50. Heidegger, *The Essence of Truth*, 193.

51. Ibid.

52. Heidegger's interpretation of *allodoxia* explicitly counters Schleiermacher's translation of the term as "*Verwechselung*," in other words, as erroneously mistaking or confusing two things. By contrast, for Heidegger *allodoxia* refers to an exchange of one determined thing for another in a process of opining one thing *in terms of* or *as* something other. What thus can take place in *allodoxia* is that by taking one thing as another, opining may also take it as something that it *is not*. Whereas understanding *allodoxia* as a confusion of one thing for another does not do justice to the simultaneous full presence of two things in the mental act of opining, the apophantic structure of conceiving of one thing by way of another presupposes that "the object of *doxa* is as it were two objects (*amphotera*)" (*The Essence of Truth*, 196).

53. It is tempting to associate *allodoxia* with Prototagas' doctrine that all is in motion and that everything is without distinction, constantly becoming something else, not even having the time, as it were, to ever become other.

54. With the term *phyle*, or tribe, Socrates refers, of course, to the religious, corporate, and military divisions of the Greek cities—divisions which, at least at their origin, were based on ties of ethnic kin, and several of which made up each city. To speak of the tribe to which Protagoras belongs is thus also to insinuate that there is at least one more such tribe. For our context, it may be interesting to recall that Cleisthenes' far-reaching reform at the end of the fifth century BC of the Athenian *polis* did away with the old *phylai* and reorganized them in a way that more democratically reflected the actual citizen-body. Only for a few sacred purposes were the old *phylai* allowed to survive. In short, the use of the term by Socrates seems also to connote the obsoleteness of archaic and nativist positions.

55. Monique Dixsaut, *Platon. Le Désir de comprendre* (Paris: Vrin, 2012), 87.

56. Parmenides is to be associated with sophism as well, to the extent that the Megarian school of Euclides, which took its main doctrine from the Eleatics and in particular from Zeno, also practiced eristic sophistry in a merely negative sense, with its disregard for truth and intention only to destroy the opponent.

57. Plato, *The Collected Dialogues*, 922 (128c3–5).

58. See Benardete, "Theaetetus Commentary," 142.

59. To accomplish this kind of thought that would truly be in the middle of extremes, the thinker would, on the level of theoretical thought, have to exercise what in the context of the statesman's art is called "true measure."

60. According to Friedländer, in the rebuttal of Theaetetus' second answer to the question about what knowledge is—namely, true opinion—the need to account for the possibility of false opining already forces Socrates to take on Parmenides. Though he did not dare examine the latter before, it is made clear here that without overcoming the rigid concept of the Parmenidean distinction between knowing and not knowing, no answer to the question of falsehood is possible. See Friedländer, *Plato*, 177–178.

61. And, in turn, when taking on Parmenides, Protagoras would then serve as the horizon for an examination of the former. Socrates' resistance to subjecting Parmenides to the promised interrogation can perhaps also be explained by his unwillingness to accord Protagoras such a privilege.

62. Polansky, *Philosophy and Knowledge*, 160.

63. Schleiermacher translates *aiskune* as *Scheu*, to be in awe before someone whom one holds in reverence.

64. Let us also remind ourselves of the definition of shame in the *Laws*: it is the fear of "getting a bad reputation from some unworthy act or speech" (*The Collected Dialogues*, 1246 [647a1–2]).

65. In the *Laws*, Plato refers to parricide as among the "most abominable of all forms of homicide" (*The Collected Dialogues*, 1431–1432 [872d6]). See also Book IX of the *Laws*, where Plato writes that if a man could die more than once, justice would require someone responsible for parricide or matricide to be put to repeated deaths (1428–1429 [869a–c]).

66. Socrates forces Theodorus, a friend of Protagoras who despises "bare speeches"—his qualification for philosophical speeches—at least for a while into the discussion about the underpinnings of Protagoras' argument. But is the inclusion of an other in speech, and even giving him a lead in speaking, not also an acknowledgment that speech is speech only if there is a constitutive place for the other?

Chapter Two

1. Friedländer, *Plato*, 150.

2. Taylor, *Plato: The Sophist and the Statesman* (Toronto: Thomas Nelson and Sons Ltd., 1961), 23–24.

3. Cornford holds that "critics have made too much' of this "alleged 'eclipse of Socrates' by the Eleatic Stranger" (*Plato's Theory of Knowledge*, 169). However, this view not only downplays the dramatic effect of Socrates' silence in the dialogue but also minimizes the role played by the Stranger.

4. Only toward the end of the dialogue does the Stranger come to realize that Theaetetus' nature is such that, without having to be persuaded by speeches, it is drawn by itself to what is true. See 265d8–e3.

5. Ernst Moritz Manasse has pointed out that in the late dialogues the Stranger renounces Socrates' concern with fighting for the souls of his interlocutors, thus signifying a complete change of the philosophical intention of the form of expression that is the dialogue. See Manasse, *Platons Sophistes und Politikos. Das Problem der Wahrheit* (Berlin: Siegfried Scholem, 1937), 67.

6. Taylor, *Plato: The Sophist and the Statesman*, 251.

7. Campbell, *The Sophistes and Politicus of Plato*, xvi. Campbell even holds that, in the late dialogues, Plato is "striving after a philosophy of the concrete, and endeavoring to substitute real and fruitful inquiry for barren logical exercitations" (xv).

8. In *Minos*, a dialogue about the law (*nomos*), Socrates defines the latter as correct and true opinion and, as such, as a dis-covering or finding out (*heuresis*) of what is. In other words, the task of the philosopher is one of finding out what is lawfully and appropriately distributed (*dianome*) to each by the statesman in a *polis*. See Platon, *Oeuvres Complètes*, Vol. 13, Part 2 (*Dialogues Suspects*), trans. Joseph Souilhé (Paris: Les Belles Lettres, 1930), 90, 95.

9. Although in ancient Greece, "the free" refers to those born within the city and enjoying civil rights, as opposed to the slaves who are strangers without rights, here the distinction refers not literally to slaves (*douloi*) but to those within the *polis* whom Socrates in the *Theaetetus* compares to domestics or household slaves (*oiketes*), because in public life they are subservient to the judges in the assemblies, and their lives are dominated by the hourglass. See 172c8ff.

10. Fulcran Teisserenc, *Le Sophiste de Platon* (Paris: Presses Universitaires de France, 2012), 15. As Cornford suggests, in a dialogue on the philosopher, Plato would presumably have gathered up all the loose threads in the *Sophist*. See Cornford, *Plato's Theory of Knowledge*, 168–169, 183, 215, 268, 323.

11. For the constitutive function of the gap between oneself and oneself for thinking, see Teisserenc, *Le Sophiste de Platon*, 158.

12. Is it possible to bring the problematic of time raised in the *Theaetetus* to bear on the problematic of promise?

13. Although the Greeks distinguished two main types of strangers along the interior/exterior divide—the non-citizens inseparable from the city (*metoikoi*) as opposed to the cultural others (the barbarians, who themselves were divided into geographically and culturally excentric strangers distinct from those who were welcomed by the Olympic community, and those who lived in proximity and in contact with the Greeks, the *perioikoi*)—the differentiation does not stop there. For a detailed sociological and historical examination of the status of the stranger

throughout the history of Greece, see Marie-Françoise Baslez, *L'Etranger dans la Grèce antique* (Paris: Les Belles Lettres, 1984).

14. Plato, *The Collected Dialogues*, 17. For a detailed discussion of Socrates' presentation of himself at his defense *as* a stranger, see Anne Dufourmantelle and Jacques Derrida, *Of Hospitality*, trans. R. Bowlby (Stanford, CA: Stanford University Press, 2000), 13–21.

15. Henri Joly, *Études platoniciennes: La question des étrangers* (Paris: Vrin, 1992), 41–42.

16. The *Laws* is a dialogue among strangers, the *xenos Athenaios*, the *xenos lakedaimonios*, and the *xenos Knosios*. Is it a mere accident that Plato's inquiries into the laws of the commonwealth take place between strangers, who not only mutually refer to one another as foreigners, but at the same time also "uproot" one another? Let me also note that, in the version of the *Laws* that Aristotle was familiar with when he wrote his treatise on *Politics*, the discussion leader was not the Athenian Stranger but Socrates (1265b19). Only in our version of the *Laws* does Plato seem to have changed the names, thus also making it possible for him to be construed as the mouthpiece of that dialogue.

17. Plato, *The Collected Dialogues*, 418.

18. Ibid., 419. See also Monique Dixsaut, *Le Naturel philosophe: Essai sur les Dialogues de Platon* (Paris, Vrin, 2016), 560–562, and *Platon*, 53, 61–62.

19. In the *Laws*, the Athenian is also addressed by his hosts simply as *o xene*, or as *o xene Athenaie*, but in distinction from what occurs in the *Sophist*, he in turn apostrophizes his hosts by this vocative as well. In contrast to the *Sophist*, which is a dialogue between a stranger and his Athenian hosts, the *Laws* is a dialogue among parties who are strangers to one another. Further, the Athenian stranger confronts his host with an unsparing critique of Cretan and Lacedaemonean law. "Your cities," he tells them, "are organized like armies, not like societies of town dwellers" (*The Collected Dialogues*, 1263).

20. All the participants of Plato's dialogues are highly dramatized figures, as Debra Nails has shown in *The People of Plato: A Prosopography of Plato and Other Socratics* (Indianapolis: Hackett Publishing Company, 2002). Why, then, has the figure of the Stranger from Elea not received the same attention as the other protagonists? For Wolfgang Wieland, "the namelessness of the Stranger signals the lack of significance of the reality context" in Plato's late dialogues, and their increasing abstraction from such a context, and consequently the interlocutor's role is also reduced to one of merely formal affirmation or negation of conceptual distinctions that could equally well have been made in a lengthy discursive speech (*Platon und die Formen des Wissens*, 82). But whatever the value of that argument, the fact remains that Plato's recourse to a stranger in these dialogues intimately shapes the argument itself, and his foreignness is furthermore highlighted by the contrast in which the other well-individualized participants of the two dialogues stand to him.

21. The same is the case in the *Statesman*, where he is also the main speaker. Here, too, we do not learn anything personal about him. Plato does not provide us with any physical characteristics of the Stranger, as he does at times for his protagonists. For example, Theaetetus, in the dialogue that bears his name, is depicted as having "a snub nose and prominent eyes" (*The Collected Dialogues*, 917). If the great portraitist, as Hans-Georg Gadamer characterizes Plato, refrained from giving a vivid portrayal of the Stranger, it is certainly because he intended for him to have a certain abstract quality (see Gadamer, "Plato als Porträtist," in *Gesammelte Werke*, Vol. 7 (*Plato im Dialog*) (Tübingen: J.C.B. Mohr, 1991)). For the abstract quality of the foreigner in general and the abstract nature of the relation to foreigners, see Georg Simmel, *Soziologie. Untersuchungen über die Formen der Vergesellschaftung* (Munich & Leipzig: Duncker & Humblot, 1922), 511.

22. See *Theaetetus*, 163b3–5. The Stranger must speak Greek, or be able to do so, otherwise he could not perform the job that, as a stranger, he is to accomplish. Let me also note that no reference is made to the Stranger's attire. Only in the case of his being a barbarian would such a reference have imposed itself.

23. Liddell and Scott, *A Greek-English Lexicon*, 69.

24. Rather than in the heartland of Greece, it was in the Ionian cities, made up moreover of very heterogeneous populations, that the first wave of Greek philosophy, the Ionian philosophy of nature, was born. The second wave originates on the Western edge of the Greek domain. In other words, Greek rational thought does not spring from its "own" soil; furthermore, it was formed by refugees, expatriates, or strangers.

25. See Nestor-Luis Cordero, "Introduction," in Platon, *Le Sophiste*, trans. Cordero (Paris: Flammarion, 1993), 17.

26. For the history of the translation of the passage in which Theodorus introduces the stranger as "different from" or as "a comrade of the circle of Parmenides and Zeno," see Nestor-Louis Cordero, "Annexe I," in Platon, *Le Sophiste*, 281–284.

27. Jean-Luc Nancy therefore wonders whether "the Stranger is *truly* from Elea, from this faraway place, *ton ekei topon*, a utopic place perhaps, atopic, no doubt" ("Le Ventriloque," 318).

28. Of the four types of strangers that Plato distinguishes in Book XII of the *Laws* to be welcomed in his newly created ideal state, none fit the Stranger in the *Sophist*, especially not the first kind who come to the city for business reasons, and of whom Plato says that they are in no way to introduce any innovations. Not even the fourth type, a visitant who in the uncommon event would "be a counterpart of our own observers from another country," and whose avowed object would be "either to see for himself some excellent features superior in the beauties to be found in other societies, or to reveal something of the sort to another state," compares to the Eleatic stranger. The two other types of permitted visitors from abroad are "observers in the literal sense of the word; they come for the sights to be beheld by the eye and the musical displays to be enjoyed by the ear," and

"those who come from other countries on business of state" (*The Collected Dialogues*, 1498 [952e–963e4]).

29. Émile Benveniste, *Dictionary of Indo-European Concepts and Society*, trans. Elizabeth Palmer (Chicago: Hau Books, 2016), 294.

30. Gadamer, "Dialektik ist nicht Sophistik—Theätet lernt das im 'Sophistes,'" in *Gesammelte Werke*, Vol. 7 (*Plato im Dialog*), 347, 353. See also Stanley Rosen, *Plato's Sophist: The Drama of Original and Image* (New Haven, CT: Yale University Press, 1983), 64.

31. Teisserenc, *Le Sophiste de Platon*, 15.

32. Like Young Socrates, there are a number of silent characters in Plato's dialogues, except that Young Socrates will eventually become the interlocutor of the Stranger in the *Statesman*. The presence of silent characters in dialogues, who can only be seen but not heard, would seem to be further evidence of Gilbert Ryle's argument that the dialogues were not only meant to be read but also performed at the Dionysian Games. See Ryle, *Plato's Progress*.

33. As Rosen notes, rather than asking *who* the Stranger is, the question should be *what* the Stranger is (*Plato's Sophist*, 62).

34. Ryle, *Plato's Progress*, 28–32.

35. Jean-François Mattéi, *L'Étranger et le simulacre: Essai sur la fondation de l'ontologie platonicienne* (Paris: Presses Universitaires de France, 1983), 152.

36. Is this not an instance of Plato's "preference for words belonging to the tragic period of Greek poetry" in his later dialogues, to which Lewis Campbell has drawn attention? See Campbell, *The Sophistes and Politicus of Plato*, xxx–xxxi.

37. Liddell and Scott, *A Greek-English Lexicon*, 1189.

38. Benveniste, *Dictionary of Indo-European Concepts and Society*, 293.

39. Plato, *The Collected Dialogues*, 1316.

40. After having defined the obligations toward aliens in the *Laws*, Plato continues: "the gravest of offenses, whether against landsmen or aliens, is always that done to a suppliant [*hiketes*], for the god in whose name the suppliant made his appeal when he obtained a promise keeps jealous watch over the sufferer, and thus he will never suffer his wrongs unavenged" (*The Collected Dialogues*, 1316). Thus, *xenia* has also to be clearly distinguished from another institution in ancient Greece that dealt with supplicants from abroad, the institution of *hikesia*. Whereas Zeus Xenios presides over the institution of *xenia*, and is the god on whom the Greeks could also call in order to find hospitality when abroad, Zeus Hikesios was the god of aliens seeking protection, asylum seekers, and fugitives. Another institution, that of the *agorai*, was presided over by Zeus Agoraios, the god of those seeking understanding in the political arena.

41. These references have, of course, drawn the attention of many commentators, most recently Sylvain Delcomminette, who seeks to assess their importance for the dialogue as a whole. See Delcomminette, "Odysseus and the Home of the Stranger from Elea," *The Classical Quarterly* 64, no. 2 (2014).

42. Socrates' association of the Stranger with a god, and thus with someone who might be in the position to judge the Athenians' conduct morally, is certainly a reference to the impending trial of Socrates, as John Sallis has pointed out. However, I believe that it is also necessary to link this reference to what the Stranger says later in the dialogue about the philosopher as a free and just man. See Sallis, *Being and Logos: Reading the Platonic Dialogues* (Bloomington: Indiana University Press, 1996), 457.

43. Refutation, as the Stranger argues later in the dialogue, is the most important and the highest form of education by which the soul is purified of its ignorance. It must be distinguished from the art of contradiction (eristics) that, in the fifth definition, will be shown to be one aspect of the sophist. But the art of refutation also seems to resemble that of the sophist as developed during the sixth *diairesis*, and the Stranger is thus forced to acknowledge a "sophistics noble and grand in descent" (231b10–11). However, the overall thrust of the *Sophist* consists in showing that, indeed, the sophist practices only a sham version of this art, whereas the philosopher can truly be characterized by it. It is also in this context that Plato compares the sophist and the philosopher to a wolf and a dog, respectively (231a7).

44. As several commentators have pointed out, Theodorus' reply, which shows that he has no sense of the difference between polemics and refutation or, in Rosen's words, "between immoderate and moderate refutation," is further evidence of the fact that he is *only* familiar with the art of the sophist, which he has left behind for the solid knowledge of mathematics, and not with the art of the philosopher (*Plato's Sophist*, 64). By holding that the man is in no way a god but, as a philosopher, certainly godlike, he may also have missed out on the Stranger himself who, as a foreigner, is by definition accompanied by a god.

45. Arnaldo Momigliano notes that, even during the Hellenistic Age, "[t]he Greeks remained proudly monolingual as, with rare exceptions, they had been for centuries. It was not for them to converse with the natives in the natives' languages." And this remained the case even though, as he adds, they did have "a basic sympathy for foreigners. We know how Herodotus, one of the founding masters of ethnography, was ready to declare 'barbarian' customs superior to the Hellenic ones. But it was a cool, ultimately self-assured, look at foreign civilizations. There was no temptation to yield to them. In fact there was no desire to get to know them intimately by mastering foreign languages. It was observation from outside . . . What emerges [from it] is the superiority of the Greek love of freedom" ("The Fault of the Greeks," *Daedalus* 104, no. 2 [1975], 12, 15). Let me add here that it is Plutarch who, standing up for the cause of his ancestors, accuses Herodotus of all kinds of lies and fabrications and of besmearing the memory of Greek ancestors; even doubting whether he was a Greek at all, Plutarch labeled him a "pro-barbarian [*philobarbaros*]" ("On the Malice of Herodotus," in *Moralia*, Vol. 11, trans. Lionel Pearson and F. H. Sandbach (Cambridge, MA: Harvard University Press), 23).

46. Considering the frequent accusation that the ancient Greeks distinguished themselves from all non-Greeks—with the latter as "barbarians," understood in the modern sense as lacking culture, and thus demonstrating cultural arrogance—it needs to be pointed out that this accusation is, scientifically speaking, incorrect. However, this does not mean that no prejudice against the so-called "barbarous peoples" existed. But, as the Stranger holds in the *Statesman*, the popular division of mankind into Hellenes and barbarians is as absurd as if cranes, which were considered to be the most intelligent animals, claimed that all other animals, including humans, were brutes (263d3–e2). To conclude this remark, I wish to quote Taylor, who writes in *Plato: The Sophist and The Statesman* that "we today do worse than make a mere ethnological oversight if we allow ourselves loosely to put Jews, Arabs, Persians, Chinese, Japanese, Malays together under the label 'Orientals,' and then proceed to facile generalizations about the limitations of the 'Oriental,' his incapacity for self-government, or for physical science, or what you please. We are running the risk of cultivating an insular self-conceit which may do us untold harm in a hundred ways, and we need to be taught the lesson Plato enforces in his pleasantry about the reflective crane, by discovering, for example, that the Chinese, in turn, lumps *us* all together as outlandish 'ocean-men' " (201).

47. Jean-François Mattéi, *Le Procès de l'Europe: Grandeur et misère de la culture européenne* (Paris: Presses Universitaires de France, 2011), 49–50.

48. François Hartog points out that, "for the Greeks of the fifth century, royalty was despotic and a barbarian leader was bound to be royal" (*The Mirror of Herodotus: The Representation of the Other in the Writing of History*, trans. Janet Lloyd (Berkeley: University of California Press, 1988), 171; see also 200.

49. Plato, *The Collected Dialogues*, 1026 (262c10–263).

50. Delcomminette, "Odysseus and the Home of the Stranger from Elea," 536.

51. Rosen, *Plato's Sophist*, 140.

52. However well taken Delcomminette's suggestion is, the Stranger's confutation of Parmenides also implies that, as the home of philosophy, Elea is also at stake in the rebuttal in question. Some of the reasons at the heart of the Stranger's criticism of Parmenides' doctrine—I refer in particular to his qualification of the doctrine as a myth, or as local talk—also applies to Elea as the name for such a home.

53. Joly, *Études platoniciennes*, 22.

54. Gadamer, "Dialektik ist nicht Sophistik," 355.

55. Ibid., 357.

56. Socrates' question about whether the Stranger's philosophical companions think of the three names as designations for one thing, or as names for three different kinds (*gene*), links the question of what the philosopher, the sophist, and the statesman *are* from the start of the dialogue to the question of *logos*—that is, to the question of the elementary constituents of intelligibility that will be the object of the central part of the dialogue.

57. It is likely that Plato never wrote this dialogue because, in the process of establishing what the sophist is, this dialogue, as well as the *Statesman*, explains in the same breath how the sophist and the statesman respectively differ from the philosopher and, thus, provides hints at what the philosopher and philosophy are. Indeed, as Reiner Wiehl explains, this is so because the inquiry into the nature of the sophist is already informed by the Stranger's doctrine of the "greatest kinds," according to which the "look" of Sameness (*tauton*) implies a concern with the look of Difference (*heteron*). Of course, it does not follow that these dialogues therefore fully exhaust the nature of philosophy. See Wiehl, "Einleitung des Herausgebers," in Platon, *Der Sophist*, trans. Otto Apelt (Hamburg: Felix Meiner Verlag, 1985). The nature of philosophy remains all the more unexhausted if, as I will suggest, this differential determination of philosophy culminates in the Stranger's grounding of philosophy in the doctrine of the "greatest kinds," a doctrine that cannot be complete.

58. The very fact of the sophist's existence as a multifaceted and elusive animal, hiding and slipping away, making his capture almost impossible, is already proof that, in a way, Non-being has being.

59. Taylor, *Plato: The Sophist and the Statesman*, 46, 85.

60. Joseph Socher, *Über Platons Schriften* (Munich, 1820); Wincenty Lutosławski, *The Origin and Growth of Plato's Logic* (New York: Longmans, Green, and Co., 1897), 384–385.

61. Concerning the term "categories," Cornford writes, "Plato never uses the word, and Aristotle, who does use it, considers it inapplicable to any of the five Kinds" (*Plato's Theory of Knowledge*, 276).

62. What is new is that, in the *Sophist*, ideas concern the minimal discursive forms or concepts without which, and without whose interrelation, no rational speech would be possible. But since these ideas are as immutable as the distinct ideas—the good, the just, the beautiful, and so forth—distinguished in the earlier works, there is continuity as well between their earlier and later conception. However, to assure their indispensability for any rational order, Plato, in the *Sophist*, no longer has to locate them in some intellectual region distinct from the concrete world in order to dramatize their universality, but can determine them as intrinsic to concrete discursive speech.

63. Taylor, *Plato: The Sophist and the Statesman*, 7–8; see also 82, 89. Whether this discovery is that of God, and of "the full significance of personality," as Taylor holds, is another question.

64. Campbell, *The Sophistes and Politicus of Plato*, xxii–xxv.

65. Ibid., xxx–xxxvi.

66. In the *Statesman*, the Stranger also distinguishes two kinds of virtue that it is the statesman's task to interweave.

67. Taylor, *Plato: The Sophist and the Statesman*, 73.

68. Jacob Klein writes, "It is this guise of 'madness' that the Stranger of Elea seems to adopt now: it is his new—and true—face," the face of the philosopher (*Plato's Trilogy*, 38)

69. It is true that the notion of *koinonia* of the ideas or forms is already mentioned at 476a in the *Republic*, but besides concerning their relation among themselves, as well as the communion with actions and bodily things, the emphasis here is, Manasse remarks, on their purity and unmixed nature (*Platons Sophistes und Politikos*, 35).

70. Dixsaut, *Platon*, 167–168. In the *Sophist*, Plato does not go beyond his previous conception of ideas, Dixsaut holds; he seeks only to explain how isolated ideas can communicate (150–157). However, does the possibility of communicating not presuppose a disponibility of the ideas to do so that had not been thematized in the *Republic*, the *Phaedo*, or the *Phaedrus*? As opposed to the Good, which unifies the different ideas, the notion of *koinonia* indeed suggests a more developed concept of ideas.

71. I am grateful to Bharani Kollipara for reminding me that the way the Stranger broaches the question of Non-being builds on Plato's own developments regarding the intelligibility of Being itself and, thus, his efforts to extend the mandate of philosophy beyond what Parmenides accomplished.

72. The two forms of mimetic art are premised on either faithfully copying the exact proportions of a thing or, for the sake of illusion, changing them. The Stranger's embarrassment in locating the sophist in one of these kinds mirrors the difficulty encountered in the sixth division, where at least the noble sophist became almost indistinguishable from the philosopher. Indeed, as regards mimesis, the Stranger is also confronted with a noble mimesis as opposed to a deceitful one.

73. See Georg Wilhelm Friedrich Hegel, *Hegel's Lectures on The History of Philosophy*, Vol. 2, trans. Elizabeth S. Haldane and Frances H. Simson (London: Routledge & Kegan Paul LTD, 1994), 65–66. Although Hegel's critique of Parmenides in the Greater Logic—namely, that in cutting Being off from all relation to otherness by distinguishing it absolutely from Nothing, it becomes impossible to proceed from within Being as a beginning to something else, except by linking it to "something extraneous, something *outside* it"—is clearly indebted to the Stranger's refutation of Parmenides, Hegel nevertheless does not draw out the consequences of the fact that this criticism comes from a Stranger (*Science of Logic*, trans. A.V. Miller (London: George Allen & Unwin Ltd., 1969), 95. Indeed, as a "disciple" of Parmenides, his critique and refutation of the doctrine does not come from the outside but rather, as that of a stranger, from within that very doctrine.

74. The Stranger certainly aims at greater methodological rigor when, in the context of the division (and naming) of kinds into forms, he observes that "it seems, there was some ancient and uncomprehending idleness among those earlier in regard to the division of the genera by species, so that no one even tried to divide" (267d6–8).

75. Apart from originating in Elea, it could still be held that the Stranger belongs to a younger generation of Eleatic philosophers. Parmenides is his mental "father." With respect to Socrates, whose death is imminent and who fades into

silence after the introductory remarks, the Stranger seems also to be a somewhat younger person. In turn, he is a "father" to Theaetetus, who, at times, is apostrophized in the dialogue as "my boy," or "my child." At the beginning of the *Statesman*, the old Socrates says of the young Socrates, who is silently present for the whole dialogue, that he is believed to have some sort of kinship with him, since they are alike in looks and bear the same name (257d1–258a3). The young Socrates, who will succeed the old one, is thus also an addressee of the Stranger's speech and will be formed by his discourse. The generational dimension of the dialogue is evident, and is intimately linked to the pedagogy and the teaching of a rejuvenated philosophy to a new generation. See also Gadamer's "Dialektik ist nicht Sophistik," which consistently stresses the pedagogical nature of the Stranger's teaching.

76. Friedländer, *Plato*, 261.
77. Ibid., 250, 262.
78. Dixsaut, *Platon*, 143.
79. Dufourmantelle and Derrida, *Of Hospitality* 7–9. But if, as a "foreign son," the Stranger takes the parricide of father Parmenides upon himself, does he not do this as a proxy for what would have been a native son, such as Plato, thus making his invitation among the Athenians a ploy for them to discharge themselves from the guilt that inevitably must come with such a deed?
80. Benveniste, *Dictionary of Indo-European Concepts and Society*, 294. Benveniste continues by adding that the institution in question thus interrupts the "permanent situation of mutual hostility which existed between peoples or cities."
81. Nancy, "Le Ventriloque," 311.
82. Through this madness, the Stranger reveals himself to be a—or *the*—philosopher. The kind of dialectical analysis of Parmenides that the Stranger performs hereafter will lead to the declaration that, in seeking for the sophist, they have instead stumbled upon the philosopher (253c8–11).
83. Theodor Gomperz, *Griechische Denker. Eine Geschichte der antiken Philosophie*, Vol. 2 (Leipzig: Von Weit und Comp., 1902), 456.
84. Teisserenc, *Le Sophiste de Platon*, 14.
85. Significantly enough, at the beginning of the *Sophist*, Socrates invokes the conversation that he attended as a juvenile with the already frail Parmenides (217c2–7). According to his account, subsequent to his own inadequate interrogation of the status of the ideas, the main part of the conversation consisted in the thinker giving an example of the kind of dialectical and mental gymnastics, and dry-as-dust exercises, that one must master before all philosophical examination. Ironically, Parmenides' formal exhibition of the grueling requirements for all philosophical investigation—that is, the model of a two-way question–answer exercise in which the consequences of both a proposition and its negative are derived—orients the Stranger's own critical examination of Parmenides' understanding of Being and Non-being in the *Sophist*. In spite of his fierce critique of Parmenides' statement that one can speak only of Being, the outline of the requirements of dialectical

thinking is the horizon within which the parricide of father Parmenides takes place. Indeed, since in the *Parmenides*, "Parmenides is all the time drawing consequences, legitimately or illegitimately, from propositions that hinge on the formal or 'common' concepts, including those listed as 'Greatest Kinds' in the *Sophist*, it is arguable that in the *Sophist* itself Plato is gropingly beginning to explore what we, but not yet he, can identify with the implications, incompatibilities, and compatibilities that hold between propositions in virtue of the 'common' concepts that they embody" (Ryle, *Plato's Progress*, 142). See also Paul Natorp, *Plato's Theory of Ideas: An Introduction to Idealism*, trans. Vasilis Politis (Sankt Augustin, Germany: Academia Verlag, 2004), 260–261.

86. Plato, *The Collected Dialogues*, 931.

87. Rosen, *Plato's Sophist*, 282. Since the Stranger's recasting of the notion of Non-being as Otherness does not necessarily imply a rejection of Parmenides' conception of Non-being as the non-conceivable contrary of Being, there is in principle no parricide involved in his refutation. Nonetheless, even if the Stranger takes issue with Parmenides only to make use of the Parmenidean concept of Non-being to introduce Otherness, Plato's emphasis on the Stranger's refutation as a refutation of *father* Parmenides, and thus as something resembling a parricide, must be taken seriously. See Cordero, "Introduction," 55–56. In my reading, it is also necessary to distinguish the parricide of Parmenides from an Oedipal or sacrificial act by his physical or spiritual sons intent on inaugurating a new philosophical order. In a way, one could argue that insofar as the Stranger demonstrates that Parmenides' thesis, because of its aporetic nature, is a thesis that cannot be upheld—or, rather, that could never have been upheld—Parmenides would not have been a father to be sacrificed in the first place. To put it bluntly, Parmenides would never have been a father, strictly speaking, making sacrificial parricide unnecessary. But above all, the Greek concept of sacrifice would not allow one to construe the parricide as a sacrifice in a Judeo-Christian sense.

88. See Gadamer, "Das Vaterbild im griechischen Denken," in *Gesammelte Werke*, Vol. 6 (*Griechische Philosophie II*) (Tübingen: J.C.B. Mohr, 1985). I think that the *Sophist* reveals a clear connection between the parricide of Parmenides and the deep shake-up of the traditional image of the father in fifth- and fourth-century Greece. During that time, in which no experiences were avalilable for orientation in the new world that opened up, a large gulf arose between the generations of the attical leadership. Not only did the older generations realize that the younger generations found themselves in a new world in which everything could be put into question, but the younger generation felt abandoned by the older one, which could no longer provide them with standards for orientation. As Christian Meier remarks, the resulting disdainfulness of the younger generation for the older one started with a contempt for their fathers (*Athens*, 516–517, 519).

89. Stanley Rosen feels justified in dismissing Jacques Derrida's interpretation of the dialogue and, in particular, his extension of the problematic of parricide to

the question of writing. This is not least because, along with most other commentators of the *Sophist*, Derrida also speaks of the Stranger's radical interrogation of the Parmenidean thesis as a parricide. See Rosen, *Hermeneutics as Politics* (New York: Oxford University Press, 1987), 79–82; and Derrida, *Dissemination*, trans. Barbara Johnson (Chicago: University of Chicago Press, 1981), 163–165.

90. If this point is viable, then the originality of Rome (and thus of Europe) as basing its identity on the transmission of the accomplishments of another culture, as Rémi Brague has argued, would have been preceded in a much more radical way by Greece itself. See Brague, *Eccentric Culture: A Theory of Western Civilization*, trans. Samuel Lester (South Bend, IN: St. Augustine's Press, 2002).

91. Arendt, *Between Past and Future*, 124.

92. Arendt writes, "The great Greek authors became authorities in the hands of the Romans, not of the Greeks. The way Plato and others before and after him treated Homer, 'the educator of all Hellas,' was inconceivable in Rome, nor would a Roman philosopher have dared 'to raise his hand against his [spiritual] father,' as Plato said of himself (in the *Sophist*) when he broke with the teaching of Parmenides" (ibid., 124).

93. In antiquity, the title of the dialogue, *Sophist*, was followed by a subtitle: *On Being* (*peri tou ontos*). See Cordero, "Introduction," 20.

94. Natorp, *Plato's Theory of Ideas*, 265. After having recognized that the notions of both Being and Non-being are perplexing because none of the ways they have been determined allow one to say what they are without falling short of what they are in themselves, the Stranger broaches the question of how "we address on each occasion [a] same thing with many names" (251a6–7). He then adds, "in accordance with the same speech, we lay down each as one [thing] and then again we go on to speak of it as many and with many names" (251b2–4). With this, the explicit question of the *logos* and its "categories" is anticipated.

95. Plato scholars have repeatedly sought to identify the various currents of philosophizing that the Stranger takes on, and there exists a lot of disagreement on which particular historical figures or schools, if any, they can be identified with. For the argument that I am trying to make in this chapter, but also for reasons of competence, I need not, and cannot, take a stand in this respect. However, even though Plato describes these different views in a way that may not always be historically correct, they are not therefore necessarily of his invention. I agree with the majority of scholars who hold that the references are to real persons and currents in the fifth century.

96. The question of which historical figures or currents are meant by Plato when he opposes the earthborn giants to the friends of the forms, the corporealists to the idealists, poses a number of difficulties, especially with regard to the friends of forms; hence, there is not much agreement among Plato scholars on this matter. At first, the *eidon philoi*, because of their love of ideas, could easily be mistaken for Megarians, and even identified with Plato himself, but apart from the fact that they

sever (*khoris*) the ideas entirely from anything corporeal, thus not allowing for any participation of the sensible in the intelligible, the persons in question must belong to a different group, most likely the Pythagoreans with their doctrine about mathematical figures. See Taylor, *Plato: The Sophist and The Statesman*, 44–45. However, it has also been suggested that these "idealists" might be members of Plato's own Academy. See Natorp, *Plato's Theory of Ideas*, 289, 292–303.

97. One can call this a battle between a materialist and an idealist view about Being as long as one does not understand "idealist" in a modern sense. Indeed, the gods acknowledge corporeal existence.

98. See Rosen, *Plato's Sophist*, 213.

99. Friedländer, *Plato*, 266.

100. See also Rosen, *Plato's Sophist*, 216.

101. I have so far avoided, and plan on continuing to avoid, the controversy regarding the historical references of the different philosophical positions critically engaged by the Stranger, since the issue does not really bear on my argument. However, I would like to note that since the thinkers opposed to the materialists in the battle of the giants are referred to as "the friends of the species" or forms (248a4), they are often taken to be the representatives (in the Academy) of the Platonic theory of the ideas. Be that as it may, these friends of the ideas advocate a total separation of the intelligible from the corporeal, which is entirely at odds with the Platonic notion of participation (*methexis*).

102. The Stranger's statement that he and Theaetetus must search for a pathway through the aporetic impasse "as fittingly as we can" also highlights the finitude and always provisional nature of what is thus established as universal.

103. Plato admits of such doubleness explicitly in the case of the Same (256a11–b6). I recall that the problem of falsehood did not find a satisfactory answer in the *Theaetetus*. However, I do not seek to argue how the Stranger's demonstration according to which accounting for falsehood requires a rebuttal of Parmenides' assertion that Non-being is not, and that it *is* in a certain way, paves the way for a successful account of the possibility of false opining and falsehood. I simply want to point out that, since for every *eidos* or species, " 'that which is' is extensive, but 'that which is not' is infinite in multitude" (256e8–9), the notion of *to pseudes heteron*—that is, of false (because lacking being) otherness—represents the possibility of falsehood and deceit, and is thus crucial to such a demonstration.

104. Gadamer, "Dialektik ist nicht Sophistik," 359. To interpret Plato's contention about what is said of something—in this case, all the other things that are implied *immediately* or in the same breath by the notion "human being"—as a first sketch of a theory of predication amounts to reading Plato through Aristotelean, if not post-Fregean, eyes. I subscribe, by contrast, to Rosen's reminder that "[t]he first step in reading Plato is to put aside our Aristotelean spectacles" (*Plato's Sophist*, 7).

105. If what Plato advances about predication and the nature of propositions seems, from an Aristotelean and modern perspective, to be imperfectly developed,

this is perhaps not by accident; for, does not the Platonic concern with the weaving of forms, their *symploke*, in meaningful discourse, pursue only another problematic in which predication is one of the various ways in which such meaningfulness can be accomplished?

106. It is in this existential, rather than formal logical, sense of a community of the ideas through their participation in one another that Manasse's parlance of the "logicization" of the ideas by the Stranger must be understood.

107. Indeed, if no thing whatsoever can be conjoined with another, one would not even be able to hold that Motion and Rest have being, which would make it impossible to say that things change or are at rest. In the same breath, none of the ontological views that the Stranger discusses would be possible. To hold that nothing can be connected to something else is, further, a position that contradicts itself because, to make the claim, one cannot avoid the use of the term "being." But if, by contrast, everything combines with everything, then one would have to assert that Motion is at Rest and vice versa. This is impossible, as the Stranger concludes, "by the greatest necessities" (252d9–10). See also 259c8–d10.

108. The combination of the *gene* or *eide* as discursive intelligibilia is the central problem of the *Sophist*. With the systematic exploration of their interconnection, Plato also raises an issue that his earlier elaborations on the ideas in the *Phaedo*, the *Republic*, and the *Pheadrus* not only did not address but that also radically changes their nature. Is it by accident that he puts a stranger in charge of this reconsideration of the nature of the ideas?

109. For a compelling criticism of the application of the term "categories" to the Platonic Forms, or Kinds, and the confusion to which it leads, see Cornford, *Plato's Theory of Knowledge*, 268–276. Cornford forcefully makes the point that "Plato was not concerned with propositional forms; his Dialectic studies realities, and his conception of these realities was radically different from Aristotle's" (268).

110. Rosen writes that they are "hardly the 'most important' or 'greatest' in an exclusive sense; one might argue that terms like 'one' and 'many' stand on a par with the examples chosen by the Stranger" (*Plato's Sophist*, 264). According to Taylor, "[i]t is never said that the list of the *universalia universalissima* is complete, though later Platonists, like Plotinus in *Ennead* vi. 1–3, treat them as a complete list of Platonic 'highest universals,' or categories" (*Plato: The Man and His Work*, 389).

111. Teisserenc, *Le Sophiste de Platon*, 138.

112. For anything to be what it is, it must participate in the forms of Being, Sameness, and Otherness. If, notwithstanding that Motion and Rest do not meet the same criteria of universality, the Stranger lists them among the greatest of the genera, it is for historical reasons, Teisserenc argues; namely, it is "in order to inscribe the new ontology into a certain faithfulness to the philosophical tradition, at least, to its Platonic reinterpretation which opposes the partisans of mobility to those of rest" (ibid., 114).

113. Rosen, *Plato's Sophist*, 245, 281.

114. After having suggested that the knowledge in question is the philosopher's knowledge, the Stranger holds that it belongs to dialectical knowledge "to divide according to genera and not to believe either the same another [*heteron*] species or if it is other the same [*tauton*]" (253d1–3). With this reference to dialectics and *diairesis*, the knowledge in question would seem at first indistinguishable from the one practiced by Socrates; yet, apart from the fact that the Stranger's divisions of the sophist's "look" were interrupted by an ontological reflection before it could be resumed, thus suggesting a new understanding of division, the reference to the categories of the Same and the Other with respect to the process in question seems to hint at a crucial difference between what Socrates and the Stranger call philosophy. The dialectics that the Stranger here associates with philosophy is already informed by the eidectic alphabet that he is in the process of elaborating. In the Stranger's ensuing words, "whoever is able to do this, perceives adequately one look (*idea*) stretched in every way through many, though each one is situated apart, and many (looks) other than one another comprehended on the outside by one (look), and one (look), in turn, bound together into one through many wholes, and many (looks) set apart and distinct in every way—and this is to know how to discern according to genus, in which way the (genera) are severally capable of sharing and in which not" (253d5–e3). As the Stranger's statement acknowledges, dialectic and division involve several other types of forms, such as the One and the Many. Some of these forms, however, such as Internality and Externality, are not explicitly addressed in the *Sophist*.

115. Gadamer, "Dialektik ist nicht Sophistik," 361.

116. Ibid.

117. As forms, all of them are "extensively different" (255d4) from one another, other than Being in particular and, as a result, Non-being (256d12–e6), even though all forms participate in the form of Being, and Being is thus distributed across all the forms. Being, for its part, is itself said to be "other than all the rest" (257a1–2). But what, then, does it mean to speak, as many commentators of the *Sophist* do, of the genres as genres of Being? The Stranger establishes that speech or discourse (*logon*) is a genre of Being and that to deprive oneself of it would mean to deprive oneself of philosophy (260a5–7), since philosophy as an account-giving is "devoted to the look (*idea*) of that which is" (254a8–9). This account-giving takes place by way of the other forms, which thus can be labeled, as the Stranger himself labels them, as forms of Being.

118. Teisserenc, *Le Sophiste de Platon*, 92.

119. Ibid., 93. See also 111.

120. If the Stranger does not adhere to this order, it is because the nature of an *eide* or *gene* cannot, as Sallis has pointed out, be determined in separation from those others with which it is in communion (*Being and Logos*, 510–511).

121. I will not comment on the extremely complex nature of this community, which the Stranger refines (255e–257a). However, I would like to linger for a

moment on the Stranger's argument in which "Other" is established as a form in its own right. In order to show that "Other" is a fifth kind and not just another name for Being, the Stranger says that "some of 'the things which are' are spoken of by themselves [*auta kath'hauta*], and some are always spoken of in relation to different things [*alla aei legesthai*]" (255c14–16). This, however, would not be possible "if 'that which is' and 'the other' were not extensively different" (255d3–4).

122. Joly, *Études platoniciennes*, 95.

123. For foreignness and alterity to become connected, other questions first had to be broached, questions that did not arise for the Greeks of that time—in particular, Joly notes, the question of "the human being in his universality, and that of the human other in his or her singularity" (ibid., 40). Of course, this does not mean that the Greeks did not inquire into the particular marks that constitute the individuality of a human being. A case in point is Socrates' discussion in *Theaetetus* of what accounts for the particular individuality of the human being as opposed to a generic thing such as a wagon (207a–208d). Although, in the dialogue on the *Sophist*, Plato inquires into the human genre of being rather than a particular human other as an other, that the sophist is referred to as a slippery, complex, and multifaceted animal or beast, almost impossible to nail down, is perhaps also indicative of the Greeks' limits for conceptualizing human alterity. In the Stranger's efforts to surround the sophist, the Socratic method of division reaches its breaking point.

124. From a contemporary perspective it is, of course, tempting to refer to him, as Mattéi does throughout his work, as the Other. Mattéi writes, "Only the Stranger is the Other. The other of Parmenides as well as the other of Socrates" (*L'Étranger et le simulacre*, 159). He goes as far as to assert that the Stranger in the *Sophist* "is characterized from the first lines on as *heteros*, 'other,' other than Socrates, who has invited him for an encounter with his Athenian friends and who passes the word onto him" (*Le Procès de l'Europe*, 87). I assume that Mattéi confuses *heteros* with Theodorus' reference to the Stranger as a *hetairos*, meaning an associate, companion, or disciple of Parmenides. However, as far as I can see, these two Greek terms are not related.

125. Natorp, *Plato's Theory of Ideas*, 280–281 (translation modified). In the original German, the passage reads, "Das Andre ist das Andre *des* Andern. Der Grieche versteht durchaus die Andersheit als *Gegenseitigkeit*; er sagt nicht, wie wir: Das Eine—das Andre, sondern: das Andre—das Andre. Ist *A* gegen *B*, so ist nicht minder *B* gegen *A* das Andre, *sein* Andres. Damit ist schon gegeben, daß die Andersheit nicht sowohl scheidet als *verbindet*. Die Abgrenzung wird Angrenzung, die Grenze vermittelt den *Denkübergang*" (*Platos Ideenlehre: Eine Einführung in den Idealismus* (Hamburg: Felix Meiner Verlag, 1994), 308.

126. Ibid., 281.

127. By "displacing from its center the Parmenidean genre of Being, by attaching the genre of Non-Being to it, and by conferring to the latter the eminent dignity of the Other, *to heteron*," it would seem "as if the unheard-of encounter of

strangeness, and even of the 'foreignness' of the central character, with *alterity* as a generic category of all thought and all discourse, true or false, inaugurated at the same time a philosophy that comes from abroad, a mode of philosophizing otherwise, and a new way of showing that it is not possible to think the Same without the Other" (Joly, *Études platoniciennes*, 13).

128. See Benardete, *The Argument of the Action: Essays on Greek Poetry and Philosophy* (Chicago: University of Chicago Press, 2000), 335.

129. This is, of course, the position of Emmanuel Levinas. See Derrida, *Writing and Difference*, trans. Alan Bass (Chicago: University of Chicago Press, 1978), 89.

130. Ibid., 127.

131. See also Dufourmantelle and Derrida, *Of Hospitality*, 61.

132. Diès writes that Non-being "expresses only the essential alterity of Being, and of every being, in relation to everything else" ("Notice," in Platon, *Le Sophiste*, *Oeuvres Complètes*, Vol. 8, 288). Being is other than everything else, but Diès implies that it enjoys this otherness only insofar as it is that which can only be defined by itself. This understanding of the alterity of Being does not take the Stranger's parricide seriously enough. The Stranger's point is that Being is other because it participates in the form of Otherness; thus, it is what it is not on the basis of itself but, precisely, in that it is always *heteron ti*, that is, always in a differential relation to what it is not.

133. The Stranger continues, "so we'll not concede the point, whenever it's said that a negative indicates a contrary, but only so much, that the prepositioning of 'not,' general and particular, reveals something of everything else than the names that come after it, or rather than the things (*pragmata*), whatever they are, for which the names uttered after the negative are laid down" (257b10–c5).

134. Teisserenc, *Le Sophiste de Platon*, 133–134.

135. Cornford, *Plato's Theory of Knowledge*, 208.

136. That *absolute* Non-being cannot be a form has been convincingly argued by Rosen. Indeed, an awareness of the context in which the Stranger refers to "the species of 'that which is not' " (258d6–e1), even though absolute Non-being cannot be a form—that is, while evoking the stakes of the debate with Parmenides—makes it futile to elaborate on the possible meaning of what a form of Non-being could amount to.

137. Or should we say that, like opposition, hierarchy is also judged to be a derivative mode of relating?

138. Hegel, *Hegel's Lectures on The History of Philosophy*, Vol. 2, 65–66.

139. Liddell and Scott, *A Greek-English Lexicon*, 893, 943.

140. Rosen, *Plato's Sophist*, 284.

141. Ibid.

142. Friedländer, *Plato*, 274.

143. And therefore, the possibility of a nonrelational concept of otherness had to be excluded, while at the same time opening the space for the consideration of noncategorizable otherness.

144. Needless to say, the qualification "divine" has no religious sense in this context.

Chapter Three

1. Taylor, *Plato: The Sophist and the Statesman*, 245–250.
2. Ibid., 250.
3. Ryle, *Plato's Progress*, 285.
4. Manasse observes that the parallel between the statesman and the philosopher hits one's eyes through one word: *sumploke* (*Platons Sophistes und Politikos*, 210–211).
5. Cornelius Castoriadis, *On Plato's Statesman*, trans. David Ames Curtis (Stanford, CA: Stanford University Press, 2002), 14.
6. See Catherine H. Zuckert, "Who's a Philosopher? Who's a Sophist? The Stranger V. Socrates," *The Review of Metaphysics* 54, no. 1 (2000), 65.
7. If the sophist looks so much like the philosopher, is it not also because the philosopher—or more precisely, the Socratean philosopher—is also a bit of a sophist? I will not further examine this point, except to say that it unmistakably shows the Stranger's criticism to also be directed at Socrates' understanding of philosophy.
8. Yet, as Monique Dixsaut has pointed out, in distinction from the sophist, the public speaker does not use the *logos* in the same way as the latter. This does not imply the destruction of the *logos*. See Dixsaut, *Le Naturel philosophe*, 558. I add that with his short and private speeches, the sophist also resembles the philosopher. But the deeper reason for his lack of resemblance to the philosopher (and vice versa) lies with the sophist's use of eristics exclusively to refute his opponent, and thus to prove his superior skills, whereas the philosopher uses the method in order to arrive at something that can be agreed upon as true. Any further examination of the issue demands an elaborate exploration of how eristics and dialectics relate on the basis of the differences of the Socratic method in the earlier and later dialogues.
9. See, for example, Harvey Ronald Scodel, *Diairesis and Myth in Plato's Statesman* (Göttingen: Vandenhoeck & Ruprecht, 1987), 50–52.
10. Campbell, *The Sophistes and Politicus of Plato*, xix.
11. Taylor, *Plato: The Sophist and The Statesman*, 85.
12. Castoriadis, *On Plato's Statesman*, 48.
13. See Xavier Marquez, *A Stranger's Knowledge: Statesmanship, Philosophy & Law in Plato's Statesman* (Las Vegas, NV: Parmenides Publishing, 2012), 183–184.
14. Diès, "Notice," in Platon, *Le Politique, Oeuvres Complètes*, Vol. 9, lx.
15. Meno's response to Socrates—according to which he was completely perplexed and paralyzed by the latter's questions regarding the nature of virtue, namely, that if he "behaved like this as a foreigner in another country, [he] would most likely be arrested as a wizard"—also shows that only in Athens could a foreigner, without being arrested, dare put established doctrines into question as radically

as the figure of the Stranger in the *Statesman* does (*The Collected Dialogues*, 363 [80b5–6]). This is one of the reasons why the dramatic structure of the dialogue calls for a stranger to develop a conception of political art that casts even Plato's own previous stance into question.

16. Marquez is one of the very few to have paid attention to the Stranger's evocation of wonder and its call for philosophical reflection, although he does not recognize that this form of wonder is at the origin of a specific form of philosophical thought (*A Stranger's Knowledge*, 277, 300). As we know from the myth that the Stranger tells, the cosmos, as ordered matter, progressively reverses into chaos once the demiurge Cronus retires, bringing about a period that corresponds to the age of Zeus—the period when the cosmos, in the form of our world, needs to care for itself. The wonder expressed by the Stranger is in relation to life under Zeus—that is, life in cities, and thus political life, in which memory of the age of Cronus guides human beings and maintains the stability of the cities. The wonder that Socrates brings up in the *Theaetetus* is about the cosmos in the age of Cronus, as it were. The enigma regarding the stability of the cities is explained by the memory of the divine order of the first epoch, which is the foundation of the law of the city.

17. From the dialogue of the preceding day on the sophist, the attendants present during the discussion of the statesman know, of course, what they are asking the Stranger to do for them. It is therefore worth noting that already, at the opening of the dialogue, Socrates thanks Theodorus for having introduced him to the guest from Elea. In turn, Theodorus asks the Stranger to gratify them by also elaborating what defines statesmanship.

18. Let us also recall that students in the Academy were not taught only mathematics but politics as well, which was taught on the basis of geometrical methods. As Joly remarks, "the geometrization of the political thing, based on a redefinition of territory and space, the calendar and time, of calculus and number, constituted the principle of Cleisthenes' reform, and was at the origin of the democratic structures of the city." Furthermore, he adds that "Plato pursues this tradition by invoking geometry as the fundamental science for political science but he also separates himself profoundly from it" (*Le Renversement Platonicien: Logos, Episteme, Polis* (Paris: Vrin, 1994), 305.

19. As Benardete notes, Young Socrates "does not know anything about statesmen, just as Theaetetus had never seen a sophist" ("Eidos and Diaeresis in Plato's *Statesman*," *Philologus* 107, nos. 3–4 (1963), 193.

20. Ryle, *Plato's Progress*, 285.

21. This question is all the more warranted in light of Socrates' imminent death.

22. In the elenctic-maieutic process that drives the Platonic dialogues, the questions that Socrates addresses to his interlocutors take different forms, from a formal or rhetorical perspective. One such form is the following, which I borrow from the *Republic*:

SOCRATES: "This, then, would be one of our proofs, but examine this second one and see if there is anything in it?"

GLAUCON: "What is it?" (580d).

Glaucon is thus invited to respond to a proof before he even knows what it is! This type of question does more than just build suspense. It is a type of question that presupposes that the addressee is able to anticipate or, more precisely, to "see" what follows necessarily from something that has been established. This type of question occurs, perhaps, more frequently in the *Statesman* than in any other of Plato's dialogues. If this is correct, then Young Socrates' repeated requests that the Stranger explain what he means would be testimony to his constant failure to "see" the logical implications of previously established insights.

23. Marquez's point is that, since "political knowledge has and can have no permanent place in the political community, it is always a 'Stranger's knowledge.'" Regarding true statesmanship, it consists in the insight that the genuine statesman "must remain a stranger to his creation"—in short, that, once he has founded the city and made it secure enough to survive without him, he also withdraws (*A Stranger's Knowledge*, 8, 335).

24. Rosen remarks that the methodological rectifications reflect the Stranger's progressive awareness of "the excessive theoretical ambition, or the attempt to capture human life in the grid of *diaeresis*. The Stranger is not just educating Young Socrates. Socrates is punishing old Socrates. He is educating and punishing himself" (*Plato's Statesman: The Web of Politics* (South Bend, IN: St Augustine Press, 2009), 74.

25. Let me note that in ancient Greek, *zoōn* signifies both a living animal and a portrait.

26. For the notion of *skiagraphia*, in particular in the *Republic*, see Plato, *The Collected Dialogues*, 827 (602a–e).

27. For this synergetic ideal, see Wieland, *Platon und die Formen des Wissens*, 80.

28. Michel Narcy, "La Critique de Socrate par l'Etranger dans le *Politique*," in *Reading the Statesman: Proceedings of the III Symposium Platonicum*, ed. Christopher J. Rowe (Sankt Augustin: Academia Verlag, 1995), 228.

29. Plato, *The Collected Dialogues*, 511 (265e1–3).

30. Rosen, *Plato's Statesman*, 17.

31. Mitchell Miller, *The Philosopher in Plato's Statesman* (Las Vegas, NV: Parmenides Publishing, 2004), 76.

32. Ibid., 77.

33. Rosen asks: "Do natural kinds—or as we now say, classes—always exist in complementary pairs, like even and odd numbers?" (*Plato's Statesman*, 28).

34. In distinction from dividing mankind into parts such as the Hellenes and the Barbarians, dividing it as a genus into males and females would be a division in accordance with species (262c10–263a2).

35. Taylor, *Plato: The Sophist and The Statesman*, 202. Taylor goes on to discuss in detail the mathematical joke.

36. See also Diès, "Notice," in Platon, *Le Politique*, xviii–xix.

37. In the *Timaeus*, Plato makes the two classes—true opinion and mind or reason (*nous*)—into "a great principle," before introducing a third class, the *khora*. He writes, "We must affirm them to be distinct, for they have a distinct origin and are of a different nature; the one is implanted in us by instruction, the other by persuasion; the one is always accompanied by true reason, the other is without reason; the one cannot be overcome by persuasion, but the other can; and lastly, every man may be said to share in true opinion, but mind is the attribute of the gods, and of very few men. Wherefore also we must acknowledge that one kind of being is the form which is always the same, uncreated and indestructible, never receiving anything into itself from without, nor itself going out to any other, but invisible and imperceptible by any sense, and of which the contemplation is granted by intelligence only. And there is another nature of the same name with it, and like to it, perceived by sense, created, always in motion, becoming in place and again vanishing out of place, which is apprehended by opinion jointly with sense" (*The Collected Dialogues*, 1178 [51d–52a7]). In the *Statesman*, the distinction pertains also to two forms of knowledge, but there, true opinion is seemingly as rare a commodity as *episteme*! What is more, it is construed as the legitimate counterpart in the practical domain to what *episteme* is in the theoretical domain.

38. Undoubtedly, in the *Meno*, Plato already distinguished "correct opinion [*orthen doxan*]" or "true opinion [*doxa ara alethes*]" (97b6–11), which is a divine gift for statesmen, from knowledge, which results from recollection. Even though true opinion is "as good a guide as knowledge for the purpose of acting rightly" (97b9–10), knowledge "is something more valuable than right opinion" (98a5–6) (*The Collected Dialogues*, 381–382). In the *Statesman*, the distinction between both remains intact, but by endowing public affairs with a logic specifically its own, true opinion, I hold, helps Plato to forcefully cement the independence of the political domain from philosophy. Marquez writes, "We might say that Plato in the *Statesman* is exploring the possibility of divorcing philosophy from politics" (*A Stranger's Knowledge*, 20).

39. In the *Laws*, the title of government is attributed to six agencies, if not seven, all of which are said to be in conflict with one another. One of these is that of the father or mother over their offspring and the family. His or her government does not represent a model for the wise men's supreme claim to rule the ignorant, which instead belongs to statesmanship (*The Collected Dialogues*, 1284–1285).

40. If, as Lewis Campbell holds, the knowledge of the statesman would "essentially be the same whether applied to a state or of a household," it would be difficult to explain the paucity of true statesmen, since anyone of the many household heads could take his position (*The Sophistes and Politicus of Plato*, iii).

41. Having thus divided all insightful knowledge into discriminating and injunctive knowledge, the question arises where philosophy fits in. It cannot fit into discriminative knowledge because, unlike the latter, it does not come to an end after having discriminated its insights. Contrary to the logician, the philosopher—like the statesman—is not quit of that into which he has gained insight after having critically examined it. Especially because philosophy is geared toward a knowledge produced in common, it seems to be closer to that of the statesman. But it is more than questionable whether philosophy, as the science of free men (as it has been called in the *Sophist*), is injunctive. And if it is injunctive, in what sense is it so?

42. The Stranger remarks that "it's desirable for those who are doing anything in common to be unanimous" (260b10–11).

43. Narcy, "La Critique de Socrate par l'Etranger dans le *Politique*," 231.

44. Ibid., 232.

45. Miller, *The Philosopher in Plato's Statesman*, 54, 115.

46. Euripides' *Orestes* from 408 seems to be a most perfect record and critical exposure of the opportunism and demagogy that reigned in Athens during that period. When judging Plato's remarks regarding the philosopher's unwillingness to participate in the affairs of the state, one should not overlook the actual total failure of the elite in Athens in those years.

47. Hannah Arendt, *The Human Condition* (Chicago: University of Chicago Press, 1958), 221–230.

48. For this reason, once his job is done, the statesman can withdraw. But because he is a human being, and therefore not a supreme authority—such an authority is perhaps the law—anyone, if he or she musters the necessary skills, can in principle be a statesman.

49. Although the problematic that, in the *Statesman*, compares to that of Non-being in the *Sophist* is that of just measure, I wonder whether the "big myth" and "the ancient stories" (*ta palai lekhthenta*) (268d8–e11) that the Stranger resorts to do not parallel what in the *Theaetetus* has been said about Homer and the tragedians. In the *Theaetetus*, the tragedians were held to lend authority to the more recent doctrines of Protagoras. Admittedly, the "big myth" told by the Stranger in the *Statesman* is largely his own invention, but does it not also radically put into question all theocratic accounts of statesmanship?

50. Plato, *The Collected Dialogues*, 1434 (875c3–6).

51. Unlike the enlightened tyrant and the philosophical legislator who, according to Book IV of the *Laws*, both possess a natural endowment (*phusei*) that predisposes them to their mutual task, the statesman has not been produced by nature. The *basileus politicus* of the *Statesman* must be distinguished from both the philosopher-king and the legislator (*nomothetes*): *together* with the enlightened autocrat, the *nomothetes* creates the ideal state. See Plato, *The Collected Dialogues*, 1301–1302 (710e7–9). However, in Book X, in the context of a critique of pre-

Socratic natural philosophy, Plato takes issue with the belief, attributed to "prose writers and poets," that there is no connection between nature and statesmanship (*politike*) (1445 [889d7–890a9]).

52. As Dixsaut observes: "For Plato, the human being is not a political animal, shaped by nature to live with his likes within a city" (*Platon*, 216; see also 218, 223). Is this not also the gist of the myth about the age of Cronus? Only when the human animals are forsaken by the gods do they have to learn how to live together. Needless to say, in order to conceive of a commonwealth in its radical uniqueness, it must be uncoupled from even this negative relation to the theological.

53. In Book II of the *Laws*, the Athenian stranger tells Clinias, the Spartan, that his "cities are organized like armies, not like societies of town dwellers; you keep your young men in herds [*agelaioi*, which was also the name of the groups formed by young boys of the same age under the supervision of older young men] like so many colts at grass in one troop" (*The Collected Dialogues*, 1263 [666e1–3]). Being made up of herds—with the distinction, however, that apart from the fact that herds are not entities in which one is educated to become a good citizen, universal militarization serves to secure their physical existence though there is no god anymore to provide for them as herds—the Spartan cities are thus to be understood as the anachronistic surviving herds of a forgone age.

54. Taylor, *Plato: The Sophist and The Statesman*, 209.

55. Furthermore, so do all the existing political regimes which are imitations (*mimema*) of Cronus' mythical house-hold.

56. Taylor, *Plato: The Sophist and The Statesman*, 215. A *syntheke* is an agreement, eventually a covenant or treaty. *Politon* is the genitive plural of the noun "citizen" (*polites*). Therefore, a *syntheke politon* is an agreement, a treaty, and arrangement of citizens, which—in democratic Athens—is taken in the citizen assembly.

57. It is true that Plato, in the *Laws*, does not observe this distinction in the same way as it is observed in the *Statesman*. Although all living creatures, human beings included, "are chattels of the gods," "all good as they are [*aristoi*]," the gods not only nurture but also care for them (*The Collected Dialogues*, 1458 [902c2]).

58. With this, the myth not only sets the stage for the ensuing distinction of the art of caring into forcible, tyrannical "care" on the one hand, and the art of the statesman whose science exclusively concerns voluntary human caretaking on the other, but also its distinction from all the arts that are merely concerned with the material needs of human beings.

59. Rosen, *Plato's Statesman*, 177–178.

60. Many commentators have pointed out that in the *Statesman* Plato lets the Stranger take on the paradigmatic role that mathematics enjoys elsewhere in Plato's thought, particularly in the *Republic*, although there too Plato emphasizes the intrinsic limits to mathematics that cause it to be only a propaedeutic to philosophy. Undoubtedly, philosophy in a proper sense—that is, starting with Platonic philosophy—could emerge only as a result of the discovery by mathematics of an ideal,

purely intelligible realm. But from a philosophical perspective, the intrinsic limits of mathematics are linked to its inability to account for the existence of mathematical idealities. It takes them as given and self-evident, but it never inquires into their status as idealities. It also must be pointed out that the Stranger does not entirely do away with mathematics. When distinguishing the two methods of measurement, for example, the first method based on arithmetical methods is discarded for the benefit of a superior type of measurement, which is certainly no longer arithmetical, but which is not therefore simply non-mathematical. As Joly has shown, the latter is informed by geometrical proportionality (see *Le Renversement Platonicien*, especially 262–271, and 320–321).

61. Sallis, "Beginnings–," in *Plato's Statesman: Dialectic, Myth, and Politics*, ed. John Sallis (Albany, NY: SUNY Press, 2017), 14.

62. It is here that one can behold the Stranger's pedagogical approach: by encouraging Young Socrates to divide the subject in a dichotomous fashion, which must inevitably result in absurd conclusions, he makes him aware of the shortcomings of a mathematical and theoretical approach to an issue such as politics.

63. The Stranger's myth explains how the arts came into being after the world was forsaken by Cronus, not simply in order to restore the golden age but to create a similar world—one, however, relative to the human being.

64. In the *Laws*, Plato returns to the metaphor of weaving in order to describe, if I understand correctly, how the fabric of a state is made up by an intertwinement of the citizens who are to be magistrates and have been provided with a code of laws, and those citizens who have been only lightly tested by education. Here Plato emphasizes the difference between the warp and the woof much more than in the *Statesman*. The warp is made up by citizens who are the officials, those who fill the magistracies (*The Completed Dialogues*, 1320–1321).

65. For a different reading of what the standard achieves, see Miller, *The Philosopher in Plato's Statesman*, 66–67.

66. See ibid., 64.

67. Rosen, *Plato's Statesman*, 119.

68. At one point, after having established that all becoming needs a mean, the Stranger also speaks of "the becoming of the mean [*metriou genesin*]" (284d7–8). How is this to be understood? Does this mean that, in distinction from the immutable and eternal ideas with which theoretical knowledge is concerned, the mean with respect to which what is of the order of becoming is judged, is itself something belonging to this very order?

69. In Benardete's words, "The being of nonbeing is to nonbeing as the measure of the mean is to the arithmetical measure" ("Statesman Commentary," in *Plato's Statesman*, 115).

70. Friedländer writes, "The phrase 'learned minds' is read correctly as referring to the Pythagoreans, yet perhaps we are to think not only of the Pythagorean schools in distant Sicily, but also of the Pythagorean tendencies within the Academy

itself [. . .] the critique points to that philosophical school to which Plato is so deeply indebted in his thinking about mathematics and natural science, and about the nature of measure as well" (*Plato*, 291–292).

71. See 284d1–9.

72. For the connection of justice as *dike* to the precise and complete entity of a polity, see also Plato, *The Collected Dialogues*, 1337 (757e2–3).

73. When the Stranger affirms that the true royal art is not rule-bound, which scandalizes Young Socrates, he makes it clear that laws in human affairs are not the last instance, as are the ideas brought to light in the theoretical realm by a method modeled mathematically. If understood as timeless, laws in the order of becoming hinder the mediation that a genuine statesman has to accomplish between the universal and the particular.

74. "And on women too [*kai tas archousas*], Glaucon said" (Plato, *The Collected Dialogues*, 772 [540c3–6]).

75. Ibid., 1377 (805e5–8).

76. Leo Strauss, "Plato," in *History of Political Philosophy*, eds. Leo Strauss and Joseph Cropsey (Chicago: University of Chicago Press, 1987), 73. Let me also point out that at the precise moment the Stranger introduces weaving as a paradigm for statesmanship, he calls upon Zeus. Addressing himself to Young Socrates, he avers, "Do you want, by Zeus, Socrates, if we don't have any other ready at hand—well, do you want at any rate that we choose the art of weaving?" (279b1–3). For weaving as a masculine art, see especially John Scheid and Jesper Svenbro, *The Craft of Zeus: Myths of Weaving and Fabric*, trans. Carol Volk (Cambridge, MA: Harvard University Press, 1996).

77. Needless to say, if weaving is only the paradigm for the political art for lack of a more fitting one, there are limits to what it can establish about the political art. After all, for what is engendered through the statesman's art, the very ordinary and common art of weaving is an example that falls short of the grandeur of what the latter accomplishes. Furthermore, if the paradigm in question is only a paradigm, and moreover a paradigm for want of a better one, then it does not allow one to argue that the statesman is a craftsman. Let us not lose sight of the fact that the statesman's art has been defined as injunctive. *Qua* paradigm, weaving is supposed to bring to the fore within statesmanship a knowledge that is inherent in actions such as weaving, but that in no way is identical with them.

78. The parallel between the art of clothmaking—in which weaving plays the biggest part—and that of caring for the cities consists first in this: that each is named on the basis of what it accomplishes, and is different from the other only as regards the kind of protection it provides. Furthermore, in the same way that the art of weaving consists mostly in weaving cloaks, from which it receives its name, so the royal art receives its name (*politikes*, civil) from its care for the cities.

79. See also Campbell, *The Sophistes and Politicus of Plato*, xiv.

80. Let us also point out that even though on occasion Plato compares the statesman to a captain, this comparison does not hold because in the distinction

from all captains who vouch only for the safety of their passengers and the cargo, a true statesman betters an existing state and its members. See *Gorgias* 511d–512b5, in *The Collected Dialogues*, 293–294.

81. See Miller, *The Philosopher in Plato's Statesman*, 107.

82. Such weaving also requires, of course, the rejection of what cannot be made into the necessary antagonistic threads out of which a city is formed.

83. Plato, *The Collected Dialogues*, 1330.

84. Undoubtedly, the rejection of some who are judged unfit to be members of a polity appears highly problematic, especially given the emphasis I have put on fundamental democracy. Yet, from Plato's time to the present, in Western and non-Western parts of the world alike, all communities are based on exclusion. As Zygmunt Bauman has shown in *Liquid Times: Living in an Age of Uncertainty* (Cambridge, UK: Polity Press, 2007), waste in terms of human beings is perhaps today more than ever a factual product of (both failed and well-functioning) states. An all-inclusive polity, if it is not to be totalitarian, is also a contradiction in terms because a polity presupposes a limit. For Plato, this limit is formed by those who refuse to be others, or who are incapable of relating to others. As demonstrated by the Stranger's theory regarding contrary virtues, a polity rests on the relation of its members to each other as others, and has no chance of survival except through the complete interlacing of its members on the basis of a relation of their contrary characters. One can argue, of course, that the way he conceives of otherness is too narrow, and that it is necessary to open up otherness to conceptions that are not merely framed by opposition and complementarity. But this does not mean that any concrete polity would be capable of exhausting all the possible ways in which a relation to an other can be forged. A polity approaches its limit when an other refuses to be included, and thus resists being made into an other. Whoever rejects the types of relation between others—as others accepted in a concrete society—positions him- or herself at the limit of this society. The right to exclude oneself is the right not to be an other, a right that a fundamental democracy must recognize. However, this is a right that makes sense only with respect to the togetherness from which someone withdraws, and is thus still a negative way of being part of it. By contrast, the real and structural problem of a polity concerns those who cannot even afford to claim for themselves the right of not belonging to a specific form of social interrelatedness.

85. This analogy is also the limit of the paradigm, since the weave that human beings form on the basis of their contrary characters and virtues is one in which they let themselves be formed, as opposed to the warp and the woof, which do not enter by themselves the web into which they are made to interlace. However, since human beings are not pure souls but bodily beings, they need a statesman to "make" them enter the political fabric.

86. The "human bonds" are above all marital in nature. This understanding of human bonds presupposes the distinction earlier in the dialogue between mixed and pure generation—that is, between generation by genera with one another, such

as horses and monkeys, and unmixed or pure generation, of which human generation is one example among others. Bonds (*desmoi*), it would seem, are possible and necessary only within species that are, in dichotomous fashion, divided through the middle from within themselves.

87. How is one to conceive of this activity of "instilling," especially if Plato uses it to designate the defining activity of the statesman? But does this term—"instilling"—therefore necessarily have a unique meaning? Schleiermacher translates the term as "*einbilden*" (literally, to form into); Diès as "*imprimer*" (to imprint); Fowler as "implants." According to Liddell and Scott, *empoien* means to make in, to put in, to foist in, to produce, or to create in. Does the preposition *em* or *en* mark a significant difference from *poien*, to make? Since the expression concerns the souls of the citizens to be woven together into a city, it certainly refers to a making within the soul, as opposed to a making that makes something out of them. But only the context permits one to interpret the verb in a way that distinguishes it from the meaning of "to make," "to cause," or "to produce."

88. Does this not also suggest that the thus formed contrary virtues weave themselves together because virtues are ultimately one—that is, one virtue?

89. Undoubtedly, wool fibers twisted into hard and soft threads can be said to be predisposed to interlacing, but they cannot be said to accomplish such interlacing by themselves. As all paradigms do, set next to what they are to illuminate, the paradigm of weaving can only shed light on it, but does not establish its full identity. For a careful reading of the term *paradeigma* in the dialogue, one that also pays close attention to the Greek word itself, see James Risser, "The Art of the Example in Plato's *Statesman*," in *Plato's Statesman: Dialectic, Myth, and Politics*, ed. John Sallis, 172–174.

90. Manasse adds, "In the case of the statesman the concept of weaving is no longer descriptive in a neutral sense, but itself already ethically determined, and applies exclusively to the 'true' statesman" (*Platons Sophistes und Politikos*, 210).

91. In spite of the citizens' self-weaving, injunction is still necessary because as humans they are, after all, bodily creatures.

92. "Hermes asked Zeus in what manner he was to bestow these gifts [of respect for others and a sense of justice] on men. 'Shall I distribute them as the arts were distributed—that is, on the principle that one trained doctor suffices for many laymen, and so with the other experts? Shall I distribute justice and respect for their fellows in this way, or to all alike?'

'To all,' said Zeus. 'Let all have their share. There could never be cities if only a few shared in these virtues, as in the arts. Moreover, you must lay it down as my law that if anyone is incapable of acquiring his share of these two virtues he shall be put to death as a plague to the city'" (Plato, *The Collected Dialogues*, 320 [322d2–4]).

93. Ibid., 1398 (832b10–c7).

94. The many, *plethos*—apart from meaning a great number, a multitude of people, a mass—has, of course, also the connotation of populace and mob. But from the argument that even a few cannot possibly create a polity, it follows with necessity that a multitude is even less capable of doing so. Only one is capable of the art in question. See also the *Statesman*, 297b10–c5, where the same point is forcefully made one more time.

95. Plato, *The Collected Dialogues*, 1404 (712e10–713a2).

96. Ibid. (713a2–5).

97. Manasse, *Platons Sophistes und Politikos*, 78. Manasse continues, "Insofar as the one who acts is a knower, he is free from all handed down tradition, and that means locating him as a point of rest within time. This implies taking a decided position against all traditionalism, that is, against the belief in the unquestionable authority of what has become."

98. In Book XI of the *Laws*, Plato links the precision involved in lawgiving to that of the good archer. He writes that "the law like a good archer [*toxotes*] must in each case take careful aim at its mark; it must be exact in determining the magnitude of the correction imposed on the particular offense, and, above all, the amount of compensation to be paid" (*The Collected Dialogues*, 1484 [934b4–7], translation modified).

99. See Wieland, *Platon und die Formen des Wissens*, 162–163.

100. Ernst Kapp, "Theorie und Praxis bei Aristoteles und Platon," in *Ausgewählte Schriften*, eds. H. and I. Diller (Berlin: de Gruyter, 1968), 167–179.

101. Does this mean that once the statesman has been found, a return to the problematic of self-rule could be envisaged?

102. In the discussion of the various political regimes, it is interesting to note that the Stranger does not valorize any particular regime. In his discussion, the Stranger approaches these forms from within the horizon of popular representations of them, which is also the standpoint of the uncritical Young Socrates. As demonstrated by the criterion of the one, the few, and the many, monarchy, oligarchy, and democracy are in essence forms of factional strife, and are thus internally corrupt. Even democracy as understood on the basis of popular criteria is simply a regime in which the poor dominate the rich.

103. Among the commentators, it is specifically Marquez who has highlighted the withdrawal of the statesman once his task has been accomplished. At first, undoubtedly, by the very position he occupies a statesman seems to relate to his subjects as a stranger. Yet, when his task has been accomplished and he folds himself back into the multitude of citizens, he shows himself to be one like them. In the same way that the Stranger questioned the Athenians' distinction of themselves from the barbarians, he thus seems to question the assumption, based on the myth of Cronus, that in the current age of Zeus a statesman is a godlike figure. As Honig observes, "If the foreign-founder must leave after the work of founding is done, that

need stems from the very foreignness that so enables foreign-founders" (*Democracy and the Foreigner*, 25). Even if the statesman is a citizen rather than a foreigner, as a founder he is a foreigner of sorts, and must thus, once he has completed his task, take his leave by disappearing within the multitude of the citizens he has united into a commonwealth.

Bibliography

Agier, Michel. *L'Etranger qui vient. Repenser l'hospitalité*. Paris, Seuil, 2018.
Arendt, Hannah. *Between Past and Future: Eight Exercises in Political Thought*. New York: Penguin Books, 2006.
Arendt, Hannah. *The Human Condition*. Chicago: University of Chicago Press, 1958.
Baslez, Marie-Françoise. *L'Etranger dans la Grèce antique*. Paris: Les Belles Lettres, 1984.
Bauman, Zygmunt. *Liquid Times: Living in an Age of Uncertainty*. Cambridge, UK: Polity Press, 2007.
Benveniste, Émile. *Dictionary of Indo-European Concepts and Society*. Translated by Elizabeth Palmer. Chicago: Hau Books, 2016.
Benardete, Seth. *The Argument of the Action: Essays on Greek Poetry and Philosophy*. Chicago: University of Chicago Press, 2000.
Benardete, Seth. "*Eidos and Diaeresis in Plato's Statesman*." *Philologus* 107 (1963): 193–226.
Benardete, Seth. "*Theaetetus Commentary*." In *Plato's Theatetus: Part I of The Being of the Beautiful*. Translated by Seth Benardete. Chicago: University of Chicago Press, 1986.
Brague, Rémi. *Eccentric Culture: A Theory of Western Civilization*. Translated by Samuel Lester. South Bend, IN: St. Augustine's Press, 2002.
Burnyeat, Miles. *The Theatetus of Plato*. Indianapolis: Hackett Publishing Company, 1990.
Campbell, Lewis. *The Sophistes and Politicus of Plato*. New York: Arno Press, 1973.
Campbell, Lewis. *The Theaetetus of Plato*. New York, Arno Press, 1973.
Castoriadis, Cornelius. *On Plato's Statesman*. Translated by David Ames Curtis. Stanford, CA: Stanford University Press, 2002.
Cole, A. T. "*The Apology of Protagoras*." *Yale Classical Studies* 19 (1966): 101–118.
Cordero, Nestor-Luis. "Introduction." In Platon, *Le Sophiste*. Translated by Nestor-Luis Cordero. Paris: Flammarion, 1993.
Cornford, Francis MacDonald. *Plato's Theory of Knowledge*. London: Routledge & Kegan Paul, 1935.

Delcomminette, Sylvain. "Odysseus and the Home of the Stranger from Elea." *The Classical Quarterly* 64, no. 2 (December 2014): 533–541.
Derrida, Jacques. *Dissemination*. Translated by Barbara Johnson. Chicago: University of Chicago Press, 1981.
Derrida, Jacques. *Writing and Difference*. Translated by Alan Bass. Chicago: University of Chicago Press, 1978.
Desjardins, Rosemary. *The Rational Enterprise: Logos in Plato's Theateteus*. Albany, NY: SUNY Press, 1990.
Diès, Auguste. Platon, Œuvres *Complètes*. Translated by Auguste Diès. Paris: Les Belles Lettres, 2012.
Dixsaut, Monique. *Le Naturel philosophe: Essai sur les Dialogues de Platon*. Paris, Vrin, 2016.
Dixsaut, Monique. *Platon. Le Désir de comprendre*. Paris: Vrin 2012.
Dufourmantelle, Anne, and Jacques Derrida. *Of Hospitality*. Stanford, CA: Stanford University Press, 2000.
Friedländer, Paul. *Plato, Vol. 3: The Dialogues. Second and Third Periods*. Translated by Hans Meyerhoff. Princeton, NJ: Princeton University Press, 1969.
Gadamer, Hans-Georg. *Gesammelte Werke*, 9 Vols. Tübingen: J.C.B. Mohr, 1991.
Gomperz, Theodor. *Griechische Denker. Eine Geschichte der antiken Philosophie*, Vol. 2. Leipzig: Von Weit und Comp., 1902.
Hartog, François. *The Mirror of Herodotus: The Representation of the Other in the Writing of History*. Translated by Janet Lloyd. Berkeley: University of California Press, 1988.
Hegel, Georg Wilhelm Friedrich. *Hegel's Lectures on the History of Philosophy*, Vol. 2. Translated by Elizabeth S. Haldane and Frances H. Simson. London: Routledge & Kegan Paul Ltd., 1994.
Hegel, Georg Wilhelm Friedrich. *Science of Logic*. Translated by A. V. Miller. London: George Allen & Umwin Ltd., 1969.
Heidegger, Martin. *The Essence of Truth: On Plato's Cave Allegory and Theaetetus*. Translated by Ted Sadler. New York: Continuum, 2002.
Honig, Bonnie. *Democracy and the Foreigner*. Princeton, NJ: Princeton University Press, 2001.
Joly, Henri. *Études platoniciennes: La question des étrangers*. Paris: Vrin, 1992.
Joly, Henri. *Le Renversement Platonicien. Logos, Episteme, Polis*. Paris: Vrin, 1974.
Kahn, Charles. "Plato's *Charmides* and the Proleptic Reading of the Platonic Dialogues." *Journal of Philosophy* 85, no. 10 (1988): 541–549.
Kapp, Ernst. "Theorie und Praxis bei Aristoteles und Platon." In *Ausgewählte Schriften*, edited by Hans and Inez Diller, pp. 167–179. Berlin: de Gruyter, 1968.
Klein, Jacob. *Plato's Trilogy: Theatetus, the Sophist and the Statesman*. Chicago: University of Chicago Press, 1977.
Liddel, Henry George, and Robert Scott. *A Greek-English Lexicon*. Oxford: Oxford University Press, 1968.

Lutosławski, Wincenty. *The Origin and Growth of Plato's Logic*. New York: Longmans, Green, and Co., 1897.
Manasse, Ernst Moritz. *Platons Sophistes und Politikos. Das Problem der Wahrheit*. Berlin: Siegfried Scholem, 1937.
Marquez, Xavier. *A Stranger's Knowledge: Statesmanship, Philosophy & Law in Plato's Statesman*. Las Vegas, NV: Parmenides Publishing, 2012.
Mattéi, Jean-François. *L'Etranger et le simulacre: Essai sur la fondation de l'ontologie platonicienne*. Paris: Presses Universitaires de France, 1983.
Mattéi, Jean-François. *Le Procès de l'Europe: Grandeur et misère de la culture européenne*. Paris: Presses Universitaires de France, 2011.
Matthews, Gareth B. "A Puzzle in Plato: *Theaetetus* 189b–190e." In *Philosophical Analysis: A Defense by Example*, edited by D. S. Austin, pp. 3–15. Dordrecht: Kluwer Academic Publishers, 1988.
Meier, Christian. *Athens: A Portrait of the City in Its Golden Age*. Translated by Robert and Rita Kimber. New York: Henry Holt and Co., 1998.
Meier, Christian. *A Culture of Freedom: Ancient Greece and the Origins of Europe*. Translated by Jefferson Chase. Oxford: Oxford University Press, 2012.
Meier, Christian. *Entstehung des Begriffs 'Demokratie'. Vier Prolegomena zu einer historischen Theorie*. Frankfurt: Suhrkamp Verlag, 1970.
Miller, Mitchell. *The Philosopher in Plato's Statesman*. Las Vegas, NV: Parmenides Publishing, 2004.
Miller, Mitchell. "Unity and *Logos*. A Reading of *Theaetetus* 201c–210a." *Ancient Philosophy* 12, no. 1 (1992): 87–111.
Momigliano, Arnaldo. "The Fault of the Greeks." *Daedalus* 104, no. 2 (1975): 9–19.
Nails, Debra. *The People of Plato: A Prosopography of Plato and Other Socratics*. Indianapolis: Hackett Publishing Company, 2002.
Nancy, Jean-Luc. "Le Ventriloque." In *Mimésis. Des articulations*, edited by Sylviane Agacinski et al., pp. 271–338. Paris: Aubier-Flammarion, 1975.
Narcy, Michel. "La Critique de Socrate par l'Etranger dans le *Politique*." In *Reading the Statesman: Proceedings of the III Symposium Platonicum*, edited by Christopher J. Rowe, pp. 227–235. Sankt Augustin: Academia Verlag, 1995.
Natorp, Paul. *Platos Ideenlehre: Eine Einführung in den Idealismus*. Hamburg: Felix Meiner Verlag, 1994.
Natorp, Paul. *Plato's Theory of Ideas: An Introduction to Idealism*. Translated by Vasilis Politis. Sankt Augustin: Academia Verlag, 2004.
Niehues-Pröbsting, Heinrich. *Überredung zur Einsicht. Der Zusammenhang von Philosophie und Rhetorik bei Platon und in der Phänomenologie*. Frankfurt/Main: Klostermann, 1987.
Plato. *The Collected Dialogues*, edited by Edith Hamilton and Huntington Cairns. Princeton, NJ: Princeton University Press, 1980.
Plato. *The Being of the Beautiful: Plato's Theaetetus, Sophist, and Statesman*. Translated by Seth Benardete. Chicago: University of Chicago Press, 1986.

Platon, *Minos*, in *Oeuvres Completes*, Vol. 13, Part 2: *Dialogues Suspects*. Translated by Joseph Souilhé. Paris: Les Belles Lettres, 1930, pp. 75–102.
Plutarch. "On the Malice of Herodotus." In *Moralia*, Vol. 11. Translated by Lionel Pearson and F. H. Sandbach, pp. 2–132. Cambridge, MA: Harvard University Press, 1979.
Polansky, Ronald M. *Philosophy and Knowledge. A Commentary on Plato's Theaetetus*. Lewisburg, PA: Bucknell University Press, 1992.
Risser, James. "The Art of the Example in Plato's *Statesman*." In *Plato's Statesman: Dialectic, Myth, and Politics*, edited by John Sallis, pp. 171–181. Albany, NY: SUNY Press, 2017.
Rorty, Amélie Oksenberg. "A Speculative Note on Some Dramatic Elements in the Theaetetus." *Phronesis* 17, no. 3 (1972): 227–238.
Rosen, Stanley. *Hermeneutics as Politics*. New York: Oxford University Press, 1987.
Rosen, Stanley. *Plato's Sophist: The Drama of Original and Image*. New Haven, CT: Yale University Press, 1983.
Rosen, Stanley. *Plato's Statesman: The Web of Politics*. South Bend, IN: St Augustine Press, 2009.
Ryle, Gilbert. *Plato's Progress*. Cambridge: Cambridge University Press, 1966.
Sallis, John. *Being and Logos: Reading the Platonic Dialogues*. Bloomington: Indiana University Press, 1996.
Sallis, John. "Beginnings–." In *Plato's Statesman: Dialectic, Myth, and Politics*, edited by John Sallis, pp. 1–14. Albany, NY: SUNY Press, 2017.
Scheid, John, and Jesper Svenbro. *The Craft of Zeus: Myths of Weaving and Fabric*. Translated by Carol Volk. Cambridge, MA: Harvard University Press, 1996.
Scodel, Harvey Ronald. *Diairesis and Myth in Plato's Statesman*. Göttingen: Vandenhoeck & Ruprecht, 1987.
Simmel, Georg. *Soziologie. Untersuchungen über die Formen der Vergesellschaftung*. Munich & Leipzig: Duncker & Humblot, 1922.
Snell, Bruno. *Die Ausdrücke für den Begriff des Wissens in der vorplatonischen Philosophie*. Berlin: Weidmannsche Buchhandlung, 1924.
Socher, Joseph. *Über Platons Schriften*. Munich: 1820.
Stenzel, Julius. *Studien zur Entwicklung der Platonischen Dialektik von Sokrates zu Aristoteles*, 3rd edition. Stuttgarts: B.G. Teubner, 1961.
Strauss, Leo. "Plato." In *History of Political Philosophy*, edited by Leo Strauss and Joseph Cropsey, pp. 33–89. Chicago: University of Chicago Press, 1987.
Taylor, A. E. *Plato: The Man and His Work*. New York: Meridian Books, 1956.
Taylor, A. E. *Plato: The Sophist and the Statesman*. Toronto: Thomas Nelson and Sons Ltd., 1961.
Teisserenc, Fulcran. *Le Sophiste de Platon*. Paris: Presses Universitaires de France, 2012.
Waldenfels, Bernhard. *Topographie des Fremden. Studien zur Phänomenologie des Fremden*, Vol. 1. Frankfurt/Main: Suhrkamp, 1997.

Wiehl, Reiner. "Einleitung des Herausgebers." In Platon, *Der Sophist*. Translated by Otto Apelt, pp. vii–xli. Hamburg: Felix Meiner Verlag, 1985.

Wieland, Wolfgang. *Platon und die Formen des Wissens*. Göttingen: Vandenhoek & Ruprecht, 1982.

Zuckert, Catherine H. "Who's a Philosopher? Who's a Sophist? The Stranger v. Socrates." *The Review of Metaphysics* 54, no. 1 (2000): 65–97.

Index

Agier, Michel, 165n31, 166n33
Anaxagoras, 8
Arendt, Hannah, 5, 82, 109, 126, 128, 185n92
Aristotle, 13, 53, 68–69, 83, 89, 91, 116, 181n61, 186n104–105, 187n109

Bauman, Zygmunt, 199n84
Bazlez, Marie-Françoise, 175n13
Benveniste, Emile, 59, 61, 78, 183n80
Bernadete, Seth, 11, 24, 40, 98, 164n14, 192n19, 197n69
Brague, Rémi, 185n90
Burnyeat, Myles, 39, 166n1

Campbell, Lewis, 53, 69, 116, 166n1, 167n11, 170n27, 175n7, 178n36, 194n40
Castoriadis, Cornelius, 112, 116
Cebes, 8
Cicero, 56
Cleisthenes, 6, 173n54, 192n18
Clinias, 19653
Cole, A. T., 173n45
Cordero, Nestor-Luis, 177n25–26, 184n87, 185n93
Cornford, Francis MacDonald, 101, 169n20, 172n41, 175n3, 175n10, 181n61, 187n109

Crito, 56
Cronus, 4, 127, 131–135, 151, 154–155, 158, 192n16, 196n52, 197n63, 201n103

Delcomminette, Sylvain, 65, 178n41, 180n52
Deleuze, Gilles, 171n37
Derrida, Jaques, 78, 98, 165n31, 176n14, 184n89
Desjardins, Rosemary, 166n4, 168n19
Diès, Auguste, 12, 116, 190n132, 200n87
Dionysius, 10
Dixsaut, Monique, 43, 70–71, 77, 176n18, 191n8, 196n52
Dufourmantelle, Anne, 176n14

Empidocles, 25
Epicharmus, 25
Euclides of Megara, 65, 166n1, 174n56
Eunomia, 15
Euripides, 195n46

Frege, Gottlob, 186n104
Freud, Sigmund, 78
Friedländer, Paul, 51, 86, 104n3, 174n60, 197n79

Gadamer, Hans-Georg, 66, 93, 177n21, 1182n75
Glaucon, 192n22, 198n74
Gomperz, Theodor, 80

Hartog, François, 180n48
Hegel, Georg Wilhelm Friedrich, 74, 102, 182n73
Heidegger, Martin, 41, 173n52
Heraclitus, 25, 27, 47, 87, 168n19, 169n20
Hermes, 200n92
Herodotus, 64, 179n45
Homer, 25, 27, 42–43, 47, 61–62, 169n21, 185n92, 195n49
Honig, Bonnie, 15, 201n103

Janus, 5
Joly, Henri, 56, 65, 97, 189n123, 192n18, 196n60

Kahn, Charles, 165n21
Klein, Jacob, 23, 171n35, 173n49, 181n68
Kollipara, Bharani, 182n71

Levinas, Emmanuel, 98, 190n129
Liddell, Henry George, 60, 200n87
Lutoslawski, Wincenty, 68–69

Manasse, Ernst Moritz, 150, 155, 175n5, 182n69, 187n106, 191n4, 200n90, 201n97
Marquez, Xavier, 119, 192n16, 193n23, 194n38, 201n103
Mattéi, Jean-François, 60, 189n124
Meier, Christian, 5–6, 14, 164n7, 184n88
Melissus, 45, 49
Meno, 191n15
Miller, Mitchel, 118, 122, 127, 138, 167n5, 197n65
Momigliano, Arnaldo, 179n45

Nails, Debra, 176n20
Nancy, Jean-Luc, 11, 164n17, 165n31, 177n27
Narcy, Michel, 127
Natorp, Paul, 83, 97, 183n85, 185n96, 189n125
Niehues-Pröbsting, Heinrich, 164n13
Nikolopoulou, Kalliopi, 171n36

Oksenberg Rorty, Amélie, 172n42

Parmenides, 2–4, 11, 24–27, 39, 43–50, 57–58, 64–65, 67, 70–72, 74–84, 88, 91, 93–94, 96–97, 99, 101–102, 104–108, 116, 128, 136, 139, 146, 168n19, 169n21, 174n56, 174n60–61, 180n52, 182n73, 183n79, 183n79, 183n82, 183n85, 184n87–89, 185n92, 186n103, 189n124, 189n127, 190n136
Plotinus, 187n110
Plutarch, 179n45
Polansky, Ronald M., 27, 48, 166n4, 167n5, 171n34
Protagoras, 20–29, 31–37, 42–50, 59, 71, 77, 112–113, 116, 127, 137, 151, 167n11, 168n13, 168n18–21, 169n23–25, 170n28, 171n31–32, 171n34, 171n37, 172n40, 173n53–54, 174n61, 174n66, 195n49
Pythagoras, 139, 185n96, 197n70

Risser, James, 200n89
Rosen, Stanley, 65, 81, 103, 121, 138, 178n33, 179n44, 184n89, 186n104, 187n110, 190n136, 193n24, 193n33
Ryle, Gilbert, 60, 111, 164n15–16, 169n24, 178n32

Sallis, John, 134, 179n42, 188n120
Scheid, John, 198n76
Schleiermacher, Friedrich, 172n40, 173n52, 174n63, 200n87

Scodel, Harvey Ronald, 191n9
Scott, Robert, 60, 200n87
Simias, 8
Simmel, Georg, 177n21
Skemp, J. B., 139
Snell, Bruno, 167n10
Socher, Joseph, 68
Solon, 14, 165n27
Stenzel, Julius, 17
Strauss, Leo, 141, 163n3
Svenbro, Jesper, 198n76

Taminiaux, Jacques, 127
Taylor, A. E., 19, 22, 68–69, 111, 116, 132–133, 180n46, 181n63, 185n96, 187n110, 194n35

Teisserenc, Fulcran, 54, 59, 91, 175n11, 187n112
Terpsion, 166n1

Waldenfels, Bernhard, 164n9
Wiehl, Reiner, 181n57
Wieland, Wolfgang, 163n3, 176n20, 193n27

Xenophanes, 83

Zeno, 11, 45, 57–58, 64, 174n56
Zeus, 15, 127, 131, 134, 141, 143–144, 151, 154, 178n40, 192n16, 198n76, 200n92, 201n103

www.ingramcontent.com/pod-product-compliance
Lightning Source LLC
Chambersburg PA
CBHW020654230426
43665CB00008B/438